AF225456

Triangle of One Hundred Years Wars

JJ Klaas

UJ Press

Triangle of One Hundred Years Wars

Published by UJ Press
University of Johannesburg
Library
Auckland Park Kingsway Campus
PO Box 524
Auckland Park
2006
https://ujonlinepress.uj.ac.za/

First published 2023

https://doi.org/10.36615/9781776453092

978-1-7764530-8-5 (Paperback)
978-1-7764530-9-2 (PDF)
978-1-7764605-0-2 (EPUB)
978-1-7764605-1-9 (XML)

This publication had been submitted to a rigorous double-blind peer-review process prior to publication and all recommendations by the reviewers were considered and implemented before publication.

Copy editor: Luke Perkins
Cover design: Hester Roets, UJ Graphic Design Studio
Typeset in 10/13pt Merriweather Light

Contents

Dedication

This book is dedicated to my selfless visionary teachers of Zanyokwe Primary School, Thembelani Secondary School, and HH Majiza High School in Qoboqobo (Keiskammahoek). Despite having started schooling at age eleven, they instilled confidence in me to believe that I was capable beyond imagination. I also dedicate it to my remarkable inspirational lecturers of the University of Fort Hare, University of Oklahoma in the United States and the University of Cambridge in the United Kingdom.

Gratitude

Had it not been the remarkable support, understanding and sacrifice of Dr Sino Nocwaka Klaas the daughter of Manzana and our children Lizwi, Linamandla and Olothando, I would not have completed the book. Thank you my amazing family.

Acknowledgement

I owe my identity to the women and men who moulded the essence of who I am. I was fortunate to have walked on the shoulders of incredible people. I remember my late father, *"Mvulane"*, who instilled a strong sense of self-reliance. I am grateful to my mother Nofundile who named me Jongi in order to look ahead as well as my late aunt Nomkhitha who gave me the second name Joseph, *"the gifted son of Jacob"*. My late maternal grandfather, Namangile Sabalele, *"Jwarha"*, was my pillar from whom my African identity was rooted.

I cannot forget my maternal grandmother Khonjiwe, the daughter of Jusayi from *"amaQwathi"* clan who looked after the multitudes of us as her grandchildren. I am grateful to Zatshoba Kenny Poho, *"Bhelekazi"*, the guardian during my teenage years. She brought me up like a young Prince destined to make a difference and to always utilize available opportunities to the best of my abilities.

Growing up at kwaRharhabe in the village of Zanyokwe in Qoboqobo in the Eastern Cape Province of South Africa, provided me with the rare privilege to witness the beauty of a solid African society centred on the core values of selflessness, pride, patience and hard work. I would watch with awe the remarkable disposition of the notable pillars of the village such as Zinzo Gantsho, *"Tshawe"*, Jongilanga Chweba *"Ngwane"* and Mcheya Matinise *"Thole."* Furthermore, I acknowledge the role played by the humble elders of the Presbyterian Church at Mkhubiso village in my life, such as Mongezi Makoyi *"Jikijwa,"* Mzimkhulu Sankqele *"Rhadebe,"* Kenneth Jonga *"Letha"* and Zipho Goba *"Mbathane"*.

Academically, I am grateful to Mr Thembela Kwinana *"Ntshele"* my compassionate teacher as well as Mr Duma Mxoli and the late Mr Khaya Mabuya whose voices I can still hear today. The late Professor Mbulelo Vizikhungo Mzamane, *"Msimango"*, was an exceptional academic who laid a solid foundation of excellence and Africanness.

Had it not been for these incredible patriots, who carried me during the different phases of my life, I would not have become an African with a deep sense of understanding of our history, driven by the optimism of hope and determination.

The idea to write this book emanated from intense and frequent conversations with Professor Loyiso Nongxa *"Mband' eXhalanga"*, a mathematician with a PhD from the University of Oxford, United Kingdom and the former Vice Chancellor of Witwatersrand University. He triggered my interest by lending me a book written by Noel Mostert, titled *The Frontiers* in early 2020. I used the Covid-19 lockdown period to start my reading and writing process. Professor Nongxa was delighted to see the final product of this book.

I am thankful to Professor Ncedile Saule *"Msuthu"* for sharing his reflections and insight on the broader cultural and historical aspects of amaXhosa in the context of wars of resistance and conquest.

During the writing process I shared my thoughts from time to time with a circle of wonderful thinkers to ascertain whether my approach, focus and relevance of the work were aligned. Thank you Mr Sango Ntsaluba, Professor Luvuyo Wotshela, Mr Thabo Makupula, Dr Philani Nongogo, Ms Noloyiso Caga, Mr Mzukisi Skenjana, Mr Themba Nganda, Ms Sivuyisiwe Masiza Vumazonke and Mr Monde Duma for your validation.

I am grateful to the librarian of the Cory Library at Rhodes University, Ms Vathiswa Nhanha, who assisted me in accessing the primary source material both in print and online, as well as the librarian of the Howard Pim Library at the University of Fort Hare, Mr Simphiwe Dlephu, who helped me to access some of the rare books. Finally, I am thankful to Ms Kefilwe Makhanya for her remarkable efforts in editing my book as well as Mr Luke Perkins through UJ Press.

Foreword from the Royal House of AmaXhosa Nation

The book *"Triangle of One Hundred Years Wars"* provides an incredibly gripping and riveting South African historiography, chronologically articulated through an endogenous lens by a native South African. It chronicles a record reflective of the fundamental historical events within the southern part of Africa. The narrative delineates the adroitness of the visionary leadership of amaXhosa given the successes and failures on the protracted wars etched in the Eastern Cape region.

The book offers a considerate and uplifting rare historical account by an African historian *uMsuthu*[1]. It illuminates an unflinching narrative characterised by the compelling drive of relentless resistance of amaXhosa, who found themselves in the coalface of the British encroachment in the Eastern Cape region, at the beginning of the nineteenth century. Among other things, the book articulates the purposive and visionary actions undertaken by King Hintsa Aa! Zanzolo[2] in defence of his nation, as well as the unparalleled gallant fortitude of the descendants of Prince Rharhabe such as Prince Ndlambe, Prince Maqoma and King Sandile.

To this end, the book illuminates our understanding on salient attributes about the Southern African Nation's Royal House of amaXhosa legendary reputation and perseverance in their persistent fight during the one hundred years wars of resistance. The book is likely to be a must-read by all South

---

1   Msuthu in this context refers to the author from the amaMvulane clan. AmaMvulane belong to the clans who emigrated to the Eastern Cape centuries ago originally coming from Lesotho hence they are called abeSuthu.

2   The royal salutation Aa! Zanzolo will only be used once as a form a respect. In the subsequent reference to the King in the book one will only use King Hintsa. The book uses royal titles such as King, Queen, Prince and Princess which is consistent with the English language.

Africans and the entirety of the African continent who need to understand their aetiological tapestry as a nation and their evolution for the benefit of posterity.

Forthwith, one fancies the prospects for such scholarly knowledge be incorporated into South Africa's education system curricula so that younger generation may begin comprehending what an indispensable contribution done by their forebears. They will learn about how their forebears sacrified their lives through sweat and blood in the battle fields into bringing about all that is at least worthwhile about the South Africa we see today.

In the context of the amaXhosa-led wars of resistance against a relentless colonial assault, we owe patronage to the Royal Dynasty of amaTshawe[3].We remain indebted to the craft of this erudite exposition that has captured the remarkable accounts of an indefatigable spirit of amaXhosa Nation in the context of the complex history of South Africa.

Indeed, it elucidates the horrendous acts of conquest by colonialists to dispossess the indigenous people of their inalienable asset. Thus, with this book, *uMsuthu* has taken us through a journey of a reconstructionist paradigm of learning, unlearning, and relearning about South Africa's history.

By Prince Zolile Burns-Ncamashe (MP) Spokesperson and Advisor of Amarharhabe Kingdom and South African Deputy Minister of Cooperatative Governance and Traditional Affairs.

---

3   AmaTshawe are named after Tshawe the son of King Nkosiyamntu. Tshawe usurped the Kingdom of amaXhosa from Cirha his brother, the designated heir to the throne. Since then the descendants of amaTshawe had remained in the throne of the Kingdom of amaXhosa until the present day.

Prologue

On the 3rd of October 1935, Italy, under the leadership of Benito Mussolini, invaded Ethiopia. The surprise attack by 200 000 soldiers led by Field Marshal Emilio De Bono was launched from the coast of Eritrea. The Ethiopian army disintegrated under sustained heavy artillery. On the 7th of May 1936, Italy announced the annexation of Ethiopia. Emperor Haile Selassie was compelled to go into exile.

The main reason behind the unprovoked invasion was to avenge the historic Ethiopian defeat of Italy in the Battle of Adwa on the 1st of March 1896. Ethiopia, under the decisive leadership of Emperor Menelik II, took a stand in the strategic mountainous terrain of Adwa. About 6000 Italian soldiers were killed and around 4000 of them were captured as prisoners. The historic defeat of Italy defined Ethiopia as the only African country that was never colonised.

This incident illustrates the significance of history in the building and celebration of national pride and collective identity. About 40 years after the historic defeat by an African country in Adwa, the wound was still raw in Italy; hence Mussolini avenged it as a form of atonement in order to salvage Italian national pride. By the same token, the South African historiography, which had been largely inclined towards the dominant narrative of European conquest and civilization, failed to inspire African students because nothing much had been written about significant African victories in the pre-colonial era, during and post-colonial era. The defining War of Mlanjeni of 1850-1853, which stands out as the longest, deadliest and costliest war ever fought between Africans and Europeans in Sub-Saharan Africa in the nineteenth century, was also omitted from the dominant and official history of South Africa.

One moves from the premise that history is an important discipline which, among other things, is instrumental in the construction of patriotic identities and consciousness in relation to how past historical events shape the present socio-economic conditions. We cannot be proud of who we are; the language we speak and the identity and cultural values we have; if we cannot trace these to our history and create connections to the present.

It is unfortunate that our official written history provided no inner insight about the significant contributions of Africans and their heroism in the wars of resistance and emancipation. It is against this background that one deemed it imperative to embark on this journey of attempting to revisit our history in an effort to provide critical perspectives on some of the defining historical events of nineteenth century Southern African history, in the context of African wars of resistance against European Imperialism.

In the South African context, the debate about land will remain an abstract academic exercise if we cannot trace it to the concrete historical traceable events of the dispossession, displacement, dehumanization and commodification of Africans as instruments of cheap labour. For instance, it is of paramount importance that the current generation must know and learn about the first British-led ethnic cleansing in Southern Africa that was carried out in 1811-1812 against amaXhosa between Nxuba (Fish) River near Makhanda[1] (Grahamstown) and Xelexwa (Gamtoos[2]) river near Gqeberha[3]

---

1   At the time of the British occupation of the Cape Colony in 1806 and during the war of 1811-1812, the place was not Grahamstown. It was only named Grahamstown after the expulsion of amaXhosa in 1812. In October 2018, Grahamstown was renamed Makhanda, the name of the warrior of amaXhosa who died on 25 December 1819, after he led amaXhosa in the battle of Grahamstown on 22nd April 1819.

2   According to Pettman (1920) and Raper (1989), there is a likelihood that the name Gamtoos originated from the Gamtouers/Gamtouws the name of one of the Khoe tribes in the region.

3   In 1820, the city was named Port Elizabeth by Sir Rufane Donkin (1773-1841) the British Governor of Cape Colony in 1820 - 1821. Elizabeth was the name of this wife who died in India. In 2019, the Eastern Cape Geographical Names

(Port Elizabeth), by Colonel John Graham on instructions of John Francis Cradock, the British Governor of the Colony between 1811 and 1814.

History provides answers to the questions about why the Khoe and San people are a small minority on the margins of the South African society. South Africans should know that as the native inhabitants of the Cape, the Khoe and San people were subjected to systematic state-sponsored extermination during the era of the Dutch colonialism from mid-1600s until the latter part of the 1800s.

Most historical books as well as online resources, such as the military history of South Africa, often glorified wars in which the Europeans achieved decisive victories such as the Battle of Grahamstown on 22 April 1819, yet little has been written about the agonising War of Mlanjeni, where the British Empire suffered the highest number of casualties in comparative terms.

A critical re-examination of the Nongqawuse phenomenon (1856-1857), is conducted in this book in the context of the wars of resistance and the introduction of the highly lethal and contagious European cattle lung sickness (1854-1857) that coincided with the governorship of Sir George Grey in the Cape colony between 1854 and 1861. Revisiting Nongqawuse is intended to elucidate some of the fundamental, related events of historical significance that have been ignored in pursuance of a particular colonial narrative that portrayed amaXhosa as victims of their own actions.

Furthermore, the book contributes to the elucidation of the deeper analysis of the dominant Euro-centred historical narrative often packaged as official knowledge in the school textbooks. It examines how such a highly skewed and biased alien narrative of the official history impacted the cognitive construction of African identities.

Committee recommended that Port Elizabeth be renamed Gqeberha, the original African name of Baakens River that runs through the city. On 23 February 2021, the name change was gazetted by the South African government.

Although History was one of my major subjects for my undergraduate degree at the University of Fort Hare, at the time I was under immense pressure to study for the purpose of obtaining good grades. About two decades later, I developed a desire to revisit this subject, driven largely by the desire to understand our history in relation to some of the dominant narratives regarding the contributions of Africans and the distorted portrayal of the wars of resistance and the Nongqawuse phenomenon.

The journey of relearning and reconstructing our own history from an African perspective was an extraordinary one, as it provided a rare encounter of historical consciousness by going back in time in an attempt to reconstruct an African narrative. I was able to link the remarkable bravery and incredible fearlessness of King Hintsa, who offered himself as a sacrificial lamb to the invading British army in order to save his people, with the subsequent heroic acts of contemporary Anti-Apartheid activists. Among them were Mangaliso Robert Sobukwe (1924-1978), Nomzamo Winnie Madikizela Mandela (1936-2018), Mlungisi Griffiths Mxenge (1935-1981), Nonyamezelo Victoria Mxenge (1942-1985), Thembisile Chris Hani (1942-1993), Bantu Stephen Biko (1946-1977), Matthew Goniwe (1947-1985), Sicelo Mhlauli (1949-1985), Sparrow Mkhonto (1951-1985), Fort Calata (1956-1985), and many Africans who sacrificed their lives in the struggle for total emancipation.

Preface

The second British occupation of the Cape Colony in 1806, marked the beginning of the greatest agonising wars of resistance fought between Africans and the Europeans in Southern Africa in the nineteenth century. The book is anchored in some of the significant historical events during the time when Africans and Europeans were locked in wars in the triangle between Gqeberha, Graaf Reinet and Gcuwa.

The triangle stood out as a highly-contested centre, as attested by the battlefields of relentless wars of resistance that lasted from 1779 until 1879. The significance of the triangle is the fact that it was the staging ground of some of the major tragic acts of conquest in the history of South Africa in the nineteenth century. It was the scene of the British execution of ethnic cleansing of amaXhosa in 1811-12 between Xelexwa river and Nxuba River, the massive construction of forts and military posts that were meant to withstand the resolute resistance of amaXhosa, the outbreak of the longest and deadliest war fought between Africans and Europeans in Sub-Sahara Africa in the nineteenth century, and the landing of the highly lethal European cattle lung sickness that decimated about 80% of the herds of amaXhosa.

This book is an attempt to revisit the natural disposition of Africans in the context of the century-long wars of resistance, the larger part of which were fought between amaXhosa and the British colonial establishment. One of the major contributions of this book is the comprehensive examination of the War of Mlanjeni that has been omitted from the dominant official South African historiography of both the twentieth and the twenty-first century. The events indicate that the British conquest of Southern African was never a 'walk in the park' over docile submissive natives; it was attained through the sweat and blood of some of the greatest resistances demonstrated by Africans, who were capable, innovative and visionary.

Chapter One is a critical examination of the natural disposition of amaXhosa as one of the Southern Nations who endured the brutality of British Imperialism in Southern Africa. This Chapter examines the kind of people that amaXhosa were, what enabled them to withstand one hundred years of resistance, and what vital lessons can be learnt from such harrowing endurance.

Chapter Two maps out the initial series of resistance wars led by amaXhosa during the first three decades of the British occupation of the Cape Colony. What stood out during this period was the first British ethnic cleansing in 1811-12; the controversial reign of King Ngqika in enabling the British conquest and the role of Wesleyan missionaries in fomenting a war which culminated in the agonising unceremonious death of King Hintsa, the supreme royal aristocrat of amaXhosa; as well as the exodus of amaMfengu from Gcuwa (Butterworth) to Ngqushwa (Peddie).

Chapter Three explores in detail the defining War of Mlanjeni from 1850 to 1853, known as the longest, deadliest and costliest encounter of intense armed resistance in the history of Southern African wars of resistance in the mid-nineteenth century. The war overstretched the British Empire; and thus resulted in the surrender of the jurisdiction beyond Orange River in January 1852 to Andries Pretorius; the collapse of the government of Prime Minister John Russell[1] in February 1852; the sinking of the Birkenhead in Cape Town in February 1852, with 445 officers meant as reinforcements for the war; and the dismissal of General Harry Smith, the Hero of Aliwal as the Governor of the Cape Colony and Henry Somerset the Commander of the British army.

Chapter Four is a critical review of the Nongqawuse phenomenon in the context of the wars of resistance against

---

1   Lord John Russell (1792-1878) served as British Prime Minister of the Whig and Liberal Party respectively between 1846 and 1852 and from 1865 until 1866. He resigned on 25 February 1852 at the time Britain was in possession of 43 colonies and battling to end the War of Mlanjeni (1850-1853) (The Guardian February 1852).

British encroachment in the vicious struggle for land and domination. The purpose of this review is to widen the Nongqawuse narrative beyond its traditional confines, as a phenomenon linked to the broader political context such as the aftermath of the War of Mlanjeni, the outbreak of the deadly European cattle lung sickness and the role of Sir George Grey, who was instrumental in breaking the backbone of resistance.

Chapter Five explores the influence of the official history textbooks as the contested pedagogy instrumental in the socialisation of African identities. It examines the ongoing complexities of subjective narratives in the construction of dominant historical narratives contained in the official History textbooks of the national curriculum. The critical review illustrated that the dominant historical narratives of the European conquest, superficial presentation of highly fragmented African history, systematic omission of heroic stories of Africans and their contributions to civilizations are some of the concerning aspects embedded in the official South African History textbooks.

Colonial Rulers of the Cape Colony: 1652 – 1912

The European colonial rulers were administrators responsible for implementation of the policies of subjugation of natives and the conquest of land. They were held accountable for failures and rewarded for the successful executions of their obligated mandates. The nature and the extent of their mandated responsibilities, the reaction and the impact of the policies they implemented and their successes and challenges, varied due to different eras and complex circumstances. In the light of that, this section is anchored on the specific governors in relation to the creation of the permanent European presence in the Cape Colony and their roles in the wars of resistance and conquest.

The arrival of Johan Petros Anthoniszoon van Riebeeck (1619 – 1677) on the Southern tip of Africa on 06 April 1652, marked the beginning of the European encroachment which was followed by the subsequent wars of resistance and conquest of Southern Africa. His ten-year exploration and the systematic establishment of an administrative town from 1652 until 1662, laid the foundations which paved the way for the continuation of the aggressive expansion of the Dutch colonial settlements which continued until 1795. His name remained the reference point associated with the official landing of Europeans in Southern Africa.

Simon van der Stel (1639-1712) was one of the notable governors during the era of Dutch colonisation of the Cape Colony. He was a man of mixed origins born by Adriaan, the Dutchman who worked for the Dutch East India Company (DEIC) stationed in Batavia. His mother Maria Lievens was a mestico born by European and Asian parents. Van der Stel was born on a sea journey to Mauritius.

During van der Stel's twenty year governorship of the Cape from 1679 until 1699, he pioneered the plantation of the vineyards at an industrial scale in areas such as Constantia and Groot as well as the establishment of Stellenbosch. He dedicated himself to the development and the consolidation of the Dutch Colony. He remained the only Dutch Governor of the Cape to be succeeded by his son Willem (1664-1733) who governed the Cape from 1699 until 1707. The towns such as Simonstown the headquarters of the South African navy, Stellenbosch and Simonsberg were named after Simon van der Stel. After retirement he did not return to his country of origin, he worked on this farm estate of Constantia until he departed in 1712.

The controversial governorship of Baron Joachim Ammena van Plettenberg (1739-1793) between 1773 and 1785 was characterised by the intensification of military campaigns against African people which were followed by the accelerated systematic extermination of the vulnerable San communities. A year after he became the Governor, large scale genocide of the San people were carried out by the armed Dutch settlers supported by enslaved Khoe auxiliary groups.

In 1774, the well-resourced commando of 250 Dutch men executed large scale massacres of San people by launching surprise attacks at the dawn in their sleeping kraals (Adhikari, 2010). During this time the San people were hunted like animals as they were shot on sight by the Dutch settlers with impunity. According to Adhikari (2010), child slavery was institutionalised in order serve the interests of the Dutch famers who were gaining more land. The relentless and the systematic institutionalized exterminations of the San were intensified in line with the Dutch East India Company (DEIC) policy of rapid expansion in search for the rich grazing land (Adhikari, 2010).

At the arrival of the Dutch settlers in mid seventeenth century there were about 30 000 San in the Cape region. The institutionalised genocide continued until the mission was accomplished in 1790's (Adhikari, 2010). As the Dutch continued to expand in their conquest of the Cape along the coast they clashed with amaXhosa on the Nukakamma/

Sundays River. The intermittent skirmishes exploded into the first war between amaXhosa and the Dutch settlers in 1779. This aspect is explored at the beginning of Chapter One.

The naming of a town Pletternberg Bay after him was tantamount to the recognition of his dark legacy of aggressive expansion of Dutch settlements to the detriment of the San communities who perished from the face of the earth. The era of Governor van Plettenberg remained one of the painful chapters of the South African history which witnessed the systematic accelerated genocide of the African San communities in order to clear the land for the expansion of the Dutch settlements.

The arrival of Governor John Francis Cradock (1762–1839) in 1811, signalled the intentions of the British establishment to expand the Cape Colony beyond the Nukakamma/Sundays River. Consequently, Cradock became responsible for implementation of the expansion policy which was carried out through the catastrophic expulsion of about 20 000 amaXhosa from the Zuurveld region between Nukakamma/Sundays River and Nxuba/Fish River. He unleashed the ruthless Colonel John Graham (1778-1821) who relished executing the British military firepower in the obliteration of amaXhosa who were caught unprepared and unfamiliar with the warfare of an established professional army of mounted soldiers with guns and artillery.

Whilst Colonel Graham was honoured by naming of a town Grahamstown in 1812, governor Cradock was also honoured by the establishment of Cradock town in 1813 as a strategic defensive buffer zone to protect the gains of the newly acquired coveted Zuurveld region. Although Grahamstown was changed into Makhanda in 2018, Cradock is still the official name of the town.

Lord Charles Henry Somerset (1767–1831) the governor of the Cape Colony from 1814 until 1826 and the member of the British royal aristocrat, intensified the consolidation of the British imprint in the Cape Colony. Somerset displayed less tolerance towards the Boers which culminated into the

Slachter's Nek Rebellion of 1815, in which a group of Boer farmers rebelled against what they perceived as the tyrannical British domination. After six Boer rebels were hanged in public in 1816 at Van Aardtspos in Cookhouse, Somerset was criticised for excessive display of authority. Also, Somerset engineered the shipping of 5000 British settlers to the Cape Colony in 1820 in order to create a strong British presence in the face of the relentless efforts of amaXhosa to reoccupy the conquered Zuurveld.

After the humiliating defeat of King Ngqika by Prince Mdushane in the battle of Amalinde in 1818, Somerset attempted to avenge Ngqika's defeat by attacking amaNdlambe. The punitive military action backfired after Prince Ndlambe resorted to relentless armed raids of the Cape Colony which were carried out at night and thus forced the European settlers to abandon their farms. Eventually, his governorship of the Cape Colony ended controversially in 1826, after he was accused of destructive autocracy and the bankruptcy of the Cape Colonial administration which was attributed to his extravagant lifestyle. Unfortunately, two years later he succumbed to stroke. The towns of Somerset West and Somerset East were named after him. In 2023 Somerset East was renamed KwaNojoli. Colonel Henry Somerset was the eldest son of Lord Somerset who fought in the wars of resistance and conquest for over three decades.

Sir Benjamin D'urban (1777-1849) was the first British governor to declare war on amaXhosa on the east of the Nciba/Kei River which resulted in the brutal murder of King Hintsa. The subsequent War of Hintsa (1834-1835) which was fought in the mountains of Mathole resulted the first defeat of the British army by amaXhosa regiments led by the courageous war veteran of the Battle of Amalinde, Prince Maqoma, the eldest son of Prince Ngqika. The governorship of D'urban became a disaster for both the British Empire and the European settlers in the Cape Colony because of the unprecedented far reaching outcomes of the catastrophic War of Hintsa. Both Du'rban and Colonel Harry Smith were fired, Adelaide province between Nxuba/Fish River and Nciba/Kei

River was dissolved, the Boers farmers embarked on a massive exodus called the Great Trek from the Cape colony to the north and the British settlers were left bitter after suffering huge losses and displacement. After he was relieved from his position he was bitter to an extent that he never returned to the United Kingdom, instead he went to Canada and remained there until he died in 1849.

General Sir Peregrine Maitland (1777-1854) the versatile British war veteran faced a situation similar to D'Urban during his governorship of the Cape Colony between 1844 and 1847. He arrived at a time of boiling tensions between amaXhosa and the British colonial establishment because of the armed commandos who conducted ruthless raids confiscating livestock deep in the territories of amaXhosa. Eventually the War of Axe in 1846 –1847 exploded. The determined King Sandile led his courageous regiments of amaXhosa in the calculated execution of what became the worst humiliating defeat of the British army commanded by Major General John Hare. The unexpected outcomes of the war became a disaster for Governor Maitland. He declared a false victory out of desperation. The British settlers were bitter because of the heavy losses they suffered from the war. In 1847, Maitland was dismissed as a Governor. His illustrious military career was shattered beyond recovery. He returned to Great Britain a broken man and later died in 1854.

Maitland was succeeded by a prominent figure in the history of the wars of resistance and conquest General Sir Harry Smith (1786-1860) who governed Cape colony between 1847 and 1852. Smith was a highly gifted and revered war veteran who fought wars in Europe, South Africa and India. He was the commander of the British army during the War of Hintsa (1834-1835). He was posted to India to redeem his military career after he was fired following the defeat by Prince Maqoma in 1835. In India he rose to prominence after the famous victory of the battle of Aliwal in February 1846. In 1847, he return to the Cape Colony as a General. The outbreak of the War of Mlanjeni in December 1850 provided him with an opportunity to face Prince Maqoma for the second time. Prince

Maqoma outsmarted Smith beyond imagination. After a series of unprecedented heavy losses in the battlefield Smith was fired. The shocking dismissal was a shattering disaster which marked the end of his remarkable career in the British colonies.

The deployment of Sir George Grey (1812-1898) in the Cape Colony between 1854 – 1861 marked a paradigm shift in the British method of conquest. Grey was the first civilian governor to be deployed in the volatile Cape colony that has witnessed unprecedented agonising wars. The governorship of Grey was characterised by the strange arrival of the highly lethal and contagious European cattle lung sickness in the Cape colony, the destruction of productive capabilities of amaXhosa which was followed by the catastrophic famine and the euphemism of Nongqawuse. Chapter four explores these matters in detail.

Dutch Governors of the Cape Colony (1652-1795)

1. 1652-1662 : Jan van Riebeeck (1619-1677
2. 1662-1666 : Zacharias Wagener (1614-1668)
3. 1666-1668 : Cornelis van Qualbergen (1623-1686)
4. 1668-1670 : Jacob van Borghorst (c1640-)
5. 1670-1671 : Pieter Hackius (-1671)
6. 1672-1672 : Albert van Breugel (-1686)
7. 1672-1676 : Jsbrand Godske (1626 -)
8. 1676-1678 : Johan Bax van Herenthals (1637-1678)
9. 1678-1679 : Hendrik Crudorp (1646 – 1720)
10. 1679-1699 : Simon van der Stel (1639-1712)
11. 1699-1707 : Willem Adriaan van der Stel (1664-1733)
12. 1707-1708 : Johannes Cornelis d'Ablaing (1663-1721)
13. 1708-1711 : Louis van Assenburg (1660-1711)
14. 1711-1714 : Willem Helot (1675-1749)
15. 1714-1724 : Maurits Pasques de Chavonnes (1654-1724)
16. 1724-1727 : Jan de la Fontaine (1684-1743)
17. 1727-1729 : Pieter Gijsbert Noodt (1681-1729)
18. 1729-1737 : Jan de la Fontaine (1684-1743)
19. 1737-1737 : Adriaan van Kervel (1681-1737)
20. 1737-1739 : Daniel van den Hengel (1699 -)
21. 1739-1750 : Hendrik Swellengrebel (1700-1763)

22. 1751-1771 : Rijk Tulbagh (1699-1771)
23. 1772-1773 : Baron Pieter van Rheede van Oudtshoorn (1714-1773) - was appointed but died en route to the Cape
24. 1773-1785 : Baron Joachim van Plettenberg (1739-1793)
25. 1785-1791 : Cornelis Jacob van de Graaff (1734-1812)
26. 1791-1792 : Johann Isaac Rhenius (1721-1811)
27. 1792-1793 : Sebastiaan Cornelis Nederburgh (1762-1811)
28. 1792-1793 : Simon Hendrik Frijkenius (1747-1797)
29. 1793-1795 : Abraham Josias Sluysken (1736-1799)

First British Cape Colony (1797-1803)

1. 1797-1798 : George Macartney (1737-1806)\
2. 1798-1799 : Francis Dundas (c1759-1824)
3. 1799-1801 : Sir George Yonge (1731-1812)
4. 1801-1803 : Francis Dundas (c1759-1824)

Batavian Republic (Dutch Colony) (1803–1806)

1. 1803-1804 : Jacob Abraham Uitenhage de Mist (1749-1823)
2. 1804-1806 : Jan Willem Janssens (1762-1838)

Second British Occupation of the Cape Colony (1806-1810)

1. 1807-1808 : David Baird (1757-1829)
2. 1808-1808 : Henry George Grey (1766-1845)
3. 1808-1811 : Du Pré Alexander, 2nd Earl of Caledon (1777-1839)
4. 1811-1811 : Henry George Grey (1766-1845)
5. 1811-1814 : John Francis Cradock (1762-1839)
6. 1814-1826 : Lord Charles Somerset 1767-1831)
7. 1820-1821 : Rufane Shaw Donkin (1773-1841)
8. 1826-1828 : Richard Bourke (1777-1855)
9. 1828-1833 : Galbraith Lowry Cole (1772-1842)
10. 1833-1834 : Thomas Francis Wade (-1846)
11. 1834-1838 : Sir Benjamin d'Urban (1777-1849)
12. 1838-1844 : George Thomas Napier (1784-1855)
13. 1844-1847 : Peregrine Maitland (1777-1854)

14. 1847-1847 : Henry Pottinger (1789-1856)
15. 1847-1852 : Sir Harry Smith (1786-1860)
16. 1852-1854 : George Cathcart (1794-1854)
17. 1854-1854 : Charles Henry Darling (1809-1870)
18. 1854-1861 : George Grey (1812-1898)
19. 1859-1862 : Robert Henry Wynyard (1802-1864)
20. 1862-1870 : Philip Edmond Wodehouse (1811-1887)
21. 1870-1870 : Charles Craufurd Hay (1809-1873)
22. 1870-1877 : Sir Henry Barkly (1815-1898)
23. 1877-1880 : Henry Bartle Frere (1815-1884)
24. 1880-1880 : Henry Hugh Clifford (1826-1883)
25. 1880-1881 : George Cumine Strahan (1837-1887)
26. 1881-1889 : Hercules Robinson (1824-1897)
27. 1881-1884 : Leicester Smyth (1829-1891)
28. 1889-1889 : Henry Augustus Smyth (1825-1906)
29. 1889-1895 : Henry Brougham Loch (1827-1900)
30. 1891-1894 : Sir William Gordon Cameron (1827-1913)
31. 1895-1897 : Hercules Robinson (1824-1897)
32. 1897-1897 : William Howley Goodenough (1833-1898)
33. 1897-1901 : Alfred Milner (1854-1925)
34. 1898-1899 : William Francis Butler (1838-1910)
35. 1901-1909 : Walter Hely-Hutchinson (1849-1913)
36. 1909-1910 : Henry Jenner Scobell (1859-1912)

References: Governors of the Cape Colony (geni.com)

Names of Towns and Rivers in the Context of the Events Described in the Book

At the time of the historical events described in this book, not all place names had been established. Certain towns and forts had not yet been established. In certain cases they had only recently been built. This book uses applicable African names and colonial names in existence at that time. The following table indicates both African and colonial names of such places.

Names of Towns

African Names	European Names
1. Cawa	Port Alfred
2. Cumakala	Sutterheim
3. Dikeni	Alice
4. Gcuwa	Butterworth
5. Gqeberha	Port Elizabeth
6. Gompo	East London
7. KwaMaqoma	Fort Beaufort
8. Kariega	Uitenhage
9. Khobonqaba	Adelaide
10. Komani	Queenstown
11. Ngqushwa	Peddie
12. Ntabozuko	Berlin
13. Makhanda	Grahamstown
14. Mkhubiso	Burnshill
15. Mnyameni	Alexandria
16. Qamdobowa	Graaff-Reinet

African Names	European Names
17. Qoboqobo	Keiskammahoek
18. Qonce	King Willim's Town
19. Xhorha	Alicedale
20. Xesi	Middledrift
21. Nyarha	Bedford

Names of Rivers

African Names	European Names
1. Qhagqiwa	Swartkops River
2. Gqili	Orange River
3. Nciba	Kei River
4. Nxuba	Fish River
5. Xelexwa	Gamtoos River
5. Nukakamma	Sundays River
6. Tsholomnqa	Chalumna River

Additional Information: Prof Ncedile Saule's oral knowledge

Chapter One

Defining Disposition of Southern Nations

"The men...were the finest figures I ever beheld: they were tall, robust, and muscular... the good nature that overspread their features, showed them at once to be equally unconscious of fear, suspicion, and treachery. A young man of about twenty... was one of the finest figures that perhaps was ever created. He was a perfect Hercules" (Barrow, 1801: 160).

1. The Forgotten History of San and Khoe

One cannot write about the Nations of Southern Africa without first acknowledging the existence, the plight and the lost history of the San and Khoe people. In as much as this book is centred on the amaXhosa-led and the British-led wars in the triangle between Gqeberha, Graaff-Reinet and Gcuwa, it is crucial to first provide a brief account of what occurred in the Cape during the first two centuries between the earliest African indigenous inhabitants and the European settlers. One moves from the premise that such a brief historical account is necessary in order to locate the essence of the earliest documented foundations of our history in the context of African wars of resistance and European conquest.

Dekker (2016) argues there is still no consensus on which appropriate name to apply to the African people who were called Hottentots and Bushmen by the Europeans after landing on the southern shores of the African continent. Patric Tariq Mellet, in his book *The Lie of 1652* published in 2020, laments the loss of land, loss of identity and the state of nothingness of the San and Khoe people. He asserts that the de-Africanisation of the San and Khoe people and their enforced assimilation into a colonially-constructed Coloured identity was tantamount to the worst cultural genocide. According to him, the earliest known major groups of people in Southern Africa were comprised of the San, Nama, Korana, Griqua, Kalanga and Cape Khoe. He noted concerns to the usage of the KhoeSan collective categorisation on the basis that the Khoe collaborated with the Dutch (later called the Boers) in the systematic extermination of the San in the eighteenth and nineteenth century. Therefore, splitting the collective definition to the San and Khoe is seen as an appropriate definition.

The San and Khoe people deserve their rightful place as the earliest indigenous people of Southern Africa. Hopefully, more archaeological work will provide additional insight into the pre-colonial history of the San and Khoe. The Dutch-led systematic extermination of the San and Khoe over a period of two centuries remains one of the darkest chapters of South African history. These African indigenous populations, with rich unique culture and vast unknown pre-colonial history, were wiped out from the face of the earth in pursuance of conquest. They left with rich stories of what life was like in Southern Africa during the pre-colonial period, what languages they spoke at the time, how they co-existed with others in a beautiful ecosystem, and the dominant features of their culture. There are probably vast forms of knowledge that they possessed, which may never be recovered again. The current generation has a responsibility and an obligation to recover any traces of that forgotten tragic history which is part of our rich heritage in one way or another.

The written accounts of the lives and the times of the San and Khoe people in the pre-colonial period are largely based on the observations made about them by those who were able to document and archive their encounters. Based on such literature, we may not be able to establish with absolute certainty who they were, what it was like to come into contact with Europeans, and how some of them survived the centuries of systematic extermination. Hopefully in future, archaeological work may provide answers to some of these questions.

Following the first British conquest of the Cape Colony in 1795, Sir John Barrow undertook an expedition into the Cape interior between 1797 and 1798. The purpose of the expedition was to explore and to identify threats and opportunities that the British Empire might encounter in the region. Barrow conducted a great deal of historical work and provided a vivid portrayal of the geographical, biological, anthropological and sociological nature of the Cape at the time.

Amongst other things, Sir John Barrow documented what we may define as the disposition and physical features of the remaining Khoe, who were almost extinct at the time. According to Barrow, *"They are mild, quiet, and timid people, perfectly harmless, honest, and faithful and though extremely phlegmatic, they are kind and affectionate to each other and not incapable of strong attachments. A Hottentot would share his last morsel with his companions"* (Barrow, 1801: 143). Probably it was because of the noble qualities they possessed that they were vulnerable to Dutch extermination.

Barrow goes further to say that the Khoe were extremely loyal to their superiors and had the ability to endure pain. He defined them as extremely lazy people who could only be awakened by terror, yet he recognised that they were excellent marksmen and valuable people in warfare. They possessed incredible observation skills, which were useful in mastering their environment. During the time of the expedition, Barrow estimated that there were about 15 000 Khoe people remaining in the Cape Colony.

A series of wars occurred first between the Dutch and the San and Khoe people. There was the First Dutch-Khoe War of 1659 to 1660, followed by the Dutch-Khoe War of 1673 to 1677, which resulted in the defeat of the large Cochoqua group in the Saldanha Bay and Boland areas. As the Dutch expanded their territories through conquest of the land, they confiscated the livestock and killed the game in order to the drive the San and Khoe people to almost total extinction. The brutality of the armed mobile commandos led to the total annihilation of the entire population of Sneeuberg San (Landau, 2010).

The successive Dutch colonial authorities continuously implemented the systematic extermination of the indigenous people in order to clear the land for European settlers. The well-armed and agile commandos were established for the purpose of carrying out mass killings of the San and Khoe both on the coast and the hinterland during different periods. They would shoot the indigenous people on sight without any form of accountability for their inhuman actions. According to Mostert (1992), the Dutch East India Company financed and supported the brutality of the commandos, whose main objective was to kill the indigenous people at every available opportunity because they were perceived as an obstacle and liability that had to be eliminated.

Towards the end of the eighteenth century and the beginning of the nineteenth, the institutionalised well-armed commandos intensified the systematic extermination of the thousands of the San people. The acceleration of the systematic genocide of the San people was triggered by the rapid expansion of the Dutch settlers along the coast and to the interior in search of the rich grazing land and the ambition to occupy and own land. The San people were perceived as the immediate threat and obstacles to the expansion of the Dutch settlements, hence they had to be exterminated.

As the Dutch continued with their pillaging from the coast to the hinterland, the survivors resorted to guerrilla warfare in an attempt to fight for their existence. As the numbers of San dwindled, their resistance weakened and the Dutch settlers gained the upper hand in engagements because they had access to better weapons and greater mobility. From time to time, women and children were spared in order to groom them for slavery, whilst large-scale genocide continued unabated throughout the eighteenth and nineteenth centuries. For instance, *"In 1774 a grand commando of 100 Europeans and 150 Khoi swept the area, killing 503 Bushmen and capturing 241. Between 1786 and 1795 there was an almost constant state of warfare in the northeast, and commandos killed 2,480 Bushmen and captured 654...*" (Stapleton, 2010: 15-16). Meintjes (1971) acknowledged that the white settlers found it difficult to recognise the San as human beings as they viewed them as a constant threat to their livestock.

To a great extent the San engaged in these endless fights for survival from a position of weakness, because they did not possess iron weapons to withstand the Dutch firepower, especially in open terrain. In 1775, the Drakenstein military entity was established for the purposes of carrying out intentional systematic extermination of the indigenous inhabitants, in order to clear the land for Dutch farmers in the interior. They were armed and mobile with horses and supplies, both for executing the depopulation process and for confiscating the livestock and children, who were assigned to the white settler farmers to be groomed as slaves. All that the earliest indigenous people of Southern Africa were able to execute were hit-and-run guerrilla tactics whose success depended on the terrain.

In the process, the San lost the battle for survival, because they lost their land and livestock. The vanquished were compelled to live an unbearable life, surviving on roots, wild fruits and hunting. They lost the collective ability to fight, as they were pursued by the commandos from a position of strength. San people perished, along with authentic accounts of their own history in the pre-colonial period as well as their language and culture.

The Khoe people, who were complicit in the extermination of the San people, were later subjected to genocide and various forms of dehumanization and slavery. Towards the end of the 1700s, systematic extermination of the Khoe was almost complete as the Dutch pursued total conquest of the southern Cape Colony. According to Omer-Cooper, *"When Governor Van Plettenberg made his tour of the frontier districts in 1778 the Khoikhoi had been practically wiped out as an independent group in the eastern frontier areas"* (Omer–Cooper, 1987: 29). Although Omer-Cooper talks about Khoe here, this is actually in reference to the San who were the victims of the Dutch-led commandos of extermination supported by the Khoe. While the Khoe were collaborators in conquest in most cases, eventually their populations were not spared either.

Besides the constant state of war for survival, the Khoe were subjected to the tragedy of an imported biological weapon of mass destruction, in the form of smallpox which reduced their populations significantly. *"Additionally, imported smallpox sharply reduced the San and Khoe population such as during the epidemic of 1713"* (Stapleton, 2010: 16). It is not surprising that in the aftermath of the devastating and agonizing war of Mlanjeni between amaXhosa and the British from 1850 to 1853, there was an outbreak of lung sickness from Europe which decimated the productive capability of amaXhosa. The European conquest of Southern Africa had to be attained at all costs. This is outlined in chapters three and four of this book.

Dutch settlers treated the colonised Khoe survivors as the wretched of the earth. Although in the pre-colonial era they lived as pastoralists, the survivors of the decades of systematic genocide were forced into hunting and eating wild fruits and roots. Later on the children were groomed into a life of slavery from an early age. According to Barrow, *"Hottentots living with the farmers of Graaff-Reinet in a state of bondage...a depressed melancholy and deep gloom constantly overspread his countenance"* (Barrow, 1801: 140). The remaining displaced and dispossessed Khoe survivors of the Dutch systematic genocide were subjected to unbearable forms of dehumanization. They were treated as sub-human.

In retrospect, the San and Khoe who survived the decades of systematic annihilation were subjected to a permanent state of ruthless slavery. In the process, they were broken down psychologically in order to destroy the will to ever think of fighting for their freedom or even dare to challenge the Europeans. When the Europeans later engaged amaXhosa in the wars of resistance, the Khoe were trained marksmen who were often placed in the frontline of the wars because their lives were perceived to be inferior to those of the Europeans.

In the process, they established themselves as vital military assets in warfare because they proved to be sharpshooters and well suited to fight in the difficult terrain of thick bushes, dangerous gorges and impenetrable forests.

The reaction of the Khoe to the wars between amaXhosa and Europeans was largely determined by their quest to survive by making use of their capabilities and familiarity with the territory as they continued to switch sides. In the war of 1811–1812 they were on the side of the British against amaXhosa. Four decades later they switched their allegiance to amaXhosa during the War of Mlanjeni out of bitterness because the British settlers resented them despite their loyalty and sacrifices they made for the British colony.

What contributed immensely to the success of Colonel Graham's ethnic cleansing of the Zuurveld was the fact that the Khoe regiments were in the forefront of the fighting, whilst the British were mainly responsible for finishing off the survivors. During Graham's execution of the scorched earth policy in the Zuurveld, it was the Khoe who were able to track and locate the secret hiding location of the sickly Prince Chungwa of amaGqunukhwebe, who was butchered on his death-bed. More information is provided on this subject in the following chapter.

Unfortunately, the Khoe's incredible performance in the battlefields, fighting for the interests of the colonialists, as well as their sacrifices neither earned them respect nor freedom. Instead, the white settlers and military personnel resented them and continued to treat them as subjects of an inferior breed. On one hand, they depended on them for farming, wars and security, but on the other hand, they hated their natural disposition of superior capabilities, especially on the battlefield. That was the sort of ambivalent relationship the white settlers had with the Khoe, which in the end characterised the complex and unpredictable relationship of loyalty and resentment between the two groups. The irony of such ambivalence was that the *"Dependence upon the Khoikhoi was so great that they were always overworked by everyone and on the assumption that they minded less than anyone else, usually given the meanest treatment"* (Mostert, 1992: 707). They continued serving as fighting machines until most of them revolted and sided with Prince Maqoma in the War of Mlanjeni from 1850 to1853. The contribution of the Khoe in that war was extremely valuable as it turned out to be the longest and deadliest war ever fought between Africans and the Europeans in Southern Africa in the nineteenth century. This war is explored in further detail in chapter three.

2. Adaptation of AmaXhosa in the Face of Existential Threat

The discipline of History is such that we learn about people, events and places in the distant past mainly through the artefacts and documented observations made by other people and structural remnants of the time. Most of what we know about amaXhosa in the historical context of Southern Africa is through oral history that has been passed from one generation to another as well as the documented accounts.

In the first quarter of the twentieth-century, John Henderson Soga, the son of the legendary Reverend Tiyo Soga, published a book *The South Eastern Bantu (AbeNguni, AbaMbo, AmaLala)* which continues to stand out as a valuable contribution to the history of Southern Nations. Professor Jeff Peires is one of the historians in the latter part of the twentieth century to have researched and written extensive scholastic works on the documented history of amaXhosa. He made use of both oral history and primary sources in compiling books and journal articles on the subject. One of his books, *The House of Phalo*, provides a detailed history of amaXhosa from the definitive period of the reign of King Phalo. In the last two decades of the twentieth century, Noel Mostert spent about ten years researching the same subject and produced an incredibly vast volume of work of 1350 pages called *The Frontiers: The epic of South Africa's creation and the tragedy of the Xhosa People.* During the same period, the Canadian historian Professor Tim Stapleton conducted extensive research and published books such as *Maqoma: the Legend of a Great Xhosa Warrior,* describing the unique role of Prince Maqoma in the Cape wars of resistance, and providing an overview of South African military history. By and large the type of work produced by these thinkers provided a solid point of departure in the development of a better understanding and critical analysis of the complex history and nuances of the wars of resistance.

Coincidentally, Professor Stapleton was one of our highly-thought-of history lecturer at the University of Fort Hare during my undergraduate studies. Also, he became one of the referees who wrote a moving commendation letter as part of my application for the Fulbright Scholarship to study for a Master's degree at the University of Oklahoma in the United States of America.

AmaXhosa fall under the category of the Bantu[1] ethnic group of Southern Africa who were found in the central-southern parts of the country in the last four centuries, whose language is the second most widely spoken in the country (Yani, 2018). Mostert (1992) reported that the fragments of pottery discovered by the archaeologists on the mouth of the Tsholomnqa[2] River in East London provided traces of the existence of Bantu people in the region as early as the seventh century.

At the height of the wars of resistance in the face of European encroachment in Southern Africa, amaXhosa were surrounded by other autonomous kingdoms such as abaThembu and amaMpondo. During some of the wars of resistance the neighbouring kingdoms provided strategic

---

1   Bantu people are comprised of various large ethnic groups such as Nguni (South Africa) Hutu (Rwanda & Burundi), Shona (Zimbabwe), Luba (Democratic Republic of Congo), Sukuma (Tanzania) and Kikuyu (Kenya) with distinct languages. They are originally from West and Central Africa and some of them migrated to Southern Africa about 5 000 years ago. Bantu ethnic groups occupy 24 countries in the Central, Southeast and Southern Africa. (Patin. et al, 2017).

2   The earliest written history of the Eastern Cape refers to this river as Chulumna which is a reflection of the European pronunciation of Tsholomnqa. The 78 kilometres long river runs from the hinterland to the Indian Ocean.

support and at times participated directly in the wars, especially in cases where their interests were affected. For instance, Prince Mapasa of abaThembu was one of the key allies of King Sandile during the War of Mlanjeni from 1850 to 1853. He was instrumental in mobilizing attacks from the northern side as far as Komani (Queenstown).

Nowadays there is a general assumption among the South African people that the African people in the Eastern Cape are all amaXhosa because of the closely intertwined relationships, to a point where such differences have become less dominant. Most importantly, the perception was largely influenced by the fact that the dominant spoken language in the Eastern Cape Province is isiXhosa. In the context of the current demographics, it is no longer possible to distinguish between amaXhosa, abaThembu, amaMpondo, amaMpondomise, amaBhaca, amaHlubi and amaMfengu from a distance and in physical appearance because of the intertwined and fluid nature of the relationships and the fact that, to a great extent, the groups are no longer confined to their compartmentalized designated locations. For that matter, most of them are either direct descendant or have blood connections linking them to the family of the Bantu people. Also, there has been close interaction and intermarriages between the various ethnic groups in the Eastern Cape. One of the ways one may trace the existence of the ethnic groups is through the clan names, whose usage and cultural attachment is still very strong and vibrant.

King Mnguni had three sons Xhosa, Zulu and Swazi (Soga 1930 & Phillipson, 1976). Then Xhosa had a son called Malangana who was succeeded by his designated heir to the throne named Nkosiyamntu. Nkosiyamntu had four sons, Cirha, Tshawe, Jwarha and Qwambe. Although Cirha was supposed to be the king as the eldest son, he was overthrown by Tshawe. Eventually, Tshawe became the King of amaXhosa.

Table 1.1 provides a brief account of the genealogy of amaXhosa as well as amaRharhabe, the extended Kingdom of amaXhosa[3], which was in the forefront of British encroachment in Southern Africa. The Kingdom of amaXhosa split into two after Gcaleka and Rharhabe, the powerful sons of King Phalo, fought in the contestation of power. Rharhabe, with the support of his father, left together with his followers and crossed the Nciba (Kei) River. Rharhabe became the founder of the extended Kingdom of amaXhosa, which was established between the Nciba River and Nukakamma (Sundays) River. Later on, the descendants of Prince Rharhabe such as Ndlambe, Maqoma, Tyhali, Xhoxho and Sandile found themselves in an unfortunate situation, having to lead the wars of resistance because of their geographical proximity to the European settlers.

According to Soga, (1930) King Sandile attained manhood in 1840 and was installed as the King of amaRharhabe in 1841. Soga defined him as a leader with an unreliable mind. He would make a decision and then later change his mind. He died in brutal encounter with British soldiers and amaMfengu in the forests of KwaZidenge during the War of Ngcayechibi between 1877 and 1879. Contrary to Soga's portrayal of Sandile, in the following chapter of this book, we see him as a courageous military strategist who decimated the British troops in the wars of 1846 to 1847 and 1850 to 1853.

When amaXhosa came into contact with the European settlers such as the military officers, the missionaries, the traders and the colonial administrators, it was an uneasy encounter because of the fundamental cultural differences, the clash of divergent political interests and the different value systems in the conduct of wars and governance. In the process of time, the growing tensions and the contestation for the sphere of influence eventually exploded into longest military confrontations.

---

3   AmaRharhabe are the extended Kingdom of amaXhosa that was established by Prince Rharhabe with the support of his father King Phalo. The amaRharhabe and the first Kingdom of amaXhosa cooperated greately during the wars of resistance.

Table 1.1:   Genealogy of the Kingdom of AmaXhosa

Genealogy of the Kingdom of AmaXhosa	AmaRharhabe the Extended Kingdom of AmaXhosa
1. King Ntu 2. King Nguni 3. King Xhosa 4. King Malangana 5. King Nkosiyamntu *Sons of Nkosiyamntu in the order of their seniority* *5.1 Prince Cirha* *5.2 Prince Tshawe* *5.3 Prince Jwarha* *5.4 Prince Qwambe* *(Tshawe displaced Cirha the Heir to the throne)* 6. King Tshawe departed in 1715 7. King Ngcwangu 8. King Sikhomo 9. King Togu *9.1 Prince Ngconde* *9.2 Prince Khetshe* *9.3 Prince Ntinde* 10. King Ngconde *10.1 Prince Tshiwo* *10.2 Prince Mdange* *10.3 Prince Hleke* 11. King Tshiwo 1670 – 1702 *11.1 Prince Phalo* *11.2 Prince Gwali* 12. King Phalo 1702 –1775 *12.1 Prince Gcaleka departed in 1778* *12.2 Prince Rharhabe departed in 1782* *12.3 Prince Tiso* *12.4 Langa departed in 1793* *(Prince Rharhabe established the second Kingdom between Kei and Sundays River supported by Phalo)*	1. Prince Rharhabe 1722–1782 *1.1 Prince Mlawu departed in 1782* *1.2 Prince Ndlambe departed in 1828* *1.3 Prince Nukwa* *1.4 Prince Cebo* *1.5 Princess Ntsusa* *1.6 Princess Khinzela* *1.7 Prince Mnyaluza* *1.8 Prince Nzwane* *1.9 Prince Sigcawu* *1.10 Prince Hlahla* *1.11 Prince Siko* 2. Prince Mlawu *2.1 Prince Ntimbo* *2.2 Prince Ngqika* *Ngqika displaced Ntimbo propelled by his mother Yese with the assistance of Ndlambe. Ngqika was later declared the royal head of the second Kingdom of amaXhosa named after Rharhabe* 3. King Ngqika 1778 –1829 *3.1 King Sandile 1821 –1878* *3.2 Prince Maqoma: 1798–1873* *3.3 Prince Tyhali: departed in 1842* *3.4 Prince Anta: 1810 –1878* *3.5 Prince Matwa 1810–1847* *3.6 Prince Xhoxho: 1815 –1878* *3.7 Prince Tente departed in 1842* *Maqoma, born from first wife, was older than* *Sandile the designated heir by birth* 4. King Sandile 1821 –1878 *4.1 King Sigonyela* *4.2 Prince Mathanzima*

Genealogy of the Kingdom of AmaXhosa	AmaRharhabe the Extended Kingdom of AmaXhosa
13. King Gcaleka 1728 – 1778 14. King Khawuta 1761 – 1804 15. King Hintsa 1789 -1835 16. King Sarhili 1810 – 1892 17. King Sigcawu d. 1902 18. King Gwebi'nkumbi d. 1921 19. King Zwelidumile 1906 -1965 20. King Xolilizwe 1926 -2005 21. King Mpendulo Sigcawu 1968 – 2019	5. King Sigonyela 6. King Velile Sandile 7. King Mxolisi Sandile 8. King Maxhoba Sandile 1956 - 2011 9. King Jonguxolo Sandile 1992 – *(In May 2021, King Jonguxolo Sandile Aa! Vul'ulwandle was officially recognized by President Cyril Ramaphosa of the Republic of South Africa as the King of AmaRharhabe, after a protracted court process that contested the downgrading of the status of the Kingdom of amaRharhabe by the Nhlapho Commission. In June 2021, King Jonguxolo was officially installed as the monarch of amaRharhabe.)*

Sources: Soga, 1930; Peires, 1981 & Wilson, 1982

Mostert (1992) observed that amaXhosa found themselves in an unfortunate situation, having to endure the most unbearable burden of waging the longest wars of resistance against an advanced and formidable enemy. Both groups had to adapt quickly to each other's different ways of conducting warfare in order to protect their interest and to survive the process of contact.

On one hand, the European manner of conducting war with Africans at the time was largely influenced by a posture of racial superiority, perceiving the latter as savages not worthy to co-exist with. The Europeans would often resort to total annihilation during wars in pursuit of land and livestock. The first military confrontation between amaXhosa and the British in the war of 1811 and 1812 was conducted with brutality and with the intention of exterminating amaXhosa. This happened after John Francis Cradock, the British Governor of the Cape Colony, instructed Colonel John Graham to expel amaXhosa from what was known as the Zuurveld region between

Xelexwa (Gamtoos) River and Nxuba (Fish) River. The policy of expulsion was implemented through the first British scorched earth policy in Southern Africa in the form of ethnic cleansing of the African people from the Zuurveld.

On the other hand, to amaXhosa, the purpose of warfare was to attain domination and absorb the defeated enemy in order to make the nation stronger. Peires (1981) noted that after the tragic death of King Tshiwo in 1715, his brother Mdange clashed with Gwali, the eldest son of Tshiwo in order to protect the young Phalo, who was the designated heir to the throne of amaXhosa. Gwali fled and took refuge in the Kingdom of Hinsati of the Inqua Khoe nation. Prince Mdange pursued him, fought and defeated Hinsati. After the defeat, the Khoe nation of Inqua people comprised mainly of ooSukwini, amaGqwashu and amaNqarhwane were never exterminated. They were absorbed and integrated into amaXhosa. Later in this section the incident will be revisited in the context of nation-building.

The British ethnic cleansing of the Zuurveld was a shattering encounter for amaXhosa, an unimaginable phenomenon alien to the established traditions of conducting warfare in Southern Africa. To their shock, the British army did not spare the sacred lives of children, women, elderly people and royal leaders. In the aftermath of the war, amaXhosa realized that if they did not adapt, they were likely to be exterminated from the face of the earth.

Peires (1976) captured the impression that amaXhosa had of the European quite well in his outstanding research work. *"The Xhosa knew that the whites despised them and they resented it. They acknowledged that European technology was superior to their own, but felt that as individuals they were equal to any Colonist they had met"* (pg 210). The ability of amaXhosa to adapt was demonstrated by the manner in which they executed their attacks in the subsequent encounters, especially the wars of 1834 to 1835, 1846 to 1847 and 1850 to 1853. The ultimate attainment of adaptability of amaXhosa against deadly British firepower was what made the difference in the wars. The wars became longer and more intensive as the British-led armies incurred higher numbers of casualties from the targeted lethal ambushes launched by combatants of amaXhosa placed in strategic areas. The use of montane forests as fortresses proved to be a masterstroke as amaXhosa were able to engage in protracted wars and thus neutralise the impact of the advancing colonial military machinery.

AmaXhosa discovered in pre-colonial times that the policy of defeat and integration was a vital one, centred on the realization that strength in numbers was a critical component of survival as a nation during the era of unpredictable wars. Also, the continued tradition of strengthening diplomatic partnerships through the institutionalization of intermarriages with neighbouring powerful kingdoms was a policy meant to establish strategic allies in the event of wars. They were not oblivious to the constant threats and possibilities of total subjugation as a nation. The systematic extermination of the San and Khoe, the fall and the disintegration of other nations such as amaNgwane of Matiwane and amaHlubi of Mpangazitha in the midst of wars was a constant reminder that survival as a nation was always a priority.

They had grave concerns about the continued foreign encroachment linked to the permanent presence of British settlers in Southern Africa. They were deeply concerned about the constant existential threat. Such concerns compelled the royal leaders and military brass to dig deep in their strategies of survival on how to repel the invading enemy. The unprecedented and continued humiliation of the royal leaders of amaXhosa in the presence of their subjects by the likes of General Harry Smith after his second return to the Cape Colony compelled the royal leaders such as Prince Maqoma to prepare for war by reaching out to potential allies. Consequently, in the War of Mlanjeni of 1850 to1853, amaXhosa were able to sustain the brutal encounter to withstand the intensity of the British firepower with the assistance and the significant contribution of abaThembu and the Khoe people.

In the process of time the British settlers resented the enduring ability of amaXhosa to mobilise other African groups and to sustain intense and highly lethal military engagement. It dawned on the colonial establishment that the united African nations had the ability to withstand the impact of superior British firepower. As the devastating wars of resistance intensified, bitterness and distrust between Africans and Europeans deepened. A red line of 'us and them' was drawn in the sand and became rooted in shaping the history of South Africa from the nineteenth to the twentieth century, as a clear distinction emerged between the indigenous Africans versus foreign Europeans, the legitimate defenders of the ancestral land and the hungry landless invaders.

It was during such trying times that amaXhosa went out to rebuild broken relationships with their neighbouring African kingdoms, which were centred on the African philosophy of *Ubuntu* which means a person is a person because of other persons and nations can fight today but tomorrow there is still room for healing, peace and co-existence based on mutual respect. However, in the case of the highly contested contacts with the European settlers, the rules of engagement had to be altered. AmaXhosa realized that Europeans had no interest in building any kind of reasonable relationships with them and African people in general. Their intentions were clear; they were in Africa to attain total domination in order to access the land, the livestock and other resources of the continent. The unpleasant reality crystallised the realization that the rules of engagement between indigenous Africans and European settlers were going to be dictated by the vicious military confrontations on the battlefield, which, in the long term, would demarcate a clear line between the landowner and slaves, and whose future generations would be prosperous and thus shape the fate of the defeated ones.

To amaXhosa, gaining leverage, respect and ascendancy on the battlefield became the defining objective in shaping the interactions with the British colonial establishment. It became clear to them that they would either survive or perish as a nation based on the outcomes of military confrontation in the battleground. Peires (1981) observed that *"The Xhosa through their long exposure to European methods of making war learned how to face firearms and how to use them to the best advantage. They adopted tactics which neutralised the massive technological superiority of their opponents... (160)."* At the time, amaXhosa had courageous leaders who marshalled their people, engaged in discreet building of alliances, executed highly sophisticated strategies and were able to sustain protracted wars in order to neutralise the enemy.

The calibre of the leaders of amaXhosa in the forefront of the wars was incredible. They had the unshakable interests of their people at heart, immense resolve and the willingness to suffer unbearable pain and even face death because they believed that true leadership embodied selflessness, fearlessness, great courage and vision. They refused to buckle in the face of the mighty British Empire and its superior weaponry.

Hence Peires (1981) noted that, *"The age of resistance was also the heroic age of the Chiefs. Ndlambe, Chungwa, Hintsa, Sarhili, Maqoma, Tyhali and Sandile may have had their faults, but they did not sell out. They stood up for their people and deserve a salute (164)."* Later in this book we shall read how Prince Chungwa was butchered on his sick-bed whilst resisting ethnic cleansing in Zuurveld; how King Hintsa made himself a sacrificial lamb by facing a gruesome death in the jaws of the British army in order to save his people; how Prince Maqoma died a lonely and miserable death on Robben Island fighting for his people; and how King Sandile was humiliated and killed during the War of Ngcayechibi.

When Sir Benjamin D'Urban amassed a colossal British army and crossed the Kei River for the first time to invade King Hintsa's Kingdom, the king demonstrated extraordinary resolve. Since this was unprovoked aggression, King Hintsa knew that the British army came to pillage his kingdom. The qualities of adaptability, self-sacrifice and fearlessness came into play again. King Hintsa willingly entered the British camp and allowed himself to be made a prisoner whilst he was buying time, sending secret messages to his people to remove and hide the cattle as far they could from the possible reach of the British army. He was prepared to die in order to save his nation.

It is not surprising therefore that a few decades later the region witnessed the emergence of highly courageous leaders of the liberation struggle such as Mangaliso Robert Sobukwe (1924-1978), Nomzamo Winnie Madikizela Mandela (1936-2018), Mlungisi Griffiths Mxenge (1935-1981), Nonyamezelo Victoria Mxenge (1942-1985), Thembisile Chris Hani (1942-1993), Bantu Stephen Biko (1946-1977), Matthew Goniwe (1947-1985), Sicelo Mhlauli (1949-1985), Sparrow Mkhonto (1951-1985), Fort Calata (1956-1957), and many others, who were subjected to unbearable sufferings and gruesome deaths. They stood for their conviction to liberate their people from the shackles of bondage that were perpetuated by the descendants of the European settlers in South Africa.

In comparative terms, the immense resistance of amaXhosa in the face of the ferocious firepower of the resolute British military establishment, stood out as one of the most extraordinary acts of courage in the history of Southern Africa and Africa. *"The century-long stalemate between amaXhosa and colonists was markedly different to any other confrontation between whites and blacks in South Africa. The only comparable largescale hostilities were the wars between the British and the Zulu, but those came when much of South Africa had already been opened up, and they did not have the tremendous long-term social and political impact of the Xhosa wars"* (Mostert, 1992: 228). It was the geographical proximity of amaXhosa to the point of highly contested contact with the advancing Europeans that led to them finding themselves having to endure the brunt of the foreign encroachment. They used their productive capabilities and the montane forests as fortresses of resistance in the neutralisation of the British firepower.

During the raging wars of resistance and conquest, amaXhosa did not only adapt their military strategies, but also assumed a particular kind of resolute psychological repositioning in the manner in which they perceived and engaged with the Europeans. Reverend John Campbell, a European missionary of Scottish origin, who was based in Cape Colony between 1812 and 1815 made interesting observations about how amaXhosa perceived the Europeans. According to him, amaXhosa maintained a strong combative disposition of self-assurance in their encounters with Europeans. As a missionary who probably managed to cultivate close relationships with the locals, he noticed that amaXhosa viewed themselves as superior to the Europeans whom they perceived as having feeble bodies and being less gifted compared to them.

Mostert (1992) also noted that, *"the Xhosa were unusually sharp and astute judges of human nature. White men were constantly confounded by their swift, embarrassing and invariably accurate assessment of personality. They themselves were masters of the expressionless response, as they were artfully serving the white man with the sort of reaction that they saw he or the situation was in need* (Mostert, 1992:765). In essence, the ability to maintain a posture of cognitive superiority to the Europeans, quick adaptability of military strategies and unparalleled resolve to resist the encroachment were some of the fundamental pillars they exhibited in order to survive as a nation.

From the continued acrimonious engagements with the Europeans, amaXhosa emerged more determined to use every available resource to resist the encroachment as evidenced in the ferocious war of Mlanjeni. *"Upon them fell the brunt of the experience of contact, violent and otherwise, with the outside world. It changed them forever and set them quite apart in experience and outlook from most of the others, except those few chiefdoms closely associated with them* (Mostert, 1992: 185)." The nature of the deadly contact compelled them to adopt a different type of mental strength, a hardened disposition and great resolve of willingness to face death. Amongst other things, they learnt to hide their true emotions and inner vulnerabilities, not to overreact to every provocation and to decide when to strike and to do so decisively. Such observations are made by Mostert (1992) as well, saying, *"The Xhosa were a shrewd and observant people and astutely equivocal when they did not fully understand a situation"* (pg 274). The royal leaders of amaXhosa deceived General Harry Smith by playing along to his antagonistic and abrasive posture when he was the British Governor of the Cape Colony between 1847 and 1852. They endured Smith's humiliation and gave him the impression that they had completely surrendered to him. At an opportune time, they avenged the humiliation, as demonstrated by the bloody viciousness, the incredible intensity and the deadly nature of the War of Mlanjeni.

Royal leaders such as Ndlambe, Maqoma, Sandile and Tyhali, the descendants of Rharhabe, played a fundamental role in the manner in which they adapted their military strategies by inflicting lethal attacks on the advancing enemy. Their astute military tactics and versatile execution of counter attacks successfully outsmarted the superior technological military machinery of the British military establishment. They stood out as the greatest masters in the art of bush warfare against the British forces in the mountains with thick bushes because of their ability in reading the enemy military tactics and strategic decisions on how and where to launch ambushes. Chapter Three on the War of Mlanjeni will show how at the right time amaXhosa leaders subjected General Harry Smith to a humiliating military defeat which marked an abrupt end to his glittering military career.

The compelling accounts made by Sir John Barrow during his expedition into Southern Africa provided a glimpse of the natural disposition of amaXhosa. *"There is perhaps no nation on earth, taken collectively, that can produce so fine a race of men as 'amaXhosa.' They are tall, stout, muscular, well made, elegant figures...The countenance of a 'Xhosa' is always cheerful; and the whole of his demeanour bespeaks content and peace of mind"* (Barrow, 1801:193-194). Barrow made the observations after his arrival in Qoboqobo (Keiskammahoek), where he was welcomed by King Ngqika , the son of Mlawu who died in a war with his father Rharhabe, the son of King Phalo.

The athletic physical appearance and the natural disposition of the men he came across provided a glimpse of what amaXhosa people looked like about two centuries ago. Inasmuch as Barrow happened to meet only amaXhosa from the branch of the Bantu people, they most probably represented what they looked like over two centuries ago, hence they had the immense endurance to overcome and to survive some of the greatest existential threats known to humankind.

In the mid-1800s, Captain W.R. King (1855), one of the British soldiers who participated in the War of Mlanjeni of 1850 to 1853, made similar observations about his engagements with amaXhosa. In his diary, which was later published as a thesis, King wrote that, *"Undoubtedly one of the finest races... women are universally well made, their symmetry being displayed to the greatest advantage by the most lofty and easy carriage, their teeth are brilliantly white, and moreover they preserve a degree of modesty..." (168)*. Whilst Barrow perfected the description of men, King rose to the challenge in the manner in which he observed and portrayed both the physical description and the natural disposition of amaXhosa women.

These historical accounts of John Barrow in this context offered a breath of fresh air compared to some of the derogatory and depressing narratives that often portrayed Africans as savages by those who had the means to document their encounters at the time. Barrow's detailed and positive accounts were not trapped in racialised narratives of 'us and them' notions of inferiority and superiority dogma. Nor did Barrow felt threatened or made comparisons in relation to the great athletic looks and the extraordinary disposition of this group of African people. He provided honest accounts and inner insight of his expedition, based on what he observed, which in a way helped him to understand the calibre and mannerisms of our African forebears. As a result, from Barrow's work, we are able to get a glimpse of the disposition and the physiological nature of amaXhosa two centuries ago.

Furthermore, Barrow (1801) went further, commenting that the customs of circumcision, disposition and belief in one God led him to believe that the origins of amaXhosa may probably be traced to the Middle East. On a similar note, King (1855) also observed that the peculiar traditions and customs of amaXhosa such as circumcision, patriarchy, polygamy and possession of cattle as source of wealth, suggest that the origins of amaXhosa are likely to be linked to the wandering Ishmaelite tribes of the Middle East.

Similarly, Meintjes (1971) observed that, based on accounts of white settlers, amaXhosa were renowned for their great physical features. *"They had beautiful manners, decorum, delicacy of speech, subtle imagery, poetic leanings and an instinctive comprehension of all the intricacies of human relationships (5-6).* To the Europeans at the time, amaXhosa came across as impenetrable people, difficult to read because of their subtle forms of communication, courageous reactions in the face of tragedy and the extent of their remarkable capabilities to sacrifice for a worthwhile cause.

3. The Solid Bonds that Held them Together

Productive Capabilities, Aristocracy, Integration, and Centre of Familyhood

To amaXhosa, cattle were the source of wealth and survival whose precious milk was the source of nutritious staple food. In times of peace the cattle were seldom slaughtered. If they needed meat they would go on hunting expeditions. In most cases they preferred to live on pumpkins, maize, corn, roots and milk from cows and goats (Barrow, 1801; King, 1855; Mostert, 1992). Mostert (1992) goes deeper to define the symbolic value, the intertwined cherished relationship and the emotional attachment amaXhosa had with their cattle, *"Cattle...were the medium of sacrifice to the ancestral spirits, linking the living with the dead. They represented the future, because they sealed the marriage bond. They represented wealth and stability... The relationship between the Xhosa and their cattle was intimate, emotional, committed and joyous...even in a head of some 500 beasts, a Xhosa could know instantly if one was missing*" (Mostert, 1992: 190). One of the causes of the greatest conflicts between amaXhosa and the Europeans was around the ownership of cattle, which was viewed by the latter as a crucial commercial commodity. Also, the cattle in war-time were the critical source of supply to the fighting men, hence they were able to sustain wars with the Europeans. The outbreak of lung sickness, which decimated about 80% of the cattle of amaXhosa just after the devastating War of Mlanjeni before the Nongqawuse saga, is explored in detail in Chapter Four of this book.

The centrality of cattle in the lives of amaXhosa was significantly intertwined with their culture, identity and nationhood. The followers of Prince Maqoma, the son of King Ngqika, who were based in what is now called Fort Beaufort, were called amaJingqi, after Maqoma's favourite ox. Also, Prince Langa, one of the sons of King Phalo named his people amaMbalu. Mbalu was the legendary ox of Prince Tiso, the older brother of Prince Langa. After the death of Tiso, Langa was installed as the leader of amaMbalu. This demonstrated the central relationship amaXhosa had with their cattle to a point where the entire nation is named after an ox (Soga, 1930).

Mostert (1992) provided an interesting narrative on the importance of milk, not just as food but as an important cultural medium. *"Its consumption provided their daily ritualistic bond between past, present and future. Each evening's milking of the cows and serving of milk from the milk sacks offered ceremonial conclusion to the day, changeless century upon century"* (pg 771). It is fascinating that milk, which may be seen as a basic necessity, had such a special value and strong cultural symbolism to amaXhosa.

Generally amaXhosa attached special value to both the domestic and wild animals around them, which they shared the environment with. They were not just commodities or means of food; there was special cultural value and symbolism attached to some of the animals. For instance, an elephant was a revered animal, equated to royal status. If it was killed, the tail and the tusks were usually handed over to the reigning prince or king. The king or the prince would not participate in the feast of the elephant, as that would be viewed as cannibalism because the royal leader was equated to the elephants. Why the elephant in particular occupied such a powerful space remains an issue for further inquiry. Was it because of its size, unique features or something far deeper than that?

AmaXhosa showed strong commitment to maintaining a solid and united nation centred on the fundamental pillars of reverence for the old and royal leaders, looking after the poor and the vulnerable, maintenance of harmonious social relationships and welcoming of strangers. The values, customs and traditions had a common objective which was to maintain bonds of association, belonging and solidarity. The cultural essence of sharing, loyalty, respect and adherence to the customs and traditions was meant to create a state of normality, nationhood and continuity. Most importantly, the survival of each group was dependent largely on the collective existence as a fundamental feature, by virtue of being an inclusive nation. That is why the kraal, compound and round huts were defining symbols of unity and inclusiveness central to nationhood, survival and continuity.

The royal leaders such as princes, princesses, kings and queens had a special place in the community of amaXhosa. At times they would convey messages through their spokespersons because they were revered. A leopard leather skin was reserved for royal leaders. During wars the lives of the royal aristocrats were spared even if they belonged to the enemy. After Rharhabe was defeated by Gcaleka with the assistance of other groups, he was captured but not killed. King Ngqika did the same after he defeated his uncle Ndlambe. Instead, Prince Ndlambe was placed under close watch in the same village where King Ngqika stayed until he escaped. That is why amaXhosa were shocked by the brutal murder of Prince Chungwa of amaGqunukhwebe and King Hintsa of amaXhosa by the British colonial authorities.

The nature, symbolism and positioning of kingship occupied a far deeper special place which transcended narrow political functions in the establishment of amaXhosa. To them the supreme royal aristocracy was not just the head of a nation but a holistic personification of nationhood and the custodian of customs and traditions. The reigning royal aristocrat stood as the bond which held the nation together whilst it remained the uncontested centre of authority.

The revered institution of kingship was often protected against possible threats to its authority, existence and continuity, hence unnecessary power struggles were often prevented and avoided. This explains why the princess who would bear a future king was married later in life in order to avoid a power struggle between the prince and the king. Unfortunately, for King Phalo, his sons Gcaleka, Rharhabe, Tiso and Langa were highly gifted characters of incredible unique personalities. They did not use their strength for consolidation of the kingdom; instead they pulled in different directions, each determined to exert his power and influence. Yet King Phalo did not manage to wield his authority and influence upon his sons. Unlike King Tshiwo and his brother Prince Mdange who built the kingdom of amaXhosa by integrating the defeated kingdoms of the Khoe, the reign of King Phalo was marked by the split of the kingdom of amaXhosa into two centres of power because of his powerful sons Gcaleka and Rharhabe.

Although Rharhabe (1715–1782) was the eldest son by birth and he was strong, energetic, highly driven and fearless, Gcaleka (1728–1778) was the designated heir to the throne by virtue of his birth from a senior house which was meant to provide the successor to King Phalo. Unfortunately, Gcaleka the son of the Princess of amaMpondo had a challenging sickly childhood experience; hence later in his life he became a devoted diviner healer, probably with the hope of getting healed in the process. Later on, after he ascended to the throne, a complicated scenario arose when he had to perform the dual responsibilities of being a leader and a divine healer who "smelt" witches. Gcaleka and Rharhabe had a contentious relationship, which eventually led to the outbreak of a civil war between them, since each had amassed followers and support of the neighbouring nations. The war became a deadly sword which cut the kingdom into two, since each son had warriors who were prepared to lay down their lives for them.

According to Soga (1930) the war was caused by Gcaleka who wanted to usurp the throne whilst his father King Phalo was still the reigning King of amaXhosa. His favourite son Rharhabe successfully stopped Gcaleka from gaining the throne through the use of force. Rharhabe had immense respect for his father's authority.

Phalo realized that there would never be peace as long as there were two bulls in one kraal. He summoned Rharhabe and assigned a considerable number of people and livestock and thus released him to extend the Kingdom of amaXhosa to the region between the Nciba and Nukakamma/ Sundays Rivers. Since Rharhabe was known for his brilliance, courage and aggression in wars, defeated small tribes between Nciba River and Nxuba River did not pose much of grave challenge to the new kingdom. Soga (1930) reported that King Phalo actually followed his son Rharhabe. In 1775, he died in his original headquarters of Tongwane, no longer ruler of the kingdom.

The decision of Rharhabe to extend the kingdom of amaXhosa on the west of the Nciba River marked the beginning of a new era in the history of amaRharhabe as well as the larger nation of amaXhosa in the context of the wars of resistance (Peires 1981). It brought the amaRharhabe component of amaXhosa to the direct frontline of European encroachment. The defining Cape Colonial wars of resistance between Africans and the Europeans in the nineteenth century were a protracted and brutal contest, mainly between the descendants of Rharhabe and the British colonial establishment. Other nations who were involved were mainly on the periphery of these wars, yet providing much-needed logistical support in order to sustain them.

At the time, the west of Nciba River region was occupied by imi-Dange, amaGwali, amaNtinde, amaGqunukhwebe, amaMbalu, San and the Khoe people before the arrival of Prince Rharhabe. Except for the San and the Khoe people, these small nations were direct branches of amaXhosa led by various princes. ImiDange originated from the leadership of Prince Mdange, the brother of King Tshiwo, who groomed and protected the young Prince Phalo from his elder brother Gwali. AmaGwali come from the lineage of Gwali, the eldest son of King Tshiwo by birth from the Right Hand House. Prince Gwali was defeated and displaced by Prince Mdange after he tried to resist the ascendancy of Phalo to the throne following the tragic death of his father King Tshiwo. AmaNtinde were the descendants of Prince Ntinde, the third son of King Togu.

AmaGqunukhwebe were the people of Prince Khwane whom he kept in a forest after they were accused of witchcraft. They were meant to have been killed, but he chose to save them. In the forest, they intermarried with the San and Khoe people and were later called the nation of amaGqunukhwebe (Soga, 1930). They were established as a nation under Prince Khwane during the reign of King Tshiwo (1670-1702). This was a reward after Khwane with the help of amaGqunukhwebe saved King Tshiwo from the jaws of defeat by amaNgqosini. They settled between Nxuba and Xelexwa Rivers. AmaGqunukhwebe lost their land after the British ethnic cleansing of the Zuurveld in 1811-12. The nation of amaGqunukhwebe is made up of clans such as ooGiqwa, ooSithathu, amaNqarhwane, ooSukwini, ooTshonyane, amaCethe and amaGqwashu (Le Vaillant, 1790) and https://iziduko.wordpress.com.

In reference to the origin of amaMbalu, Soga (1930) stated that after the death of Tiso, Langa was installed as the head of the house of amaMbalu. *"He was an unusually active man, a great hunter of the larger wild animals...a man of restless spirit and unbounded courage"* (Soga, 1930:125). He eventually attracted many followers. His people were named after Tiso's favourite ox called Mbalu, hence they were called amaMbalu. Around 1740, Langa crossed the Nciba River following imiDange, amaGwali, amaNtinde and amaGqunukhwebe.

According to Soga, amaGwali, amaNtinde and amaGqunukhwebe crossed the Nciba River in order to run away from Mdange when he was regent for the young Phalo. After Phalo became the King of amaXhosa, Mdange also crossed the Nciba River with his people in order to give space to the new incumbent to rule the kingdom without interference. All these various groups of amaXhosa settled between Nciba and Xelexwa Rivers.

Rharhabe, the energetic and restless warrior, waged war the moment he arrived in the west of the Nciba River in an attempt to subject the other nations to his authority for purposes of consolidating his kingdom. The kingdom of the San under Queen Hoho was obliterated in the process. As Rharhabe expanded his authority and influence, he defeated the San people and took ownership of the mountains of Hoho, Ntaba kaNdoda and Mathole around 1750. His greatest rivals were amaGqunukhwebe and imiDange (Peires, 1981). Eventually Rharhabe established his kingdom in the area between amaBhele, Cumakala (Stutterheim), Qoboqobo (Keiskammahoek) and Nxuba (Fish) River.

After the death of King Gcaleka from sickness, his son Prince Khawuta took over the reign of the kingdom. Rharhabe attacked and defeated Khawuta and declared himself the supreme ruler of amaXhosa (Peires 1976). The neighbouring kingdoms of amaMpondo and abaThembu were fearful of the unrestricted and powerful Rharhabe. Consequently, they fought Rharhabe and reinstated Khawuta as the king. At the time the base of his kingdom was at amaBhele near Cumakala (Stutterheim) (Peires, 1976: 252). According to Soga (1930) although the tribes of amaGwali, amaNtinde, amaMbalu, imiDange and amaGqunukhwebe resisted the growing influence of Rharhabe, his authority was felt as far as Great Nxuba (Fish) River.

Rharhabe, who was born in 1722, died in 1782 at the age of 60 together with his son Mlawu in the skirmish of Ngxogi in Xuka River with abaThembu of Prince Ndaba (Soga, 1930). Ndaba avenged the displacement he was subjected to by

Rharhabe, who assisted abaThembu of the amaNdungwane branch, the people of his wife, to displace Prince Ndaba. Rharhabe was buried near eMgwali close to Dhone. Soga (1930) defined Rharhabe as being *"a man of public weight, wisdom and superior courage"* (pg 128). At the time of his fall, his surviving children were Ndlambe, Cebo, Nukwa, Ntsusa, Khinzela, Mnyaluza, Nzwane, Sigcawu, Hlahla and Siko. At the time Prince Mlawu died, he was about to marry Nobutho.

After the tragic and untimely death of his father and elder brother Prince Mlawu in 1782, Prince Ndlambe, the second eldest son of Prince Rharhabe and Queen Nojoli of abaThembu, was left with the complex and cumbersome work of consolidating and protecting the newly established Kingdom of amaRharhabe., He took over the reigns of the kingdom as a regent, a position he held for 20 years whilst Prince Ngqika, the son of Queen Yese , was still very young. Ngqika was the preferred heir to the throne over Ntimbo, who unfortunately was a sickly prince from an early age.

Prince Ndlambe had several sons: Mdushane the father of Qasana, who later had a son, called Siyolo, Mhala the father of Makinana and Mqhayi the father of Jali. Ndlambe had other children, Siwani and Nozi, whose descendants have not been traced. Years later, Prince Siyolo played a pivotal role in the war of Mlanjeni and thus successfully blocked the vital British military supply line between Makhanda and Qonce.

Prince Mdushane, the eldest son of Prince Ndlambe, was as formidable and brilliant a warrior as his father. Mdushane rose to prominence as his father was fading due to old age. He maintained a watchful eye on King Ngqika , considering what he did to his father. In the bloody Battle of Amalinde, the forces of King Ngqika led by the young Prince Maqoma and Counsellor Makoyi, suffered a disastrous defeat at the hands of the combined forces of amaNdlambe and amaGcaleka led by Prince Mdushane (Peires, 1976; Mostert, 1992; Stapleton, 2016).

After Mdushane died in May 1829, following his father Ndlambe who departed in February 1828, he was succeeded by his son Qasana. Unfortunately, after the departure of Mdushane the formidable House of Ndlambe disintegrated. Mhala contested control of the eastern region with Dyani and managed to displace him by accusing him of witchcraft. Although Prince Mhala fought in the War of Hintsa between 1834 and 1835, he was neutral in the War of Mlanjeni between 1850 and 1853.

Mqhayi, whose homestead was in the Wesleyan Mission of Mount Coke between Qonce[4] (King William's Town) and East London, was known to be a collaborator with the British colonial establishment, probably shaped by the religious influence of the missionaries. Mqhayi clashed with his nephew Qasana after the latter participated in the War of Hintsa of 1834-1835 (Peires, 1976). Mhala was supported by his brother Mxhamli who died in the War of the Axe.

One of Rharhabe's sons, Mnyaluza, was reported to have been close to his brother Prince Ndlambe and supported him in the war against Prince Ngqika. Later on, he changed allegiance by joining Prince Ngqika until their disastrous defeat in the Battle of Amalinde in 1818. Thereafter, he crossed the Nciba River to become one of King Hintsa's closest advisors. He fled to Lesotho after the brutal murder of King Hintsa and later perished after his followers were besieged and wiped out by King Moshoeshoe (Peires, 1976).

Nozi was another brother of Ndlambe who made a living as a trader in various parts of the colony. He was known to have also visited King Moshoeshoe for gun trading purposes. He did not get on well with the colonial authorities. Princess Ntsusa, the fearless daughter of Prince Rharhabe , was famous for her terrific bravery. She was well-built and strong. As

---

4   Qonce is the African name of the Buffalo River which runs through the town to the east coast. The name was in existence before the arrival of the European settlers in the region. In 1826, it was established as a missionary station. After the War of Hintsa in 1834-35, it served as British military headquarters and later named King William's Town after King William IV (1765-1837). In February 2021, King William's Town was renamed Qonce.

a warrior, she always carried spears. She is known to have single-handedly killed seven men.

Prince Ndlambe became the rock upon which the solid foundations of amaRharhabe, the extended Kingdom of amaXhosa were laid. During Ndlambe's 20-year reign, the kingdom attained greatness and an incredible resilience to withstand the devastating impact of British encroachment, at a time when the rapid influx of white settlers in the Cape created an unfortunate situation of growing demand for land and livestock of amaXhosa. His reputation as a great leader grew, whilst at the same time he was grooming the young Prince Ngqika. In the process, Prince Ndlambe neutralised the power of the smaller nations such amaMbalu, imiDange and amaGqunukhwebe. Durign the reign of Ndlambe and later Ngqika imiDange, amaMbhalu, amaGwali, amaNtide and San and Khoe were gradually weakened in the face of the emergence of the dominant Kingdom of amaRharhabe.

Prince Ndlambe's situation was similar to the one later faced by Prince Maqoma, the eldest son of Prince Ngqika. Neither was the rightful heir to the throne, yet they were very influential in shaping and leading the wars of resistance during the time that they were regents in different periods. Their lives revolved around Prince Ngqika, who was an ally of the British establishment in pursuance of narrow interests. Interestingly, both of them had to contend with the constant challenges relating to Prince Ngqika's betrayal of the resistance in the face of European encroachment.

The life and times of Prince Ndlambe were indicative of the complex challenges of survival and continuing, defeat and triumph, betrayal and revenge that characterised the lives of royal aristocracy of amaXhosa. Early in his life he lost his pillars Prince Rharhabe and Prince Mlawu. Their sudden tragic departure parachuted Ndlambe into the unenviable position of having the enormous responsibility to build, consolidate and protect the fragile Kingdom of amaRharhabe.

Image 1.2: The rock is the royal seat of Prince Ndlambe at his headquarters in Mpongo near East London. I was directed and accompanied by Ms Nobandla Naye to the legendary place. She told me that during the drought of the 1980's, they would come to the royal seat to request rain. It would rain on the same day. The image was taken by the author on 24th April 2023. Source: Klaas, JJ. 2023.

His first baptism of fire was the betrayal by his nephew, the young Prince Ngqika, who launched an attack to ascend to power through the influence of his mother Queen Yese , at age 17. The view that Ndlambe wanted to remain in power may not be true because Prince Ngqika grew under his protection and mentoring. He could have devised surreptitious ways to have him killed if he had ambitions to remain on the throne. After Ngqika was circumcised, his mother Queen Yese influenced him to usurp power from Prince Ndlambe, who was perceived to have clung to the throne far too long. In 1795, Ngqika launched a surprise attack and captured Ndlambe whom he kept captive for years until he was saved by Prince Chungwa of amaGqunukhwebe.

The second major shocking event in Ndlambe's life was the fact that he absorbed the brunt of British firepower in the War of Resistance from 1811 to 1812, which was marked by Colonel Graham's scorched earth ethnic cleansing of amaXhosa. The calamity of the Zuurveld ethnic cleansing placed Prince Ndlambe between a rock and a hard place, in which he was sandwiched between Ngqika and the colonialists (Peires, 1976). After that, he had to navigate the troubled relationship with his nephew King Ngqika whilst simultaneously fighting the existential threat of European encroachment.

Peires (1981) observed that Prince Ndlambe expanded the Kingdom of amaRharhabe at the expense of the smaller tribes. He attacked and defeated imiDange, who resisted his father. He eliminated their formidable leader, Prince Mahote. He later overpowered amaMbalu. Prince Tshaka, the son of Chungwa of amaGqunukhwebe, remained his staunch rival whom he ultimately defeated. He established the Kingdom of amaRharhabe as a major power in the region between Nciba River, Xelexwa River and Graaff-Reinet. *"Ndlambe was by far the best soldier amongst all the Xhosa; much of his father Rarabe's military success as he struck westwards against those in his path was said to be owed to Ndlambe"* (Mostert, 1992: 269). Mostert (1992) described Prince Ndlambe as a great military genius and a man of integrity who was adored by his people. He leveraged his father's military achievements by continuing to subject smaller nations into kingdom. Following his departure on 10 February 1828, Mostert described him as a *"Perfect specimen of a powerful chief of the olden times"* (pg 608). The loss of his four sons in the War of Makhanda and Mdushane, who died in 1829, left his people with no definitive designated heir to continue his legacy.

According to Johannes Meintjes, Prince Ndlambe was a leader gifted with natural diplomacy. *"He had the ability of finding out what he wanted to know without giving much in return"* (pg 3). He was able to maintain alliances whilst he continued to build and consolidate the Kingdom of AmaRharhabe. This probably explains why Queen Yese was anxious for her young son Ngqika to usurp the throne after Prince Ndlambe established himself as the undisputed leader of amaRharhabe royal aristocracy. Prince Ndlambe laid down the solid foundations of bush warfare, which launched amaXhosa into the greatest wars of resistance during the era of the British imperialism in Southern Africa.

In the broader context of collective resistance, the ability to maintain a dignified posture of composure and fearlessness in the face of extreme danger was one of the inherent qualities amaXhosa displayed in their survival strategies against the Europeans. Considering the extreme hostility and the degree of resentment from their adversaries, it was vital to conceal their vulnerabilities and inner fears at all times. Such survival strategies were seen in the manner in which Prince Sarhili, the son of King Hintsa, reacted after learning of the barbaric death of his father, which was an astonishing and rare display of African royal aristocracy that had the strength to absorb unbearable pain. The British officers who told Prince Sarhili and the senior councillor Bhuru about the death of King Hintsa were astounded when they observed that neither one of them showed any emotional reaction. The peculiar manner of their reaction was characteristic of one of the dominant dispositions of the immense ability to endure unendurable agony, expressed through one of the idioms of amaXhosa *"Lala ngenxeba"*, which can be roughly translated as "sleep with your wound". The deeper meaning behind this idiom is the ability to conquer pain and fear in order to conceal one's vulnerability from the enemy.

While the royal aristocracy of amaXhosa faced aggressive European encroachment, which represented a threat of existential proportions, they were fully conscious and prepared to protect their people in the best possible manner. To a great extent, the royal aristocrat believed that the defining mantra of true leadership entails sacrifice and selflessness; hence Prince Chungwa and King Hintsa became direct casualties of the brutality of the European wars of conquest.

Prior to contact with the Europeans, amaXhosa practised a tradition of absorbing the smaller defeated tribes into the kingdom. To them, winning a war was not an entitlement to exterminate the other, hence during warfare women and children of the enemy were spared. They believed that war was meant to subdue, confiscate the resources and integrate the enemy. As a result, the Kingdom of amaXhosa grew and expanded their territories as they continued to defeat and absorb smaller nations. It was important to integrate and to expand for purposes of building a stronger kingdom because there was the constant threat that they could be wiped out as a nation.

It was against this background that the royal leaders of amaXhosa persevered in their efforts of strengthening the nation by absorbing their neighbours, wandering tribes, and defeated nations into a network of reciprocal social relations and a gradual system of integration. Peires (1976) noted that, *"The new areas into which the Xhosa moved were not empty and the indigenous populations were not expelled but incorporated into the Xhosa policy."* (Peires, 1976:08). The observations made by Peires (1976) are consistent with the literature pointing to the culture of inclusivity of amaXhosa, centred on patrilineage of a kinship. AmaXhosa attached a special value to the adherence to traditions, pastoral patronage, loyalty, courage and adventure.

However, the incorporation of the defeated tribes did not always work according to the plan of nation-building. The case of amaNgqosini's aspirations to the throne nearly ended the reign of King Tshiwo of amaXhosa had Khwane not saved him from defeat. Earlier on, amaNgqosinin were defeated and incorporated into amaXhosa during the reign of King Tshiwo, the son of King Ngconde (Peires, 1976). Many years later, Gaba, the royal leader of amaNgqosini, challenged the supreme authority of King Tshiwo as the reigning royal aristocrat. Consequently, war broke out between amaXhosa and amaNgqosini. Eventually amaNgqosini were defeated with the assistance of Khwane of amaGqunukhwebe.

Peires (1976) acknowledged King Tshiwo for the role he played in building the nation of amaXhosa through the integration of amaNgqosini into amaXhosa. His brother Mdange played a more or less similar role. At the time Tshiwo died on a hunting expedition, his Great Wife was pregnant. The wife took refuge at Mdange's homestead after Gwali usurped the throne. When Phalo was born, he was brought up in Mdange's compound. At the appropriate age, Mdange brought him to Gwali to take the throne as the rightful heir. A war broke out and Gwali was defeated. He ran away, taking refuge with the Khoe nation in the mountains of Nojoli. Hinsati, the Khoe leader, gave him refuge. Unfortunately, the Khoe were punished by Mdange for sheltering Gwali. The Khoe people such as ooSukwini, amaGqwashu and amaNqarhwane were eventually incorporated into amaXhosa (Peires, 1976; Mostert, 1992).

4. Queen Yese and the Descendants of Rharhabe

Since amaXhosa maintained a well-established system of alliances with the neighbouring kingdoms through bonds of intermarriages, they had relatively manageable relations with amaMpondo and abaThembu. These alliances with reliable and formidable kingdoms were critical in the event of wars with external enemies. During the war of Mlanjeni in 1850-1853, abaThembu of Prince Mapasa were one of Prince Sandile's formidable allies against the Europeans.

King Phalo, the last Supreme Royal Aristocrat of united amaXhosa, had two senior wives. The Princess of amaMpondo who gave birth to Prince Gcaleka was the Great House and the Princess of abaThembu who became the mother of

Prince Rharhabe was the Right Hand House. Later on, Prince Rharhabe married Nojoli the Princess of abaThembu, who gave birth to Prince Ndlambe. Prince Mlawu, the eldest son of Prince Rharharhabe, married Yese the Princess of abaThembu who gave birth to Prince Ngqika. In 1817, Prince Ngqika married Princess Suthu of abaThembu whose eldest son was Prince Sandile who succeeded his father as the royal head of amaRharhabe. These accounts illustrate the preferences of the royal aristocrats of amaXhosa for building of alliances with abaThembu by marrying their princesses.

Queen Yese was an extraordinary hermetic woman of many talents in the South African history. The remarkable courage, the formidable influence and the sublime brilliance of Queen Yese in shaping the Kingdom of amaXhosa, was an un astonishing phenomenon considering her gender and background. The unparalleled qualities and unprecedented achievements of Queen Yese such as to intentionally marry Prince Mlawu; to ensure that her son becomes the supreme royal aristocrat of amaRharhabe against all odds; to co-govern the Kingdom of amaRharhabe and to influence the nation to pay lobola to a man who was married to her; is still a mystery difficult to comprehend considering the deeply entrenched male patriarchy at the time. The observations about her extraordinary beautify (Barrow,1801), mystical background (Victor 2022) and her determination to co-govern the Kingdom of amaRharhabe with her son Prince Ngqika (Bezdrob, 2011) cemented her mysterious status as a phenomenal women of her generation.

The overwhelming enigmatic disposition around of Queen Yese is centred on the fact that there are no concrete historical accounts to establish whether she came from a royal background or not as well as the fact that she appeared to Prince Mlawu from a mist in the early hours during a hunting expedition. In as much as Owen (1994) acknowledged that Yese was a Princess of abaThembu, there are no direct primary sources to verify the exact details of her background and family history. Dr Stephanie Victor in her PhD dissertation of 2022 which examined the female power in the context of amaXhosa royalty, acknowledged that the origins of Queen Yese are disputed. According to her, the status of Queen Yese on whether she was an official royal wife or concubine of Prince Mlawu remained shrouded in a complex contradictory narrative. However, she noted the speculations that she was probably the daughter of a Prince of abaThembu.

There are contradictory accounts on whether her husband Prince Mlawu died in a war fighting with abaThembu or collapsed from sickness alleged to have been poisoned by Queen Yese in order to circumvent the royal succession for her son to assume the throne. Having noted that, Victor (2022) asserted that Queen Yese as a skilled mediator headed the royal house of imiNgcangathelo after the departure of Prince Mlawu. ImiNgcangathelo was the name of the favourite bull of Prince Mlawu. After she fell pregnant she fled for fear of accountability from Prince Ndlambe about the father of the child. Having a child with a man not approved by the royal traditional authority was tantamount to a serious transgression. She gave birth to a son named Matyobeni. Later on Prince Ndlambe reconciled with her on condition that she marries in order to become the respected head of imiNgcangathelo people (Victor 2022). The fact that lobola was paid to the people of the man to be married to Queen Yese was a mystery because it was against the strong customs and traditions of amaXhosa. Ordinarily, lobola was paid to the family of a woman to be married to a man, not the other way round. After the departure of King Ngqika in 1829, Prince Tyhali was deployed to assist and look after Queen Yese in her old age.

Victor (2022) asserted that despite the traditional gendered limitations at the time Queen Yese remained a decisive and influential woman as a skilled mediator, intelligent advisor, rainmaker and a powerful Queen mother to Prince Ngqika. On the same note, Anne Marie du Preez Bezdrob, 2011) in her book on Winnie Mandela defines Queen Yese as the subject of enormous influence who discharged unique unprecedented authority among amaXhosa.

In the history of abaThembu, Queen Yese stood out as the most powerful and influential woman. *"She was Tembu in origin...and said to have been a great beauty when young... Almost everything about her was extraordinary, including her marriage...was said to have appeared to Mlawu from a cloud of mist on a mountain. He took her as his wife and Ngqika was the result of the union"* (Mostert, 1992: 268). Queen Yese was clear from the beginning about whom to marry, who would become the anointed royal leader of amaRharhabe and how she would shape the kingdom. Considering the highly influential rising power of Rharhabe, Yese was aware that by associating herself with such a powerful family, she would place herself in a stronger position of influence to shape her destiny.

Prince Mlawu died in a war with abaThembu and amaQwathi together with his father Prince Rharhabe, leaving his younger brother, Prince Ndlambe, to reign as a regent, whilst Prince Ntimbo, the rightful heir, was still young. When Prince Mlawu passed away, Queen Yese was left to raise their young son, Ngqika. Queen Yese wasted no time in manoeuvring the royal traditional system of succession by displacing Ntimbo, the rightful heir to the throne, to pave the way for her son Ngqika to be the future king with the assistance of Prince Ndlambe.

Queen Yese strengthened her close relationship with Prince Ndlambe using her extraordinary exotic beauty, irresistible charisma and incredible power of influence. Having succeeded in establishing an unbreakably strong relationship with Prince Ndlambe, the alliance was sealed with a solid understanding that the young Ngqika would be the designated heir to the throne. Both of them started cultivating the ground for the subtle but systematic displacement of Prince Ntimbo. What made Queen Yese sure that Prince Ndlambe's support would yield results was the fact that as a regent, he occupied a powerful position of influence to shape the succession process in the Kingdom of amaRharhabe. The chances of successfully preventing Prince Ntimbo from ascending the throne were high. Eventually, Ndlambe successfully persuaded senior counsellors of the kingdom to proclaim Ngqika as a future monarch.

In 1795, events happened quicker than Ndlambe anticipated as Yese clandestinely orchestrated his displacement as regent due to fears that he appeared less than willing to relinquish power to her son, after 13 years in power. The young Prince Ngqika, at about sixteen years of age, ascended to the throne by displacing his uncle Ndlambe. Although Queen Yese did not publicly participate in the shocking humiliation of Ndlambe, she was the brains behind the royal coup.

The moment Ngqika was crowned as the supreme ruler of amaRharhabe, Yese further entrenched herself as practically the co-ruler of the Kingdom of amaRharhabe. Mostert (1992) observed that, *"Her position, at any rate, was of such importance that a strange and special status was created for her, which was unique in Xhosa history. To diminish the risk of suitors, a husband was found for her...the tradition was reversed. Lobola was paid for the husband and they called the husband wife and she was the husband..."* (pg 268). As stated earlier, Queen Yese was an extraordinary leader who broke the boundaries of the limited role of women in the kingdom, pioneered unprecedented practices that were alien to the customs and traditions of amaXhosa and cemented her power without hesitation or fear. She recognised no limits on how far she could go to accomplish her ambitions and desires through the skilful building of alliances, reliable networks and guaranteed loyalty.

It was reported that King Ngqika was loyal to his powerful mother. It is believed that in addition to her amazing beauty and influence, she was a powerful rainmaker (Mostert, 1992). Yese participated extensively in the political and diplomatic affairs of the kingdom in her efforts to build alliances in order to protect her son and strengthen the kingdom of amaRharhabe. She played a pivotal role in having one of the Boer leaders, Coenraad de Buys (1761-1821), reside with her at the Great Place. In the process, De Buys had a relationship with Queen Yese whilst he continued playing the role of an envoy between amaRharhabe, the second Kingdom of amaXhosa, and the European settlers.

The ascendance of King Ngqika to power occurred under the inescapable shadow of his mother, Queen Yese , who engineered her son's destiny from the beginning to the end. The controversial manner in which he usurped the throne impacted negatively on his reign through his decision-making process, especially in the formation of strategic alliances. What made matters worse for young King Ngqika was that he turned against his seasoned and experienced uncle, his mentor, the man who ensured that he became the king instead of Ntimbo, the rightful heir to the throne. The premature parachuting of Ngqika into power through the public humiliation of his uncle created a permanent animosity between them and denied the young leader a mentor who could have made him a great leader.

It was unfortunate that the controversial ascendance of Ngqika to power without the benefit of an experienced mentor was bound to create serious barriers for the young leader. Yese's decision to be the co-custodian of the kingdom created serious limitations in his ability to stand on his own, take decisions, build the kingdom and lead his people. In as much as Yese paved the way for Ngqika to be the supreme royal aristocrat of amaRharhabe, she was selfish in the process, as she also had ambitions to power and the privileges that came with it. She used her son to serve her own limited interests to the detriment of the unity of amaRharhabe and thus made the nation more vulnerable to the greater threat faced by amaXhosa at the time. Her contribution in persuading Ngqika to build an alliance with the Europeans alienated her son from the majority of amaXhosa. King Hintsa worked closely with Prince Ndlambe, who was a highly respected royal leader of amaXhosa across the Kei River. The decision to collaborate with the British establishment was largely influenced by the short-sighted objective of eliminating or neutralising Ndlambe at all costs.

At the beginning of his reign, Prince Ngqika had prospects of becoming a great and formidable leader, building on the solid foundations of Prince Ndlambe. He was renowned for his good looks. According to Meintjes, *"He was considered the flower of his race and physical beauty was remarked on by many"* (pg 4). Prince Ngqika was a leader of great aristocratic disposition, relatively tall, strongly built and with a gentle temperament. Unfortunately, his close association with the white settlers from the early stages of his reign, due to the influence of his mother, exposed him to western vices such as alcohol, which impacted negatively on his ability to lead his people.

Image 1.3: The refurbished final resting place of King Ngqika the supreme royal aristocrat of amaRharhabe. The resting place was erected on the foot of the Mathole mountain range at Mkhubiso village in Qoboqobo/ Keiskammahoek. The image was taken by the author on 29 April 2023. Source: Klaas, JJ. 2023.

Unlike most royal leaders of amaXhosa such as Tshiwo, Mdange, Hintsa and Ndlambe, Nqqika displayed tendencies that were alien to the royal aristocracy of the time. According to Peires (1981) *"Ngqika was not the sort of man who was capable of saving his honour at the expense of his material and political well–being...the Colony may have betrayed him, but they were the only friends he had, and he used his reputed influence with them to its fullest extent* (Peires, 1981:81). His violent ascendance to power at a young age was doomed to fail disgracefully after he had lost legitimacy and respect from his own people.

At age 20, King Ngqika married his first wife Nothonto, the daughter of Nxiya, from the clan of amaNgqosini of Basotho and Khoe ancestry. Around 1798, Princess Nothonto gave birth to twins Maqoma and Nongwane, at Xhukwane near Xesi (Middledrift). King Ngqika appointed his brother-in-law and witch hunter, Kota, as the guardian of Prince Maqoma. As a young boy, Prince Maqoma wore the prestigious skin of a leopard that he had killed. Later on, Prince Ngqika had several children, who were mainly boys, from different wives such as Tyhali, Xhoxho, Matwa, Tente and Anta (Stapleton, 2016).

King Ngqika felt threatened by the support offered by King Hintsa to Prince Ndlambe. In addition to his collaboration with the British colonial establishment, he made an alliance with abaThembu and married their daughter Suthu who later gave birth to Prince Sandile, the future heir to the throne. Prince Ngqika offered Maqoma the position of the Head of the Right Hand House, ensuring that he would remain the second in charge (Stapleton, 2016).

Yese's controversial relationship with Coenraad De Buys was indicative of the compromised extended Kingdom of amaRharhabe during the reign of King Ngqika. He considered the colonial establishment as an ally, when in fact it did not have his interests at heart, instead using him to access the rich land of the Kat River without having fought for it. By the time King Ngqika realized the trap he got himself into, it was too late. A considerable number of his subjects had deserted him to join Prince Ndlambe and other small kingdoms. He subsequently resorted to excessive alcohol consumption and died at an early age, leaving his children and people in a compromised position, with a broken kingdom. He was born in 1778 and passed away in November 1829.

It was only after his departure that his sons Maqoma, Tyahli and Sandile reorganised their people and mobilized other nations to take a collective and decisive stand against the invading Europeans. The fact that amaXhosa, abaThembu and the KhoeSan were able to fight as a collective in the defining War of Mlanjeni from 1850 to 1853, was a credit to the sons of King Ngqika, who mobilised for war.

Prince Maqoma emerged as a regent after the departure of his father. After he realized that Europeans regarded him as an inferior savage, he donned western clothing in order to engage with the whites on an equal basis. Mostert defined Maqoma as being *"endowed with unusual gift of mind and of command, the natural leader"* (pg 614).

He allowed his family to engage with Europeans in order to adapt to the new challenges. As part of an adaptation strategy, during the war his warriors wore European clothes to protect them from thorn bushes and *"to provide pockets for carrying ammunition"* (Stapleton, 2016: 285). During Maqoma's time, women played a supportive role during the war as messengers, peace envoys, smugglers of ammunition and as informers. Stapleton (2016) believed that the legacy and the incredible brilliance of Maqoma as one of the greatest military strategists were erased by the white settler historians in order to expunge him from history. *"The settler's typical view of Maqoma, initiated by Godlonton and inherited by Theal and Cory, continued into the apartheid era of the late twentieth-century"* (Stapleton, 2016: 04). The British historians he mentioned such as Robert Godlonton (1794-1884), George McCall Theal (1837-1919) and George Cory (1862-1935) were among some of the prominent historians of the nineteenth century whose volumes of work shaped the view of history of South Africa. However, there were concerns that this highly acclaimed body of knowledge contained deliberate distortions and omissions depending on whose history was actually narrated.

The question is: why would they be keen to portray Maqoma in a negative manner? Were they driven by resentment, considering his extraordinary contributions in the wars of resistance? Was it because of the manner in which he inflicted some of the heaviest casualties on the British forces during the wars of resistance? The War of Mlanjeni was undoubtedly the defining military theatre in which Prince Maqoma established himself as an outstanding genius who mobilized his people and marshalled his forces in the longest and deadliest war of resistance between Africans and the British in Southern Africa. What stood out about Maqoma was his extraordinary courage in the form of his great physical strength and military prowess in combating British firepower during protracted engagements. It was his relentless determination and bravery that made amaXhosa believe that they had both the intellectual and the physical ability to fight to defend their land and dignity as a nation. Maqoma proved to be a decisive and fearless leader with the ability to adopt innovative military strategies in the face of an advanced enemy with superior military power. He did not regard the British colonial military power, comprised of trained regiments, agile cavalry and deadly artillery, as something to be fearful of. He believed that mastery of the terrain and the execution of counter attacks through ambushes would neutralise the European military.

Prince Maqoma learnt from the mistakes of his father, King Ngqika, that the policy of appeasing the British colonial authorities was a futile and self-defeating political exercise. King Ngqika may have thought that the alliance with the Europeans was a strategic diplomatic plan to secure his kingdom in the face of other nations which surrounded him. Maqoma realized that taking a bold and united stand against the encroachment of the Europeans settlers who were hungry for land and the livestock of amaXhosa, was the best option under such circumstances. He knew that, as Africans, they faced a dominant opponent from whom neither appeasement nor submission was going to save them. That is why Stapleton (2016) describes Prince Maqoma as the one of Africa's greatest military leaders of the nineteenth century. Johannes Meintjies, in Stapleton (2016: 05) described Maqoma as a man who *"strides the Xhosa landscape like a giant, for few were to match his physical and mental powers and passionate nationalism, a mastermind of Xhosa aggression against the settlers."*

Among the sons of Maqoma were Makrexana, Mfazwe and Namba. In 1818 he, assisted by Counsellor Makoyi, led about 2000 fighting men in the vicious battle of Amalinde. His men suffered a harrowing defeat at the hands of Prince Mdushane, who was supported by amaGcaleka and amaGqunukhwebe. The war was so horrific that the survivors were burnt in a huge fire as an expression of anger against King Ngqika, the British collaborator. Maqoma suffered serious injuries from which it took about two years to recover (Stapleton, 2016). Prince Ngqika fled to the Winterberg Mountains. His decision to serve British interests to the detriment of his own people had alienated him from the majority of people and leaders in the region.

Maqoma witnessed the growing harassment of the royal leaders of amaXhosa, the rapid loss of land and the deep encroachment into the territories of amaXhosa. It dawned on him that the British colonial establishment was determined to strip them of their land, dignity and identity by undermining and destroying the traditional authority, which was the glue that held amaXhosa together. What Maqoma witnessed was similar to the observations made by the Nigerian novelist Chinua Achebe in his book, *Things Fall Apart*, in which he said, *"They put a knife on the things that held us together and we have fallen."* The arrival of the European settlers in the 1820s was marked by the aggressive colonial onslaught on amaXhosa in the battle for land and livestock.

Rev Henry Calderwood, in Stapleton (2016) described Maqoma as *"Evidently a man of strong good sense and decided intellect. I should suppose despise in his heart many of the white men with whom he comes in contact and who think themselves superior...in time of great emergency he is the spirit and genius of 'amaXhosa'. In troubles times he is the arm of 'amaXhosa'. His mind will always give him great power in council and he is skilful and perfectly fearless in war"* (Stapleton, 2016: 139). According to Stapleton, Calderwood discovered that Maqoma was not interested in converting to Christianity but in using missionaries as a political cover to pursue his interests. Consequently, Calderwoood became frustrated by his failure to convert Maqoma, who was always ahead of him, and he deeply resented him.

Maqoma had a dark side. When his brother Tyhali was sick, he influenced a Mfengu witch hunter to accuse Suthu of witchcraft so that Sandile could be left isolated and thus create an opportunity for him to usurp power. He also accused her of killing his father, King Ngqika. After Chief Tyhali died, Suthu was able to flee from Mkhubiso in Qoboqobo with the help of his son Sandile. The refusal of Bhotomane and Nqeno to support the witchcraft accusations saved Suthu.

Eventually, Prince Sandile replaced Prince Maqoma as the regent and became the supreme ruler of the amaRharhabe Kingdom. Prince Sandile, known as Mgolombane, was born at Mkhubiso in 1820. Johannes Meintjes, in his book *Sandile, the Fall of the Xhosa Nation*, published in 1971, presented Sandile as the last king of the independent amaXhosa, whose fall in the War of Ngcayechibi in 1877–1879, marked the final military defeat of amaXhosa after they had fought the Europeans for over 100 years. According to Meintjes, King Sandile was a tall, bearded man, with the bright eyes of a leopard.

King Sandile was a complex and enigmatic leader and the embodiment of the virtues and the vanities of the African royal aristocracy, largely shaped by the unbearable circumstances faced by amaXhosa at the time. While Meintjes (1971) presented him as an unpredictable and strange leader, born to sadness and defeat, such a characterisation failed to appreciate the more complex political challenges, the permanent state of uncertainty and survival concerns he grappled with at the time. In the aftermath of the devastating War of Mlanjeni from 1850 to 1853, the cattle lung sickness of 1854 to 1857 followed by the cattle culling to prevent the spread of the contagious lung sickness, the installation of European magistrates to replace the power of royal leaders of amaXhosa, and the death of Prince Maqoma in Robben Island in 1873 were tragic events that weighed heavily on the shoulders of King Sandile. Such events of significant magnitude had a huge impact in shaping the enduring reign of King Sandile as well as his state of mind while leading his people under an uncertain state of perpetual siege and rapid of loss of land, resources and power. The tremendous pressure of expectations to lead with very limited options may have subjected him to severe psychological strain.

Here are some of the fundamental qualities and strategies which amaXhosa applied, and which enabled them to endure the intensity of the British onslaught over one hundred years.

- They were led by generations of strong decisive leaders who were far ahead of their time in the realization of the imperatives of nation-building through integration of the defeated kingdoms and maintenance of alliances with formidable neighbouring kingdoms.
- The ownership and protection of the cattle proved to be a dependable and critical productive capability which became essential in the ability to wage and to sustain devastating wars of resistance against the Europeans.
- Building the centre of the kingdoms in fortress-like environments such as Qoboqobo was a deliberate strategy meant to neutralise the threats of invading enemies.
- Adherence to customs and traditions, reverence for the royal aristocracy and warm welcoming of strangers were key ingredients of nation-building through the creation of bonds which made people stay together.
- AmaXhosa were an advanced and organised society who valued their environment, preserved the resources and absorbed other smaller nations for the purpose of survival and development.
- Their ability to adapt was crucial in the face of advancing, highly capable Europeans whom they perceived as existential threats to their survival.

5. The Rise of African Pioneers from the Ashes of Conquest

As the British Empire completed the colonial conquest towards the end of the nineteenth century, Southern Africa witnessed the emergence of African pioneers rising from the ruins of broken kingdoms, and from dispossessed, displaced and dehumanised African societies. In the context of the Cape Colony, amaXhosa in the aftermath of the relentless century-long wars, produced pioneers whose work became the building blocks in waging the new struggle of liberation from the shackles of conquest which gained traction from the beginning of the 20th Century. Professor Mcebisi Ndletyana (2008) observed that the Cape African intellectuals of the 19th and 20th Centuries pioneered the evolution of African intellectuals who emerged as an influential middle class and who could interpret the complex challenges facing the African people. They skilfully used the newly-acquired colonial education far beyond the intended colonial objectives of African anglicisation, assimilation and intellectual slavery.

Southern African pioneers such as Reverend Tiyo Soga (1829 -1871), Dr Mpilo Walter Benson Rubusana (1858-1936) Mr John Solilo (1864-1940), Mr Mankayi Enoch Sontonga (1873-1905) and Mr Krune Samuel Edward Mqhayi (1875-1945), who emerged during and in the aftermath of the colonial conquest in the Cape colony, used the newly-acquired colonial education as an intellectual weapon to liberate Africans from the shackles of European conquest. Consequently, the nature of the significant literature they produced at the time was not an ordinary production of knowledge to appease the colonial masters, but a far deeper reflection of the vision to continue a different war of resistance, which was fought in the intellectual, spiritual and psychological domain. They refused to regard colonial education as a ladder to elitism or to an aloofness of African intellectuals in enjoying new privileges while serving their colonial masters at the expense of their own people.

Reverend Tiyo Soga was born in 1829, the year Prince Ngqika died. His father and grandfather were senior counsellors during the reign of Prince Ngqika. His grandfather was killed in the Battle of Amalinde in 1818. One of his defining legacies as an ordained black South African priest was the

Christian Hymn *Lizalis' idinga lakho*[5] (Fulfil your promise), which he composed upon his arrival on the shores below Table Mountain on a ship from Scotland in 1857. Professor Ndletyana (2008) described Reverend Soga as *"the first nationalist-intellectual and a progenitor of black consciousness"* (pg 28). After having studied in the comforts of Scotland, he was moved when he saw the suffering of Africans upon his arrival on the shores of the Cape colony. He then composed the liberating hymn, from the depth of his heart, appealing to the Creator to save the African people from the grip of oppression and slavery.

Dr Mpilo Rubusana was born in Somerset East in 1858, a difficult year following the devastating war of Mlanjeni and the deadly cattle lung sickness which came from Europe. He was born at a time the institutions of nationhood in the Eastern Cape region that held together the African people were under immense pressure from the influence of European encroachment. Rubusana was a revolutionary who co-founded Izwi Labantu (Voice of People) newspaper. Izwi Labantu was launched in East London in 1898 by a leading group of African intellectuals and activists, as a reaction to the support provided by John Tengo Jababu to the group of Afrikaner Bond conservatives. Mr JT Jabavu was the father of Professor Tengo Davidson Don Jabavu, the outstanding pioneer who played an incredible role in the establishment and the building of the University of Fort Hare. Rubusana advocated compulsory education for Africans and the use of mother tongue instruction. The collection of poems entitled *Zemnk' Inkomo Magwalandini* (Here goes your cows you cowards) stood out as a revolutionary piece of literature aimed at reviving the fight for liberation. That is why he played a pivotal role in the establishment of the South African Native National Congress in 1912.

---

5   The enduring popularity of the hymn until the present day in South Africa is a testimony of the legacy left by one of the gifted sons of the Soga family in South Africa.

John Solilo, who lived around Cradock, wrote many poems in isiXhosa. Between 1922 and 1935 he wrote and published a collection of poems. One of his greatest poems is *Mthandi Wesizwe* [6](The Patriot of the Nation), which portrays a fearless and indomitable patriot and compares this with a visionless character, a liability in other words. At the time Solilo wrote the poem, it was a few decades after amaXhosa were finally subdued by the European imperialists. Solilo was 15 years old during the last war of Ngcayechibi. He lived at a time of great challenges in which amaXhosa were subjected to dispossession, displacement, dehumanization and commodification.

The first stanza of the poem portrays the embodiment of an indomitable spirit in the face of insurmountable challenges.

Ngubani omabhongo ngelakhe ikamva?

Ngubani onegugu ziinto zakowabo,

Ohlala elinde ukubon' iint' ezintle,

Othemba linzulu, naxa kungekuhle?

The English translation of this stanza is as follows:

Who is not courageous about the future?

Who is not proud on what belongs home?

The ever optimistic one about better things to come,

The one with ingrained hope in the face of hopelessness.

This poem is a reflection of the defining disposition of the people who lived at the time, the enduring circumstances they were subjected to and the kind of extraordinary courage they

---

6 When Nelson Mandela, popularly known as Madiba, the former President of the Republic of South Africa, visited the University of Cambridge to meet the Mandela Magdalene Scholars at Magdalene College on 1ST May 2001, the author performed a spontaneous praise of Madiba reciting the first stanza's Mthandi Wesizwe. The unplanned performance became one of the highlights of the event. http://news.bbc.co.uk/2/hi/uk_news/1309216.stm

displayed in order to rise above the inhuman conditions at the height of the colonial era in the Cape colony. Solilo probably wrote the poem as a form of motivation not to surrender or lose hope no matter what was brought upon them.

Mankayi Sontonga was born in Uitenhage, one of the battlegrounds in the wars of resistance. He stood out as one of the greatest thinkers of his generation. In 1897, Sontonga composed *Nkosi Sikelel' iAfrika* (God Bless Africa) whilst working as a teacher at a Methodist Mission school in Johannesburg. The original lyrics of Sontonga's hymn are as follows:

Nkosi Sikelel' iAfrika

Maluphakanyisw' uphondo lwayo,

Yizwa imithandazo yethu,

Nkosi sikelela, thina lusapho lwayo

Yihla Moya, yihla Moya

Yihla Moya Oyingcwele

The English translation is as follows:

God Bless Africa

Raise her horn high

Hear our Prayers

God bless us, her children

Descend Spirit

Descend Holy Spirit

Sources: https://www.gov.za/ & https://en.wikipedia.org

When he composed the hymn, he was moved by the extreme suffering of African people that he witnessed whilst working in Johannesburg. The hymn was sung during the establishment of the South African Native National Congress, which later became the African National Congress, in 1912. In 1925, the organisation adopted it as its official anthem. Almost a hundred years later, the hymn was adopted as part of the national anthem of South Africa. Sontonga was an African intellectual far ahead of his time, who envisioned the liberated African continent long before it was realised.

In essence, these African pioneers of education went beyond their professional careers by using their education and the production of knowledge to provide hope, inspiration and courage to the African people in the face of the European conquest of Southern Africa. To them the conquest of Africa was not the end, but the beginning of the rise of Africans from the ashes of defeat to fight for their liberation and the repossession of their land. They emerged at a critical time in the context of the Cape Colony in which amaXhosa were trapped in the triangle of 100 years of resistance wars. To them the defeat, the loss of land and the commodification of the African people marked the beginning of a new era of a different struggle for emancipation. Finally, the revolutionary and empowering literature they generated laid the foundations for a different war of emancipation, which took shape from the beginning of the twentieth century until almost the end of the century.

Chapter Two

The Beginning of One Hundred Years Wars

"The age of resistance was also the heroic age of the Chiefs. Ndlambe, Chungwa, Hintsa, Sarhili, Maqoma, Tyhali and Sandile may have had their faults, but they did not sell out. They stood up for their people and deserve a salute" (Peires, 1981:164).

1. The African Perspective of the Cape Wars of Resistance

At the beginning of the nineteenth century, the Eastern and the Western Cape Provinces were the launching pads of the British conquest of Southern Africa. Earlier on, the Western Cape had been a Dutch colony between 1652 and 1795. During the reign of King George III, the British took the Cape Colony from the Dutch in 1795, abandoned it in 1803 and reconquered the Cape in 1806 until 1910. The first 150 years of the Dutch occupation of the Cape Colony was marked by a period of gradual expansion inland and the systematic extermination of the African indigenous inhabitants.

The first eight decades of the British expansion in Southern Africa were characterised by the agonising era of the wars of resistance and conquest between Africans and the Europeans. What stood out during that period were the vicious and deadly wars fought between amaXhosa and the British in a triangle between Gqeberha, Graaff-Reinet and Gcuwa[1]. It was from this triangle that the British policy of

---

1   The three towns Gqeberha, Graaff-Reinet and Gcuwa constitute the pillars of the triangle of the longest wars of resistance. African scholars such as Professor Ncedile Saule

ethnic cleansing was first executed from 1811 to 1812 between the Nukakamma/Sundays River near Gqeberha and Nxuba/Fish River near Makhanda. The triangle was the centre of the British massive fortification process aimed at breaking down the backbone of relentless resistance of amaXhosa. The longest and deadliest war ever fought between Africans and Europeans occurred in this triangle.

What has always been concerning in the history of these wars is the way in which they have been defined by dominant historians of European descent as *Frontier Wars*. It is of paramount importance to decolonise such Eurocentric concepts as part of the process of the deconstruction and reconstruction of knowledge systems for purposes of creating space for African contributions in the reinterpretation of our history. From an African perspective, the concept *Frontier Wars* implies that the wars were fought by opposing groups over a contested border of contact and thus placing both groups on equal terms in relation to their legitimate ownership of the contested land. Defining the San and Khoe wars of resistance against the Dutch as frontier wars is an overt distortion of history. This is also applicable to the wars fought by the British colonialists against the indigenous African populations. It is unfortunate that such distorted narratives of our history have been perpetuated for decades in order to present a particular view of conquest. Therefore, it remains an anomaly that Europeans, who landed on the shores of the Southern Africa, could be accorded an equal right to land ownership as the indigenous inhabitants.

The nature of these wars was such that the ultimate political objective of colonial conquest was not limited to the possession of the land; the system ensured that Africans remained permanently inferior through various subtle and overt forms of systematic dehumanization. The ultimate

---

believed that Qamdobowa is the original name of Graaff-Reinet. At the time of writing the book the official name of the town remains Graaff-Reinet. Gcuwa was named Butterworth after Joseph Butterworth following the establishment of the Wesleyan mission in 1827, during the reign of King Hintsa.

objective was to create a lasting psyche of inferiority complexes for generations to come, for the purpose of accomplishing both material and psychological conquest. The conquerors were fully aware that the material conquest would not guarantee their long-term security in Africa, without the completion of the psychological conquest through cognitive bondage of the mind, centred on permanent pillars of perceived European superiority and institutionalised African inferiority. For the purpose of this book, such wars are referred to as wars of resistance and conquest.

2. British Systematic Fortification of the Battle Grounds

Colonel John Graham's execution of the scorched earth policy was not only a military instrument of conquest; it was meant to send a clear message to amaXhosa about the overwhelming firepower of the British Empire, so that they would not even think of resisting the conquest. The military strategy of maximum annihilation through shock and awe was meant to subjugate amaXhosa into permanent submission. To their surprise, despite having successfully cleansed the area of 20 000 inhabitants, amaXhosa resorted to relentless guerrilla attacks, which made it difficult for the white settlers to occupy the coveted Zuurveld region between Nxuba (Fish) River and Nukakama/Sundays River. Consequently, during the governorship of Sir John Francis Cradock (1762–1839) between 1811 and 1814, the colonial power resorted to the construction of military posts and forts as a defensive deterrent to neutralise the protracted attacks.

The British policy to resort to the costly construction of a series of military posts and forts was a reaction driven by a sense of desperation to uproot the sting of the extraordinary resistance of amaXhosa against the determined colonial establishment to accomplish conquest at all costs. As the intensity of the wars increased, some of the key strategic military posts were converted into forts in order to accommodate soldiers, store supplies and military equipment. The chain of military posts and forts were linked by supply routes, which were critical during the time of war. The policy behind the military strategy was to create a state of psychological and physical permanent presence in the territories of amaXhosa, to protect the conquered areas and to serve as monitoring posts.

The British colonial establishment resented the possession of the Amathole Mountains by amaXhosa because they provided a valuable strategic advantage, which enabled them to engage in sustained lethal combat with minimum casualties, whilst they maximised their attacking prowess to the detriment of the British army. Fort Beaufort, Fort Armstrong, Fort Hare, Fort Cox and Fort Beresford in particular were strategically constructed along the impenetrable mountains of Amathole for the purpose of placing military personnel within striking range in the event of war.

Coetzee and Westby-Nunn (2019) conducted sterling work, which provided comprehensive details of the fortification of the triangle. According to them, Cradock instructed the construction of thirty fortified military posts along the Great Fish River in order to mitigate the continuous deadly attacks launched by amaXhosa after their expulsion from the Zuurveld. Despite the presence of multiple military posts, the combatants of amaXhosa were able to evade the British soldiers from a distance because of their red coats and they subsequently returned to the Zuurveld in large numbers. The thick impenetrable bushes rendered those military posts obsolete.

The military posts and forts were not only defensive positions; they served as a means of providing quick communication signals to convey intelligence information, monitor the movement of amaXhosa, store supplies and ammunition, provide support systems in the transportation of goods and military supplies, serve as places of refuge in the time of war, and as convenient areas to bury white settlers. These fortresses were often built near rivers on clear elevated areas. The construction military posts was intensified in the aftermath of the British ethnic cleansing of the Zuurveld (Coetzee & Westby-Nunn, 2019). What propelled the fortification process was the urgency to protect the conquered coveted land from imminent threats posed by the local inhabitants.

The fortification intensified again during the administration of Sir Benjamin D'Urban (1777-1849), the British Governor of the Cape Colony from 1834 until 1838 and General Harry Smith (1786-1860), the commander of the colonial forces. The decision to build more forts was triggered by the disastrous military campaigns in Qoboqobo in 1834-35, during the War of Hintsa. The failure to expel amaXhosa across the Nciba (Kei) River created a sense of urgency and desperation to build a series of bastions in order to protect the white settlers.

Fort Frederick was the first fort built in 1799 on the shores of Algoa Bay in Gqeberha after Britain's first conquest of the Cape between 1795 and 1802. It marked the beginning of the British fortification process which made the triangle between Gqeberha, Graaff-Reinet and Gcuwa the most highly fortified region in Africa, indicative of the magnitude and the intensity of the relentless wars of resistance.

Some of the notable forts built at the time, which became the contested battlegrounds of the very intense combative engagements between Africans and Europeans were Fort Hare, Fort Cox, Fort Beaufort, Fort Brown, Fort Willshire, Fort Murray, Fort Peddie and Double Drift Fort. Fort Murray was built for purpose of neutralising the resistance of Prince Phatho of amaGqunukhwebe and Prince Mhala of amaNdlambe.

Image 2.1:   This is Fort Frederick in Gqeberha. Source: Janet Szymanowski (1988) https://commons.wikimedia. org/

Fort Cox, built in Middledrift/ eXesi at the foot of the Amathole Mountains, stood out as one of the remarkable fortresses of historical significance during the era of the wars of resistance. It was the strongest fort, with an intact solid stone structure. The fort was built to keep a close watch on the Kingdom of amaXhosa located at Mkhubiso on the foot of the mountains of Amathole and Keiskamma River. It was named after Major William Cox, the tried and tested veteran of the War of 1834 to 1835 who was a reliable and favourite lieutenant of General Harry Smith. Smith deemed it appropriate to name a fort after him because of his vast knowledge of the Amathole region as well as his valuable understanding of the disposition of amaXhosa.

Coetzee and Westby-Nunn (2019) noted that the construction of Fort Cox in close proximity to the Great Place of King Ngqika was influenced by the combative approach of General Harry Smith, who was convinced that the resistance of amaXhosa was broken and therefore *"military posts should be placed in the very teeth of the enemy where they will come (to attack) and not where they dare not approach"* (pg 207). This was contrary to the view of other British officers who were

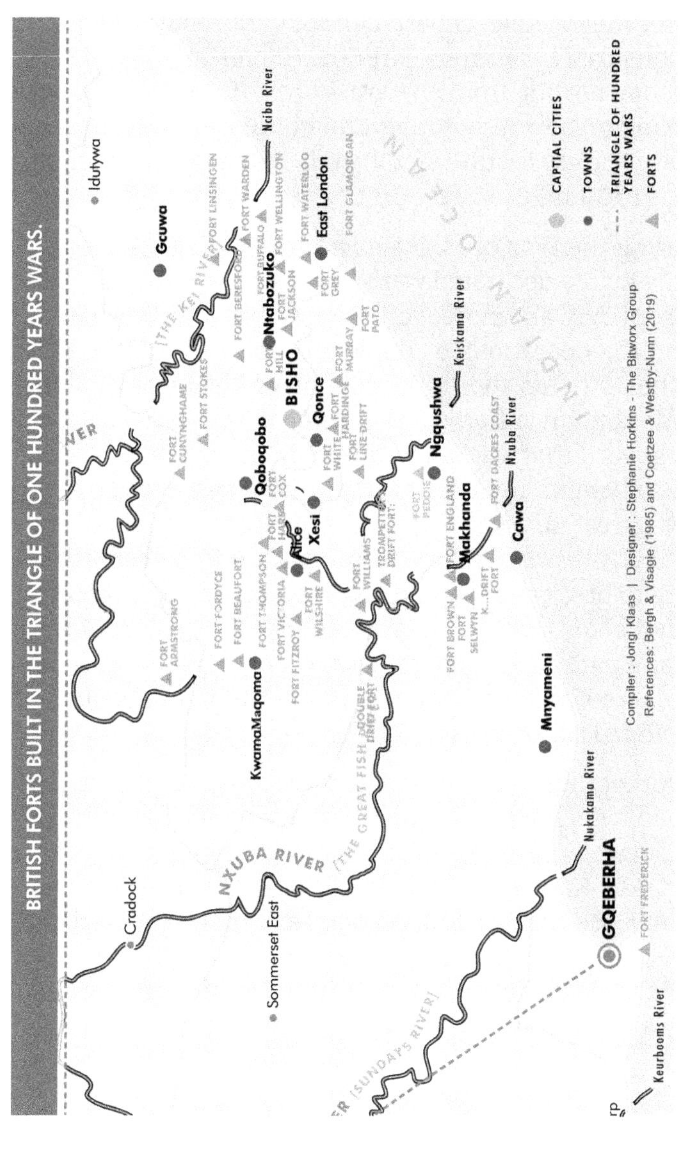

Figure 2.2: British Forts built in the triangle of one hundred years wars. Sources: Bergh, J.S. & Visagie, J.C. 1985 and Coetzee, C. & Westby-Nunn, T. 2019.

concerned that the location of the site in the bushes, with obscured views and in close proximity to the centre of power of amaXhosa, was a risky choice.

After King Ngqika departed in 1829, his body was rested a few kilometres away from Fort Cox. His resting place is still visible today not far from the gravel road from Mkhubiso to Lenye village. The Presbyterian Church built by the Glasgow Missionary Society is still standing tall on the upper ground of the village of Mkhubiso near Fort Cox.

During the War of Mlanjeni from 1850 to 1853, General Smith, the highly decorated war veteran of the British Empire, the Hero of Aliwal, chose Fort Cox as his military base to command the operations of the war deep in the strongholds of amaXhosa. To his shock, the column of Lieutenant Colonel George Mackinnon suffered a shattering defeat in the battle of Boma Pass. As if that was not humiliating enough, King Sandile led his combatants to Fort Cox. Smith's forces were crushed, and they retreated to the fort. It was an agonising experience. When Major General Somerset brought reinforcements from Fort Hare to break the siege, he was repulsed by the forces of King Sandile and suffered heavy casualties. It was only days later that Smith managed to escape Fort Cox at midnight disguised as a Khoe combatant, with the support of about 300 Khoe mounted riflemen.

Another military citadel of historical magnitude was Fort Armstrong, which was built on the range of elongated higher ground located between Elandsberg Mountains and Fort Beaufort near Katberg. At the height of the War of Mlanjeni, about 200 Khoe soldiers mutinied against their white officers and subjected Fort Armstrong to a ferocious onslaught, took the white settler survivors hostage and occupied the fortress. In February 1851, Major General Henry Somerset directed his artillery and cavalry to the obliteration of the forts in an attempt to free those who were held hostage. It is not clear how many survivors were found after the bombardment of the fortress. In essence, the construction of the military posts and multiple forts was a reaction to the resolute resistance they encountered from the courageous combatants of amaXhosa.

The legendary University of Fort Hare in Alice in the Eastern Cape Province of South Africa was named after the decorated Waterloo War Veteran, Major General John Hare, who died of a heart attack on his way back to Great Britain, following the most humiliating defeat at Fort Cox. In 1846, he led a formidable army comprised of 125 wagons with ammunition, supplies and artillery as well as British cavalry, Boer infantry, San and Khoe snipers and amaMfengu auxiliaries. The plan was to execute scorched earth tactics of total destruction of Qoboqobo in order to crush the backbone of amaXhosa resistance. When the army approached what is now known Fort Cox College at Mkhubiso in a long column, the fearless Prince Sandile, Aaa!!! Mgolombane, unleashed a deadly ambush that pulverized the army. The precision and the pace of the relentless onslaught obliterated the British-led army in one day, while the British campaign had been planned to last three months. Major General John Hare was shattered.

3. Triangle Of One Hundred Years Wars

This chapter examines the build-up of African-European wars, which culminated in the harrowing ethnic cleansing of 1811 to 1812, that was marked by the undignified departure of Prince Chungwa of amaGqunukhwebe and the unceremonious fall of King Hintsa. The era of the protracted wars of resistance fought at different intervals was an atrocious period of great uncertainty in the history of Southern Africa.

The first military engagement between amaXhosa and the Europeans occurred from 1779 until 1781. The war was provoked by Baron Joachim van Plettenberg (1739-1793), the Dutch Governor of the Cape Colony between 1771 and 1785. The war was triggered by Plettenberg's ambitions to dispossess Africans of the rich coveted land of the Zuurveld region between Nxuba (Fish) River and Xelexwa (Gamtoos) River. Zuurveld is a region with an abundance of water supported by three rivers: the Inxuba, Nukakamma (Sundays) and Xelexwa, and is suitable for livestock. The war over the Zuurveld marked the beginning of a series of African-European wars in the triangle, which continued until the fall of King Sandile in the war of Ngcayechibi in 1877-1879 (Stretch, 1988).

Prior to the arrival of the Dutch settlers, the Zuurveld was the land of amaGqunukhwebe of Prince Khwane, who were later joined by amaRharhabe of Prince Ndlambe. At the outbreak of the war, the Dutch settlers were led by Adriaan Van Jaarsveld, regarded as a highly experienced commander who was familiar with the environment. AmaXhosa who were involved in the war comprised amaGwali, imiDange, amaNtinde, amaMbalu, and Gqunukhwebe. During the war, amaXhosa made a temporary retreat from the Zuurveld and retaliated by launching unpredictable ambushes targeting the Dutch settlers. Eventually, the Dutch were defeated and amaXhosa returned to the Zuurveld.

This was the first war in which the Dutch settlers engaged amaXhosa since they landed on the shores of Southern Africa in 1652. In the first 150 years, the Dutch settlers successfully dispossessed, displaced and eliminated large populations of the San and Khoe people. The resistance they encountered from amaXhosa came as a shock to them. After the war, the Dutch settlers were left bitter by their dismal failure to expel amaXhosa from the Zuurveld.

In the following war of 1789-1793, the Dutch settlers managed to persuade Ndlambe to align with them against Prince Chungwa of amaGqunukhwebe. Prince Ndlambe joined the Dutch in order to achieve dominance over Prince Chungwa. This must have been a serious setback for Chungwa, who may have felt betrayed by his brother from the same clan of amaTshawe.

Barend Lindeque mobilized a considerable group of the Dutch commando with the intent of engaging amaXhosa in full-scale war to drive them out of the Zuurveld. At the beginning of the war, the Dutch had the upper hand, as they managed to confiscate about 2000 cattle of amaXhosa, mainly from amaGqunukhwebe and amaMbalu. More groups of amaXhosa came to Chungwa's assistance to defeat the temporary alliance. AmaXhosa reorganised themselves and retaliated, targeting farms of the Dutch settlers. In the process, they captured about 50 000 cattle, 11 000 sheep, and 200 horses. The Dutch settlers fled west of the Zuurveld.

The strategy of divide and conquer was one of the effective methods they used in the annihilation of the San and Khoe. AmaXhosa appeared to have been better organised to neutralise such forms of infiltration, except King Ngqika, the consistent British collaborator. In the case of Ndlambe, he regretted his decision, hence in the subsequent wars he stood on the side of united Africans in resisting European encroachment. In the process, Ndlambe emerged as one of the leading architects of resistance, together with his sons, some of whom died in the wars of 1818–1819.

In January 1799, the Khoe revolted against the Dutch settlers in Graaff-Reinet and in March 1799, General T P Vandeleur was sent to crush the Graaff-Reinet revolt. In April 1799, the Khoe and amaXhosa launched combined attacks targeting white settler farms as far as Oudtshoorn. This marked the third war between Africans and the Dutch settlers in the triangle of resistance. The Dutch settlers again failed to crush the joint alliance of the Khoe and amaXhosa, which proved to be too powerful for them.

In 1801, the Khoe in Graaff-Reinet launched a second rebellion led by Klaas Stuurman, Hans Trompetter and Boesak. They raided white settler farms. The commando under Tjaart van der Walt engaged the Khoi. In June 1802, Van der Walt was killed. A temporary peace arrangement was reached.

In 1806, Britain decided to reoccupy the Cape Colony based on the strategic considerations of 1795, meaning to prevent France from occupying the lucrative trade route to India. This time about 4 500 men of the British naval forces landed in Cape Town and defeated an army of about 2 000 soldiers comprised of Dutch, French, German and Hungarian mercenaries (Peires, 1981; Stapleton, 2010).

Governor John Cradock instructed Lieutenant Colonel John Graham to remove amaXhosa from the Zuurveld. At the time, amaGqunukhwebe under Chungwa were inhabitants of the rich land between Gamtoos River and Bushman's River, while amaRharhabe of Prince Ndlambe stayed in the region between Bushman's River and Great Fish River (Peires, 1981). Colonel Graham seemed to relish the opportunity of amassing a mighty force against amaXhosa. One of his well-known remarks was, *"To attack the savages in a way which I hope will leave a lasting impression on their memories"*[1] (Peires, 1981: 65).

In December 1811, Colonel Graham assembled a sizable force of about 900 regular troops comprised of 167 British dragoons, 221 British infantry, 431 Khoe infantry, a Royal Artillery detachment and 500 mounted Boer soldiers (Stapleton, 2010). His military strategy was to implement a massive attack, coupled with a vicious scorched earth policy, in the execution of Cradock's policy to drive out about 20 000 amaXhosa from the Zuurveld.

Graham organised his army into three divisions. The southern column, under Landdrost Jacob Cuyler, advanced east from the Sundays River towards the stronghold of Prince Chungwa. The northern column was commanded by Anders Stockenström, from Graaff-Reinet, whose plan was to launch an attack from the north towards Makhanda. The third column, under Graham, was to clear those running away from the war and continue to the centre of the attack.

In response, amaXhosa, under the command of Prince Ndlambe, launched simultaneous multi-pronged targeted attacks in order to disrupt and neutralise Graham's advancing three-pronged military assault. Stockenström's northern column was intercepted and wiped out by amaXhosa in one day. Graham was compelled to send a reinforcement of 500 men to assist Andries, the son of Anders Stockenström who succumbed to injuries during the war. Ndlambe took a decision

---

1   The original source is J. Cradock-Graham, n.d.RCC,VIII, p 160. Private communications from Graham, 2 Jan. 1812, RCC, VIII, p 237.)

to engage the southern column by taking a stand around the Addo bush. Eventually, Ndlambe succeeded in pushing back the advancing Cuyler's column. Graham was forced to abandon his entire military plan and cancelled the northern offensive by directing all his forces to the assistance of Cuyler against Ndlambe, who emerged as a formidable opponent following the fall of Prince Chungwa.

Ndlambe's decision to position his army in the thick forest of Addo was a calculated military strategy meant to neutralise the firepower of the British regiments by launching targeted attacks under the cover of the bushes. Most importantly his army was well position and acquainted with bush warfare. During the five-day deadly engagements, the combined British forces could not break the backbone of Ndlambe's forces, as they continued to suffer casualties while fighting in an unfamiliar and difficult terrain. Ndlambe's forces launched relentless waves of ferocious attacks in close combat.

After five days of intense engagements, Graham's forces continued to suffer increasing numbers of casualties, despite having mounted soldiers, cavalry and deadly artillery. Eventually, Graham was compelled to withdraw his forces from the cauldron of the deadly bush warfare. He diverted the attention of the army to the women, children and old people, one of whom was Prince Chungwa of amaGqunukhwebe, who was subjected to an undignified departure from his sick bed.

Professor Drusilla Yekela, the author of *The Death of Chungwa*, who taught many History students at the University of Fort Hare for decades, including the author of this book, wrote a great deal of work on the significance of the fall of Prince Chungwa. According to Yekela (2006) *"The day on which Chungwa died was one of great historical importance. This is evidenced in the oath, Ndifung' uChungw' efel' eMnyameni – I swear by Chungwa lying dead at Alexandria"* (pg 74). Chungwa died tragically, leaving behind his three sons Phatho, Kama and Kobe. The unceremonious fall of Prince Chungwa marked the defining historical imprint of the first grinding war between amaXhosa and the British-led army in the Southern Africa. The tragedy of the unanticipated fall of the revered senior royal aristocrat remains ingrained in the minds and souls of generations of amaXhosa up to the present day.

Graham, the ruthless Scottish officer, showed determination in the execution of what became the implementation of the first British scorched-earth military strategy of total destruction of property and annihilation of the inhabitants in the Zuurveld region. From that time onwards, the scorched earth military method became the British master plan that was used in the rest of the major wars in Southern African in pursuance of total conquest. This was often followed by implementation of total dispossession, forceful displacement and systematic dehumanization of the survivors. During the War of Mlanjeni and the Anglo−Boer in particular, the British resorted to the scorched-earth policy as a desperate attempt to break the backbone of resistance of their enemy.

The first war between the British army and amaXhosa in 1811-1812 caught the latter off guard because it was the first time they had to fight an enemy with advanced military methods. To amaXhosa the war was an instrument to defeat, possess and to incorporate, whilst to the British colonial establishment, the wars in Africa were methods of total obliteration with no options of co-existence. AmaXhosa perceived the deliberate mass killing of women and children during the warfare as an inhuman act, demonstrating the lowest level of savagery; an act of cowardice and desperation that was alien to the African rules of military engagement. From the shattering encounter of 1811 to 1812, it dawned on amaXhosa that they faced an existential threat of unimaginable magnitude. They either had to adapt quickly or face the prospect of complete extermination. Consequently, in the subsequent wars, amaXhosa avoided facing the British army in open terrain, as they preferred bush warfare, coupled with surprise targeted ambushes in strategic locations, meant to inflict a higher number of casualties in order to weaken the enemy.

Under such harrowing circumstances, Prince Ndlambe felt compelled to review his military strategy, because he found the shameful killing of women and children unconventional and unbearable. He organised his people to cross the Nxuba River in order to avoid incurring more casualties. This was a temporary retreat, with the intention of launching guerrilla attacks later. Graham's army seized the remaining livestock and obliterated crops and villages as well as those who were left behind (Stapleton, 2010).

The merciless British policy of ethnic cleansing of the Zuurveld marked the beginning of a new and scary phenomenon in the history of African warfare. The targeting of women and children was a catastrophic calamity of unbearable proportions. Peires (1981) captured their impression about the encounter saying, *"Total war was a new and shattering experience for the Xhosa...The purpose of war was not the destruction of productive resources, but their acquisition and absorption. The havoc brought by the Colonial forces was not only cruel but incomprehensible"* (Peires, 1981: 66). What followed such an unprecedented tragedy was the launching of relentless raids and ambushes targeting the settler communities in the Zuurveld. The British authorities retaliated by launching military attacks as far as the Kei region, in collaboration with King Ngqika, who perceived Prince Ndlambe as a threat to his kingdom. The amaXhosa combatants resorted to multi-pronged simultaneous night raids, which made the situation unbearable for the British-led army. Eventually, Cradock commissioned the construction of massive military posts along the Nxuba River.

In retrospect, despite Chungwa's repeated request for co-existence, he was ignored because Africans were treated as commodities to be disposed of at any time convenient to the colonialists. Peires (1981) also observed that the expulsion was driven by the British rejection of coexistence with amaXhosa in the Zuurveld, because they wanted to ensure complete monopoly of land ownership. The rejection of

The rejection of Chungwa's diplomatic appeals for co-existence was a clear indication that no matter how much Africans had tried to make peace with the British establishment, what mattered to them was the land and its resources and not co-existence with African people. Most of the dominant historical narrative claimed that the conflicts between amaXhosa and the European were triggered by tensions over cattle theft, usage of grazing fields and intrusions. This was basically a cover-up for the colonial policy of dispossession, displacement and dehumanization.

Most historians believe that Colonel Graham's draconian military operations laid the lasting foundations on which the British conquest of Southern Africa was pursued and accomplished. Mostert (1992) argued that *"In their different ways, General Sir John Cradock and Lieutenant Colonel John Graham had a vision of themselves as the initial architects of a new colonial society and in a very real sense it was these two soldiers who during their brief presence in South Africa began the active work of establishing a permanent British imprint upon the colony"* (pg 397). At the end of the harrowing campaign, Graham established military headquarters on a site in a town that was established and named after him. The establishment of Grahamstown, which was changed into Makhanda two centuries later, was a powerful symbol of the British presence in Africa, south of the Sahara and the military launching pad for the conquest of Southern Africa. The arrival of the British settlers in 1820 sent a clear message that the Empire had reached a point of no return in creating permanent presence in Southern Africa.

The period between 1812 and 1818 was relatively calm, as it was marked by the rise of King Hintsa, who was openly opposed to the colonial encroachment. The unpleasant alliance between the British colonialists and King Ngqika made the latter arrogant towards leaders of amaXhosa on both sides of the Nciba River. In the process, he became alienated as the majority of amaXhosa and the royal leaders resented his collaboration with Europeans which they viewed as enabling acts of conquest. Eventually, the growing tensions exploded into the outbreak of the devastating war of Amalinde in October 1818. Mostert 1992 defined it as, *"...the greatest and most terrible battle ever fought among the Xhosa themselves"* (pg 466). Ngqika's forces, under the leadership of senior counsellor Makoyi, were subjected to a resounding defeat by the combined forces of amaRharhabe and amaGcaleka, under the leadership of courageous Prince Mdushane, the eldest son Prince Ndlambe.

To avenge the defeat, Ngqika appealed for assistance to Lord Charles Somerset, the Governor of the Cape Colony between 1814 and 1826. The latter requested Lieutenant Colonel Thomas Brereton to punish Prince Ndlambe. Subsequently, Brereton assembled a large force of British, Boers, Khoe and Ngqika's remnants. Prince Ndlambe strategically refrained from engaging in the punitive war by repositioning his people to the nearby forests of Hoho. Although Brereton's forces captured a substantial number of cattle, Prince Ndlambe retrieved them through devastating raids that were launched deep into the occupied territory of white settlers, who paid a heavy price for the war. Mostert (1992) noted that the *"Large-scale raids on farms began on Christmas Day, 1818, and by the end of January 1819, much of the region of Albany, the former Zuurveld, appeared to be back in possession of the Xhosa once more"* (Mostert, 1992: 468). A number of patrolling British soldiers were subjected to horrific ambushes as their bodies were mutilated. The intensity of the attacks caused panic and abandonment of farms and white settler villages, as Ndlambe's forces continued to unleash deadly attacks in their determination to avenge the unprovoked colonial war.

Brereton came under immense pressure as he was unable to contain the devastating fireball of deadly raids, so he called for reinforcements from Cape Town, as his troops were completely overstretched and outmanoeuvred in the war, which spiralled out of control. The war that was meant to avenge Ngqika's defeat by humiliating Ndlambe turned out to be a catastrophic campaign with far-reaching consequences, especially for the European settlers, who suffered huge losses, especially loss of life. The disastrous backfiring of the war proved to be a serious miscalculation by Somerset, who underestimated the military capabilities of Prince Ndlambe. As a face-saving exercise, Lieutenant Colonel Thomas Brereton was fired and replaced by Lieutenant Colonel Thomas Willshire.

Willshire assembled 3 352 soldiers, comprising British, Boers and Khoe riflemen (Mostert, 1992). Nxele, from the side of Ndlambe, assembled about 10 000 men on the Fish River valley. On 22 April 2020, Prince Mdushane and Makhanda ka Nxele led his army to the battle of Makhanda. The regiments of amaXhosa came face-to-face with Lieutenant Colonel Willshire and chased him to the centre of the city. Unfortunately, the amaXhosa warriors were overwhelmed by the well-positioned artillery and suffered heavy casualties and they had to retreat. It was reported that after the war, Makhanda ka Nxele surrendered to the British army near Trompetter's Drift on the Nxuba River in an attempt to appease the enemy. He was incarcerated on Robben Island and never returned.

In South Africa this is the only battle that is commemorated annually. It happened to be the only war where the British army attained a decisive defeat of amaXhosa, unlike the wars of 1811-1812 and 1834-1835 where amaXhosa stood their ground. The wars of 1846-1847 and 1850-1853 stood out as the ones where amaXhosa defeated the British army in various battles, yet they are neither celebrated nor clearly narrated in the official history textbooks.

The era of King Ngqika's reign between 1795 and 1829 and the acrimonious relationship with his uncle, Prince Ndlambe, impacted negatively on the collective efforts to wage effective resistance against colonial encroachment during that period. During his reign, what mattered to him was the pursuance of power, coupled with hollow ambitions of becoming the Supreme King of amaXhosa. Ngqika was too naïve to understand that the same British colonial authorities he used to pursue his interests, in fact had bigger plans to acquire his land as they possessed the Zuurveld and Kat River during his reign and took the bold step to ship the settlers to Makhanda. It was only after his departure that amaXhosa were able to marshal collective resistance, as illustrated by the decisive wars led by his sons Maqoma, Sandile, Tyhali and Xhoxho who contributed significantly in the triangle of one hundred years wars of resistance. It explains why the wars of 1834-1835, 1846-1847 and 1850-1853 were more impactful and significant in the history of African wars of resistance.

4. First Collision between Prince Maqoma and Colonel Smith

Prince Maqoma and General Harry Smith stood as two highly gifted and capable adversaries who had a great influence in shaping the wars of 1834 to 1835 and 1850 to 1853. Both of them were determined and highly-driven characters, revered and celebrated by their people, as they both relished battlefield encounters.

Prince Maqoma's first experience of war was the bloody battle of Amalinde in 1818, which was fought between the followers of Prince Ndlambe, supported by King Hintsa, against the highly despised King Ngqika. Maqoma was seriously wounded in the battle and it took about two years for him to recover from the deep wounds. Upon the death of his father, King Ngqika, he reigned as a regent on behalf of the young Prince Sandile. In the wars of 1834 to 35 and 1850 to 1853, in which he faced Harry Smith, he stood out as an incredible military genius, with immense endurance and extraordinary capabilities to rally his people and command the war operations.

What placed Prince Maqoma, known as Jongumsobomvu, above the others, was his military genius to organise his army into small agile groups to launch multiple simultaneous attacks, in order to create a strong sense of presence everywhere; the execution of targeted deadly ambushes made possible by the strategic deployment of informers to monitor enemy movement; and the calculated implementation of the system of rotation of combatants in order to engage in a sustained war over a considerable period of time.

Image 2.3: Prince Maqoma Ah! Jongumsobomvu, the eldest son of Prince Ngqika. Source: Mostert (1992) from South African Library, Cape Town.

Harry Smith started his military career in 1805-1807 in South America. He distinguished himself in the British-French wars of the Napoleonic era in Spain between 1808 and 1814. By the time he was deployed as the commander of the colonial forces in Cape Colony, he was a tried and tested war veteran, with impeccable credentials as a disciplined, decisive and distinguished military officer. In the war of 1834-1845, where the British army crossed the Nciba River for the first time, it was General Smith who pursued King Hintsa to the banks of the Nqabarha River, which ultimately led to King Hintsa's undignified departure from the face of the earth.

Image 2.4: General Harry Smith, the Hero of Aliwal. Source: Engraved by D J Pound from a photograph by J Eastham. From the book The Drawing Room Portrait Gallery of Eminent Personages Volume 2. Published in London, 1859.

In the aftermath of the war, Smith was transferred to India, following concerns about the way in which he participated in the diabolical humiliation of the supreme royal aristocrat of amaXhosa prior to and after his departure. In India, he redeemed himself in the battle of 1845 to 1846 against the Sikhs of Punjab, in what was later known as the famous Battle of Aliwal on 28 January 1846, in which he led from the front. That is why he was often referred to as the Hero of Aliwal. Smith was the epitome of the British Empire, an ambitious, bombastic and determined soldier. At the outbreak of the war of War of Hintsa in 1834 to 1835, Smith rode his horses from Cape Town to Makhanda as commander of the colonial forces.

The war of Hintsa of 1834 to 1835 was triggered by an incident that occurred on 2 December 1834 in which Ensign Sparks led a colonial raid into Prince Tyhali's territory and seized a number of cattle. The patrol was repelled by amaXhosa combatants (Stapleton, 1992). In retaliation, Lieutenant General Henry Somerset, the son of Lord Charles Somerset, sent Lieutenant Sutton to attack Tyhali and confiscate cattle. On 12 December 1834, Sutton engaged Tyhali's warriors in an effort to capture the cattle. In the process, a bullet grazed the head of Prince Xhoxho, the favourite half-brother of Jongumsobomvu.

The injury to the young royal leader, the son of the senior aristocrat King Ngqika, infuriated amaXhosa in the Keiskamma region and pushed them to breaking point. They felt that the incremental encroachment of white settlers occupying prime lands deep in the territories of amaXhosa was bad enough. However, the colonial patrol commandos, who were a law unto themselves, operating with absolute impunity where they could shoot any Africans anywhere and confiscate cattle as they wish, became a source of frustration and anger. The shooting of Prince Xhoxho was viewed as a declaration of war; hence it triggered the outbreak of the War of Hintsa.

In the midst of mobilization for the war, Rev Kayser attempted to persuade Jongumsobomvu to refrain from war preparations. Since missionaries operated in the heartland of the communities of amaXhosa, they were strategically placed to get information and be able to take initiative in the protection of the colonial interests. One wonders what missionaries like Rev Kayser did to condemn the harassment of amaXhosa by the military commandos. Prince Maqoma made it clear to Rev Kayser that although Prince Xhoxho had not died, the shooting of a royal aristocrat was tantamount to the declaration of war, because this was an indication that their lives did not matter.

With Prince Ngqika gone, Prince Maqoma was in a position of influence as a regent to mobilise all amaXhosa to take a united stand for the first time against the colonial forces. Maqoma was still bitter about the expulsion from his land at the Kat River in 1829, which was rich, had easy access to water and was the beautiful territory of his childhood, where he established his nation of amaJingqi. He resented the humiliating expulsion, which he regarded as an abuse of power and a clear demonstration of the blatant British intention to acquire land and livestock through the use of military might. Maqoma remained determined to avenge the dispossession of his land at the right time.

In January 1835, Prince Maqoma mobilized a large army of amaXhosa with the support of his brother Prince Tyhali, as well as Prince Mhala of amaNdlambe, Prince Nqeno of amaMbalu and Prince Bhotomane of imiDange. The war marked the beginning of an all-out united onslaught against the British colonial authorities. They started off by launching multiple raids targeting the white settler farms and villages to recapture livestock confiscated by the commandos.

In response to Maqoma's declaration of war to avenge the shooting of Prince Xhoxho in February 1835, Lieutenant Colonel Harry Smith assembled an army comprised of British, Boers, and Khoe troops. He organised the army into three divisions, one column led by himself, the second one under the command of Richard England and the third led by Lieutenant General Henry Somerset. The first battle was waged on the banks of the Nxuba River. The bushy area was strategically chosen by Maqoma as the first point of the battle to engage the enemy forces from Makhanda. The encounter between the two opposing sides was brutal, intense and bloody. Maqoma's strategy was to send a small group of mounted warriors to taunt the colonial forces, and then gallop back to the thick bushes (Mostert, 1992). This strategy worked by launching deadly ambushes from the bushes and thus inflicted lethal casualties to the colonial forces. In close combat under the cover of the thick bushes, amaXhosa used their spears directly instead of throwing them at the enemy. The bush warfare was terrifying as they stood toe to toe with the colonial forces.

Maqoma launched a multi-pronged military attack on the Nxuba and Nukakamma Rivers as well as Amathole Mountains. During the war, Maqoma's army was almost everywhere in the colony. They placed military posts under siege and cut their movement and the supply lines. Maqoma's strategy was to avoid wasting resources and endangering his army by trying to invade the highly fortified military forts, which were protected by the firepower of the artillery and well-armed soldiers. Placing them under permanent siege from a distance achieved the desired purpose of confinement, whilst the rest of the combatants targeted the vulnerable settler settlements and farms. During this time, his combatants demonstrated an impressive measure of maturity and restraint by targeting white males and leaving women and children to flee on their own. They confiscated the livestock and burnt homesteads and settlement villages in order to drive the colonialists from the occupied land.

After four days of intense engagements, amaXhosa retreated in order to regroup and resume the attacks. The naïve Smith thought that marked the end of the war. He quickly declared with his inflated ego that he was the first officer in Southern Africa to win such a decisive victory over amaXhosa in four days. About three weeks after Smith's declaration of victory, amaXhosa launched attacks targeting the British troops.

Mostert (1992) observed that *"The Fish River bush in 1835 became the British army's induction into its extended experience of guerrilla warfare in the bush with an elusive, determined foe, who was highly skilled with his own weapons and within his own terrain"* (pg 694). What made this war different from previous ones was the fact that amaXhosa, under Prince Maqoma, were better organised and able to retaliate against British methods of warfare. It was the first time amaXhosa had collected a sizable number of firearms that they could use in the war. Maqoma dictated the rules of military engagement by deciding where the war had to be fought, when to retreat and when to resume attacks. As a result, the British forces were forced to adopt a reactive stance. Both the British army and white settlers found this protracted military approach laborious as it drained their energies and resources.

Sir Benjamin D'Urban, the Governor of the Cape Colony from 1834 until 1838, had to hit the ground running as the new administrator. Upon his arrival in Makhanda in April 1835, D'Urban assembled a large force of about 3 500 soldiers comprised of infantry, cavalry, British, Khoe and Boer troops. According to Cory (1919) the British Cape colonial army at the time had 27 Royal Artilleries high calibre large guns, 482 members of the 75th Regiment, 20 Royal Engineers and 226 mounted rifle soldiers. On top of all that, they were supported by the larger groups of the Khoe and the Boers.

D'Urban organised the army into four columns. Harry Smith led the first column to the Amathole Mountains, supported by the second division of Henry Somerset. Major William Cox led the third column to Fort Beaufort and the fourth division of the Boers under Commandant Van Wyk were deployed to the northern side of the Amathole Mountains (Mostert 1992; Stapleton, 2016).

During the war, the Khoe and the Boers were deployed to the frontline to engage amaXhosa in bush warfare. In the process, the British army captured cattle and laid waste to the villages by killing women and children. They embarked on relentless pillaging in the Amathole Mountains, hoping to break the backbone of resistance of amaXhosa. This was a repeat of the ethnic cleansing started by Cradock and Graham in 1811 and 1812. This time amaXhosa were more prepared and adaptable to the brutal military methods of the British army. To a great extent, the military leaders of amaXhosa were able to hide women and children from the invading army. The forces of amaXhosa excelled in counter-attacking the invading enemy forces with devastating ambushes launched from strategic locations. The purpose was not to attain decisive victory in an open warfare, but rather to inflict heavy casualties through targeted attacks in order to demoralise the army.

D'Urban and his military commanders were frustrated because they expected a traditional battle similar to the European wars instead of a bush war fought in rugged mountainous region. The cavalry and artillery of the British regular troops were useless in the face of an elusive enemy in the thick bushes and mountains. The combination of the excessively hot weather of February 1835, coupled with heavy rains, made the bush warfare conditions unbearable for the highly regimented British troops.

According to Mostert (1992) *"For the complacent victors of the Peninsula campaigns and Waterloo, aware that they held the laurels for having successfully concluded the greatest war ever fought, comfortably convinced of their martial, moral and technological superiority, it seemed a peculiar humiliation to find that what had defeated Napoleon could not easily dispose of what was considered to be merely a horde of savages"* (Mostert, 1992: 694-5). The military campaign in Amathole Mountains around Qoboqobo (Keiskammahoek), Xesi (Middledrift) and the Tyhume valley proved to be a painfully frustrating endeavour, as the sons of King Ngqika, as well as several leaders of amaXhosa from various groups, took a decisive stand through multi-pronged simultaneous attacks. The steep and rugged forest, with its deep gorges, bushy ravines and long narrow ridges offered a perfect opportunity to launch surprise attacks on the flanks of the approaching British forces. Unfortunately for D'Urban, Smith and Somerset, their artillery, cavalry and mounted soldiers failed to achieve the intended objectives in the rugged foreign terrain.

As the British troops continued infiltrating the Amathole Mountains, which were heavily populated by amaXhosa, they found deserted villages. The war in the mountains of Amathole was a futile exercise as the British army was drained by endless marches in rough territories, without making any progress in the neutralisation of the enemy. The colonial army failed to attain the envisaged victory, despite being in possession of superior firepower.

After D'Urban and his military commanders found themselves trapped in a protracted war of mutual attrition, they had to find a noble exit strategy without admitting dismal failure. They were frustrated by their failure to break the backbone of resistance, despite having burnt villages, captured cattle and killed whomever they came across during the war.

The clandestine activities and a stream of letters from a Wesleyan missionary by the name of Rev John Ayliff provided D'Urban with a plausible exit strategy from the harrowing cauldron of the war in the mountains of Amathole. In the letters of Rev Ayliff, D'Urban found a convenient reason to blame King Hintsa, the Supreme King of amaXhosa, as the mastermind behind the atrocious war. Eventually, D'Urban took a decision to disengage from the war of the Amathole mountains. He instructed Major Cox to continue with the hopeless military campaign whilst he and Smith and the larger part of the military machinery decided to cross the Nciba River to invade amaGcaleka, who were perceived to be less battle-hardened compared to more adaptable and elusive amaRharhabe. Eventually, in April 1835, the British army crossed the legendary Kei River for the first time since the occupation of the Cape colony.

The decision to abandon the agonising war in the mountains of Amathole was a matter of political and military pragmatism in order to attain a quick victory across the Nciba River. Stretch (1988) who served in the War of Makhanda in 1819, the War of 1834 to 1835 and the War of 1846 to 1847, believed that there was no evidence that King Hintsa ignited the flames of the War of 1834 to 1835. According to him, it was the white settlers and colonial military commandos who heightened the tensions through their constant humiliation of the revered royal leaders, coupled with increased incursions, deep into the territories of amaXhosa. Despite Ayliff's letters, D'Urban and Smith knew that King Hintsa was neither the aggressor nor the brains behind the war. Ayliff's letters provided them with the escape route they needed from the humiliation of their failure to break the backbone of Maqoma's resistance despite commanding a well-resourced army.

5. Missionaries in Conquest and the Exodus of Amamfengu

The war of Hintsa of 1834-1835 was a critical historical event which, among other things, cemented the controversial role of some of the Wesleyan missionaries as enabling agents in expediting the British conquest of Southern Africa, through the exploitation of vulnerabilities of African kingdoms. Many of these missionaries exploited the trust and loyalty of their converts, by soliciting vital information about the strengths and the exploitable weaknesses of the African people, as well as what kept the kingdoms together, which they used to advance the colonial interests. Such critical information placed the colonial establishment in a position of strength to exploit the weaknesses of African people in pursuance of total conquest. Sir Benjamin D'Urban's political decision to invade King Hintsa's kingdom across the Nciba River was largely justified through the series of controversial narratives generated by Wesleyan missionaries aimed at demonising King Hintsa as the instigator of the War of 1834 to 1835.

Dora Taylor, in her compelling book *The Role of the Missionaries in Conquest,* which was published in Johannesburg in 1952, under the pseudonym of Nosipho Majeke, explored, among other things, the manipulation of the precarious situation of amaMfengu, who were called Fingos by the white settlers. Taylor named Reverend John Ayliff as one of the leading controversial missionaries who played a pivotal role in influencing and facilitating the British conquest of amaXhosa. According to Taylor (1952) *"Nowhere have we a clearer example of the tactics of "divide and rule" than in the way the Rev. John Ayliff drove a wedge between the Fingos and their natural allies, the Gcaleka"* (pg 35). Taylor argued that it was at the Butterworth Mission where Rev Ayliff sowed the bitter seeds of tribal divisions whose manifestations created long-lasting fissures between amaGcaleka and amaMfengu.

Image 2.5: Rev John Ayliff. Source: Albany Museum in Makhanda, Eastern Cape.

Reverend John Ayliff was an influential Wesleyan missionary, who was placed in the Kingdom of King Hintsa. Ayliff was a strategic, patient and calculating man who, in the passage of time, fell out of favour with King Hintsa. On the surface Reverend Ayliff projected himself as a dedicated missionary, whose calling was to bring light and redemption by converting Africans to Christianity. Beneath the surface, his actual mission was to infiltrate the kingdom in order to understand and study the inner strengths and fragile vulnerabilities of the royal establishment of amaXhosa. Such vital information was critical for the British colonial authorities in their multi-pronged approach to the systematic destruction of amaXhosa. This explains why leaders such as Prince Maqoma were always suspicious about the dual role played by some of the missionaries. As for Ayliff, he was more of a British agent than a missionary, but used the latter role as a convenient cover for clandestine activities. It is tragic that in the process, his subversive activities tarnished the work of other dedicated missionaries, placed their lives at risk during the wars and undermined their worthwhile efforts.

The extent of Reverend Ayliff's infiltration went so far as converting some of the senior councillors of amaMfengu, who were in the inner circle of King Hintsa's establishment, as well as Queen Nomsa, whom he won over by curing her sick son. Winning the heart of Queen Nomsa was also strategically calculated, as the converted women of the royal houses were known to be sympathetic towards missionaries, whom they often protected in times of war. This is illustrated by the case of Queen Suthu, the wife of King Ngqika, in protecting the missionaries during the wars. Peires (1981) observed that, *"The missionaries' primary targets were some of the Xhosas' most treasured social institutions, and they met with a resounding snub...Nor was there much prospect of persuading the Xhosa to abandon polygamy and bridewealth, the cement of all social relationships"* (pg 145-6). Peires's (1981) assertion is illustrated by the manner in which the senior royal aristocrats of amaXhosa placated the missionaries by keeping them at arm's length. King Hintsa tolerated the missionaries, although he had suspicions about their activities on the basis of their history of connection with colonial authorities, which were to the detriment of amaXhosa. To him, the missionaries were not very different from the colonial agents planted to spy on amaXhosa.

Rev Ayliff fabricated a false narrative that made the British establishment believe that AmaMfengu and AmaHlubi were held in bondage as slaves by amaXhosa. Slavery was an anomaly in Southern Africa, because it was not in the culture and nature of the Southern African nations to enslave the defeated smaller tribes. According to Taylor (1952), the notion of holding others as slaves was foreign to amaXhosa. Ayliff's false narrative was contrary to how amaMfengu were treated by King Hintsa. Even some of the senior counsellors were amaMfengu. Taylor argued that King Hintsa would not have allowed his daughter to marry Prince Njokweni of amaZizi from amaMfengu, if amaMfengu were perceived and treated as slaves.

Mostert (1992) asserted that it was in the nature of amaXhosa to absorb other nations through a process of different stages of integration, *"Their tradition was that newcomers as impoverished as the Mfengu should pass through a period of clientship before becoming full Xhosa"* (Mostert, 1992: 697). Taylor (1952) also found it strange that Ayliff managed to develop a grip over amaMfengu by convincing them to turn against their allies in favour of the British. At the time, they had land granted to them by the royal rulers of amaGcaleka and were still going through the process of integration, in the way the defeated amaNgqosinin became fully integrated into amaXhosa during the reign of King Tshiwo. This was followed by the defeat and the incorporation of the Khoe people such as amaNqarhwane, OoSukwini and amaGqwashu during the reign of Prince Mdange, who acted as a regent for the young Prince Phalo, the son of his brother King Tshiwo (Peires, 1976). Dr Manduleli Bikitsha, in his unpublished document on amaMfengu dated 2019, asserted that King Hintsa's grant of land to amaMfengu who were destitute and vulnerable was a philanthropic act of Ubuntu, of giving dignity to them so that they could establish themselves as a community.

The likelihood was that the wounds from the defeat of amaMfengu in the battle of Mbholompo[2] in 1828, which resulted in the loss of their nationhood, were still raw. They were lured into the trap of hope to regain their independence as amaMfengu, and were promised land where they would fulfil their wishes. Little did they know that in the subsequent wars they were going to be used by the British, placed on the frontline and made to carry out massacres of women and children, in which they excelled especially in the battle of Mlanjeni from 1850 to 1853. At the end of those wars in 1879, the promise made by Reverend Ayliff was never fulfilled. Taylor more or less empathised with amaMfengu and the vulnerable situation they found themselves in at the time. It was easier for them, considering their recent situation, to believe in the promise of a better life under a nation presented to be more powerful than amaXhosa. Taylor (1952) argued that *"No doubt he would read to them from the Scriptures the story of how the Israelites – wanderers like themselves – received the divine promise of a land flowing with milk and honey"* (pg 35). The religious comparison of their situation and the promise for a better land to regain their nationhood went to the core of their vulnerability.

At the outbreak of the war of resistance from 1834 to 1835, missionaries such as Reverend Ayliff, Reverend Shepstone and Reverend Shrewsbury were instrumental in building a narrative which implied that King Hintsa supported the war from behind the scenes. Such a narrative was later used by the Governor, Sir Benjamin D'Urban to justify the invasion of the royal headquarters of King Hintsa whose kingdom covered the area between the Mbhashe and Xelexwa Rivers. According to Taylor (1952), Wesleyan missionaries were

---

2   Mbholompo is situated not far from the R61 road from Engcobo towards Mthatha. It is a village at the centre of Mthatha, Tsolo, Ugie and Engcobo lying below the long range of montane forests between Engcobo and Tsolo. Mbholompo is an important landmark of significant significance because it is where the nation of amaNgwane comprised of amaHlubi disintegrated.

complicit in the tragic military campaign against amaXhosa by acting as agents of the colonial authorities.

The relations between King Hintsa and Reverend Ayliff collapsed after the war started in early 1834. Mostert (1992) is emphatic in his observations that Reverend Ayliff, the self-appointed spiritual leader in the kingdom of King Hintsa, was a British agent actively gathering intelligence and conspiring against the leaders of amaXhosa. He advised amaMfengu that when the British attacked amaGcaleka they should declare their allegiance to Sir Benjamin D'Urban. Alyliff together with his family and traders were able to flee in time after a tip-off from Queen Nomsa.

That said, missionaries such as Dr John Philip, Reverend John Read and John Fairbairn, a newspaper editor, criticised the colonial authorities for the general treatment and disdain towards amaXhosa. The colonial establishment was enraged by such criticism. Reverend John Read was instructed to meet D'Urban in Makhanda, was held there against his will and became an object of humiliation by the white settlers (Mostert, 1992).

Taylor's critical observation on the role of missionaries during the era of wars of resistance and conquest is echoed by Professor Premesh Lalu in his book *The Deaths of Hintsa – Post Apartheid South Africa and the shape of recurring pasts* published in 2009. According to Lalu (2009) Rev Ayliff's controversial role at the time was also driven by personal business interests because he owned horses. Lalu asserted that the motive behind the brutal murder and mutilation of King Hintsa was not only to conquer and dominate amaXhosa, but to look at possibilities of unlocking sources of cheap African labour. Alyiff's aim of driving a wedge between amaXhosa and amaMfengu was part of that strategy to create a labour force for the white settlers, considering the fact that amaMfengu were excellent cultivators. Unfortunately, the outcomes of the war of 1834 to 1835, in which D'Urban and his military commanders failed to attain victory, coupled with large-scale destruction of the white settler farms and villages, created extreme levels of bitterness among white settlers such as John Alyiff, William Southey, Holden Bowker and many others.

Lalu (2009) asserted that the *"Repeated calls for the extermination of the native, subduing the Xhosa and confiscating their land accompanied the sense of bitterness and betrayal. The failure of ever realizing these outcomes – of pursuing a programme of genocide and unlocking potential sources of black labour – re-established a certain currency in the history of the killing of Hintsa"* (pg 73). Lalu's observations crystalize the gravity of the deep-seated hatred of the British settlers that emerged in the aftermath of their disastrous performance in the War of Hintsa. Essentially, the entire strategy of the British settlers like Alyiff to cultivate fertile ground for a wider war unexpectedly backfired because of their miscalculation of the extent of resistance and retaliation of amaXhosa; hence the repeated calls for the total extermination of amaXhosa emerged among the white settlers.

In essence, some of the missionaries were integral components of the British colonial machinery. The only difference was that most of them were the human face behind the brutality of British Imperialism in Southern Africa. They were not only involved in running missions as a cover for intelligence collection, but were also involved in running schools as well as conducting deep under-cover operations meant to eliminate threats to colonial interests. Peires (1981) made a critical observation, expressed by Prince Bhotomane, pertaining to the controversial role of missionaries, when he asked why the royal aristocrats of amaXhosa such as Prince Ndlambe, died in 1828, followed by his indomitable son Mdushane in 1829 as well as King Ngqika on the same year.

After the institutions of learning were opened for Africans, the missionaries became gatekeepers in the management of knowledge production, especially the material written by African pioneers of education. The 20-year administration of Reverend R.H.W Shepherd at Lovedale was characterised by the continued refusal to print literature perceived to be critical of the activities of the British Empire.

Although isiXhosa literature was written, it was strictly regulated. As a result, Shepherd was responsible for the loss of three manuscripts written by S.E.K Mqhayi, one of the leading pioneers of education and written language of isiXhosa, a gifted writer and incredible historian, with a strong command of language (Peires, 1981).

How amaMfengu happened to be the subjects of King Hintsa had to do with the fateful historical incident which took place at Mbholompo near Umtata in 1828. AmaNgwane of King Matiwane are Nguni speaking people who settled in Northern Natal around the White Mfolozi River. In 1818, Shaka attacked and defeated amaNgwane. They were compelled to leave their ancestral land and they travelled towards Lesotho. During their wandering journey, looking for land to settle, they came across amaHlubi of King Mpangazitha. War ensued between the amaNgwane and amaHlubi. AmaHlubi were defeated, after their leader Mpangazitha was killed. The defeat and death of Mpangazitha and several leading figures was a huge setback as amaHlubi disintegrated and ceased to exist as a united nation. Whilst a number of them were integrated into amaNgwane, others returned to Mzinyathi, led by Sidinana, the son of Mpangazitha. By that time, Dingane had replaced Shaka as the reigning leader in Natal (Ayliff & Whiteside, 1912). Some of them were incorporated into amaNgwane after the tragic departure of King Mpangazitha. AmaNgwane continued wandering as refugees until they settled temporarily near Lesotho. They fought King Moshoeshoe in an attempt to capture and occupy the stronghold of Thaba Bosiu, and failed. Later amaNgwane migrated to the south and crossed the Orange River.

Upon arrival in the Cape, amaNgwane consisted of the remnants of amaHlubi. They were attacked and defeated by the combined forces of abaThembu, amaXhosa and amaMpondo, supported by British troops, at the fateful battle of Mbholompo in August 1828. King Matiwane managed to escape with a small group, returned to Natal and was later killed by Dingane. A substantial number of them remained at Mbholompo. According to Ayliff and Whiteside (1912), after the defeat of Mbholompo, the survivors were welcomed by King Hintsa as destitute, hence they were called amaMfengu. *"Who are you? What do you want"* *They replied, 'Siyamfenguza,' which means 'We seek service,' We are destitute.' The word amamfengu, therefore means "'Hungry people in search of work'"* (Ayliff & White, 1912: 15).

AmaXhosa, at the height of King Hintsa's reign, offered to shelter and integrate amaNgwnae in line with their tradition of welcoming and sheltering destitute people. The dominant clans of amaMfengu incorporated into amaXhosa were amaZizi, amaBhele, ooNtlangwini and amaHlubi (Bikitsha, 2019). During the process of integration into amaXhosa, amaMfengu became *amabusa* to amaXhosa, meaning that they pledged their allegiance to the King of amaXhosa. They were very resourceful, as they excelled in trading and cultivation (Peires, 1981).

King Hintsa's intentions to shelter and absorb amaMfengu were not based on plans to enslave them. Peires (1976) asserted that amaMfengu were systematically integrated into amaXhosa. According to Peires (1976) *"The Mfengu were initially well-received by the Xhosa chiefs, who always welcomed the accession of new followers...The amaZizi hid their chief Njokweni for fear the Xhosa would kill him, but when he was discovered, Hintsa recognised his authority and allocated him and his people land. 66 Mfengu chiefs sat on chief's councils as councillors, and participated in important consultations. Mfengu who arrived destitute and without cattle were distributed among Hintsa's people as herdsmen in the usual manner of busa clients"* (pp 199-200). The observation made by Peires (1976) is consistent with other historical narratives that amaMfengu were integrated into amaXhosa as part of the tradition of sheltering the defeated smaller nations.

On one hand, Ayliff & Whiteside (1912) asserted that, *"The Gcalekas, influenced by their chief, Hintsa, gradually became oppressive in their treatment of the Fingos"* (pg 18). On the surface, Ayliff positioned himself as the saviour of amaMfengu from slavery; hence he influenced the British invasion. Beneath the surface, he worked to weaken the kingdom of King Hintsa by driving a wedge between amaMfengu and amaGcaleka. The actual purpose of the British invasion was to dismantle the supreme royal authority of amaXhosa regarded as the center of power and nationhood. The invasion was anchored on the false pretext presented by Ayliff that King Hintsa was complicit in the war. According to Ayliff, amaXhosa were presented as, *"...great cattle plunderers, robbing the border farmers of some of the best of the herds..."* (pg 24). Ayliff believed that amaXhosa attacked the white settlers as far as Nukakamma (Sundays) River and confiscated 100 000 cattle, 150 000 sheep and obliterated about 450 farms.

The Graham's Town Journal of 20 February, 1835 reported that Ayliff stated that King Hintsa conducted himself in a manner indicative of *"an open avowal of his hostility"* (pg 4) towards the British establishment. In this way, Ayliff deliberately targeted King Hintsa in order to divert the resentment and the anger of the white settlers towards a clear and identifiable target. This was meant to ensure that King Hintsa bore the brunt of British military firepower. Ayliff was opportunistic in exploiting the fears of the white settlers and the colonial establishment by taking advantage of the outbreak of the war of 1834 to1835 in pursuance of both personal and colonial interests.

Ayliff was determined to prove that the king had a hand in the brutal murder of a British trader named Eccles. Prior to the invasion Ayliff used amaMfengu to obtain and pass sensitive information about the kingdom to the British colonial establishment. During the invasion, he instructed amaMfengu to assemble at a particular point in order to meet the invading British army.

Ayliff & Whiteside (1912) and Theal (1912) claimed that amaMfengu left Gcuwa on 09th May 1835 destined for Ngqushwa, led by their leaders in the following sub-groups:

1.   Mhlambiso of amaHlubi who was the senior overall leader,
2.   Matomela of amaRheledwane,
3.   Njokweni of amaZizi ,

4. Nkwenkwezi of amaBhele,
5. Swana of amaGobizembe,
6. Hliso of abaseKunene,
7. Mkhuzangwe of abaYimani,
8. Nkwali of abaSwawo

Ayliff assembled amaMfengu under a huge milkwood tree called Umqwashu, where they declared a pledge of allegiance and loyalty to the British establishment. AmaMfengu were allocated land at Ngqushwa.

On the other hand, Soga (1930) argued that, *"The condition of the Fingos who sought sanctuary in Gcalekaland has been falsely represented as slavery"* (pg. 179). Soga argued that the colonial historians deliberately perpetuated the false representation of the condition of amaMfengu. According to him, following the disintegration of amaHlubi and amaNgwane, the survivors were welcomed as destitute, just like all other tribes displaced by Shaka. They were allocated land at eCeru, Ezolo near Tsomo River and Ngqamakhwe, Zingqayi and Bika and placed under their own leaders. He argued that the Europeans who stayed in Gcalekaland never presented any accounts of slavery of amaMfengu by amaXhosa. Also, amaMfengu's personal experiences in the land of King Hintsa confirmed that they were never treated as slaves. Not all amaMfengu left, because they were never treated as slaves anyway. Chief Poswa of amaHlubi and Chief Deyi of Aba-Shwawu remained behind. Soga asserted that amaMfengu arrived as destitute people in 1828 and left in 1835 in possession of 22 000 cattle.

On the same note, Spicer (1978) disagreed with the claim that amaMfengu were mistreated by amaGcaleka. Also, Legassick (2010) concluded that the resettlement of amaMfengu from Gcuwa to Ngqushwa was the outcome of the deliberate conspiracy hatched by John Ayliff, which he presented as the liberation of the enslaved people from the cruel hands of amaGcaleka.

To the British establishment, the lie was a convenient justification to uproot amaMfengu from Gcalekaland based on several reasons meantioned earlier. Such an arrangement favoured amaMafengu in the long term and gave them access to land and livestock that were confiscated from amaXhosa from time to time.

Peires argued that amaMfengu were a formidable group who maintained their cultural identity and thrived under the leadership of amaXhosa. They brought with them the usage of iron hoes and had immense skill for cultivation of the land. They excelled as traders of agricultural goods. According to Mostert (1992) amaMfengu were descendants of ironsmiths and cultivators as far back as 1500 years ago.

About two decades later, after amaMfengu settled in Ngqushwa, the British settlers resented efforts by King Sandile to establish friendly relations with amaMfengu. According to Dowsley (1932) in 1854, Lieutenant Governor was alarmed to learn that amaXhosa and amaMfengu were cultivating relations to formalise intermarriages between the two groups. The British establishment discouraged any attempts at reconciliation between the two groups due to fears of losing their ally. Sir George Grey was also alerted to the growing, younger, and more assertive generation of amaMfengu who seemed less at ease with the formalised loyalty to the British colonial establishment. Grey started the process of accelerated Anglicisation of amaMfengu in order to complete the conquest through total assimilation.

6. King Hintsa: The Epitome of African Royal Aristocracy

King Hintsa, the son of King Khawuta, was born in 1789. He reigned as the supreme King of amaXhosa between 1809 and 1835. His royal salutation was *Aaa Zanzolo!!!* He was a compassionate, visionary leader and highly revered royal aristocrat, who carried himself with a sense of enormous responsibility. In terms of natural disposition, King Hintsa was a man of extraordinary qualities, with a very astute mind which enabled him to read any situation and take appropriate decisions. Soga (1930) defined him as a man who *"possessed the sentiments of humanity common to others, holding high his chieftainship in such a manner as to retain the respect and affection of his subjects"* (pg 183). King Hintsa regarded himself not only as a King of amaXhosa but as a responsible leader bestowed with supreme authority to create harmony with his neighbours. As a supreme King of amaXhosa, his kingdom[3] was located between the Mbhashe and Xelexwa Rivers. He was a polygamist with three sons: Sarhili, Ncaphayi and Lindinxiwa, from different wives.

Sir James Edward Alexander, who was a captain in the British army, was on an expedition of discovery in Africa at the time of the war of 1834 to 1835. He accompanied the British army in the invasion of King Hintsa's Kingdom. He was present when King Hintsa approached the British camp for negotiations in an attempt to appease the enraged D'Urban and his military, whose ultimate coveted trophy was the king himself. According to Alexander, *"The great chief of the Amakosa appeared upward of six feet in height, robust and fleshy and about forty five years of age. His skin was very dark... His crisp hair was without ornament, and he wore whiskers and short beard. His nose was low and aquiline; his eyes and lips were prominent and large; though his carriage was dignified, he could not look any one steadily in the face and he had altogether a most sinister expression of countenance."* (Alexander,1837:129)

Based on Alexander's observation of King Hintsa, one could see that he was a peculiar leader with a commanding presence because of his height, his unique appearance and mannerisms. The fact that he did not maintain direct eye contact appeared to Alexander, a European, as a sign of being sinister, whilst in the African perspective it was a norm for

3   The descendants of King Gcaleka the son of King Phalo from the Great House, were always recognized as the designated senior royal aristocrats of the Kingdom of amaXhosa between Mbhashe river and Xelexwa River, even after Prince Rharhabe the son of King Phalo from the Right Hand House extended the Kingdom from Nciba River to Xelexwa River. The royal leaders of amaGcaleka and amaRharhabe always supported each during the wars of resistance except King Ngqika who deviated from the norm.

a royal aristocrat not to maintain direct eye contact with his subjects. The avoidance of direct eye contact was a noble way to keep his space and distance as a King. Alexander's description of the king is indicative of a sinister expression that was probably an indirect way of saying the King's demeanour was intimidating to them as well as to the British military commanders.

The portrait of King Hintsa was produced by Sibusiso Nxokweni based on the eyewitness description of Sir James Alexander (1837) who met the king during his expedition. Mr Nxokweni was commissioned by the author in an attempt to depict a reasonable portrait of King Hintsa.

Image 2.6:   King Hintsa. Source: The work of Sibusiso Nxokweni

SEK Mqhayi was awed by the manner in which King Hintsa conducted the trial of the twins, where each one claimed to be the eldest son. The legendary case of the twins is also based on Mqhayi's book *Ityala Lamawele* "Lawsuit of the Twins." In stanza three of the poem, Mqhayi presents King Hintsa as a God-chosen ruler and custodian of laws and customs, who must be obeyed by his people. He praised the king for allowing evidence to be presented, followed by deliberations by elders and the issuing of the final judgement in which the twins were commanded to go and build the legacy of their father Vuyisile. What mattered to Mqhayi was that he played his role excellently as the custodian of the laws and customs of amaXhosa by allowing the nation to participate in the complex marathon trial.

Mqhayi projected King Hintsa as a powerful symbol of authority in the maintenance and harmonization of traditions and customs of amaXhosa as well as the usage of traditional courts in the execution of justice. King Hintsa demonstrated compassionate and firm leadership by allowing the senior members of the kingdom to adjudicate the case before he made a final judgement on the lawsuit of the twins. Mqhayi paid tribute to King Hintsa because of the inclusive manner in which he rallied his senior counsellors in conducting the court case through his poem *Ukuphela Kwetyala (The End of the Lawsuit)* taken from Xhosa Anthology/ *Amazinga Eembongi* published in 1987. In this following section of the poem, Mqhayi defines King Hintsa as the royal anointed divine link between God and people whose authority and decision-making will always have far-reaching implications for the land and the people.

(From second stanza)
Yivani zizwe, sininik' indyebo yentliziyo,
Yivani zizwe, sinibalisele:
Ngemihla yakudala, mini kwavel' iintaba,
Kwabekw' umntu wamnye wokuphath' abanye.
Kwathiwa ke loo mntu ngumntu wegazi,

Kwathiwa loo mntu yinkonyana yohlanga.

Kwathiwa loo mntu makathotyelwe luluntu;

Aze athi yen' athobele uQamatha;

Apho kuya kuvel' imithetho nezimiselo,

Aya kuth' akuzigwenxa kungalungelelani,

Kube ziziphithi-phithi nokuphambana koluntu,

Ibe nguqukulubhede ukuphambana komhlaba,

The translation of the isiXhosa poem into English is as follows:

Listen nations to the wealth of knowledge,

Listen nations to the narration

In the ancient days of emergence of mountains

A ruler was installed to lead others.

The ruler was bestowed as a royal aristocrat

Installed as a bullock to steer the nation

Was stated to be obeyed by the nation

He will be expected to obey God.

From him the laws and rules will emerge

If he abused them, catastrophe will strike

There will be disorder and perplexity among the people

Followed by turmoil and destabilization of the land.

Source: Satyo SC (1987:06)

Abner Nyamende (2010), in the exploration of the conception and the application of justice in line with traditions and customs of amaXhosa, observed that kings like Hintsa were the centre that held the nation together in the collective execution of justice as portrayed by Mqhayi in the poem. In the case of *Ityala Lamawele*, King Hintsa withheld judgement until thorough investigations and due court processes had been followed. From *Ityala Lamawele*, one is able to see that King Hintsa, as the embodiment of the traditional royal aristocracy of amaXhosa, took his position very seriously, hence he was revered by his subjects. During his reign, amaXhosa were an established powerful nation with an inclusive functional justice system.

The revolt of amaNgqosini, which nearly destroyed the Kingdom of amaXhosa during the reign of King Tshiwo, remained a concern even after his departure. King Hintsa, the fifth royal ruler after King Tshiwo, was probably informed about what amaNgqosini were capable of, and based on what they did a century earlier. He concluded that the powerful House of amaNgqosini had to be neutralised so that he could consolidate his kingdom. King Hintsa orchestrated the surprise ambush of about seventeen senior councillors, who were caught unaware during a hunting expedition. Subsequently, the royal aristocrat of amaNgqosini was demoted to headman under King Hintsa's Right-Hand son, Ncaphayi (Peires, 1776). The destruction of amaNgqosini marked the beginning of an elimination process of immediate and potential threats to the kingdom of amaXhosa.

His next target was King Ngqika, who nearly killed his father King Kawuta, which was why he aligned himself with Prince Ndlambe. The growing animosity towards King Ngqika culminated in the Battle of Amalinde in 1818. Ngqikas's forces were obliterated by the combined armies of Hintsa and Ndlambe under the leadership of Prince Mdushane, the eldest son Ndlambe. Hintsa avenged the humiliation of Kawuta through the defeat of Ngqika in the disastrous battle.

During the reign of King Hintsa between 1809 and 1835, amaXhosa fought the first war against British colonial forces in 1811-1812, under the direct command of Prince Ndlambe. There is no available information indicating that King Hintsa supported Ndlambe in the war. A few years later, in 1818, amaXhosa experienced brutal infighting in the Battle of Amalinde, which was followed by the British retaliatory war of 1818 to1819. There is a high probability that King Hintsa supported Ndlambe in the British retaliatory war, which enabled him to mount strong counterattacks that resulted in the reshuffling of the British military command in order to sustain what turned out to be a disastrous and costly war for the British establishment.

The 26-year reign of King Hintsa witnessed the growing threat of the British colonial encroachment through military installations of forts, unprovoked wars in pursuit of land, continued displacement and harassment of amaXhosa and infiltration by hypocritical missionaries planted as agents to assess the strength and vulnerabilities of amaXhosa. In 1829, Prince Maqoma and his people were expelled from the Kat River region around Fort Beaufort which was officially named as KwamaQoma. The war of 1834 to1835 was the culmination of the growing tensions that were heightened by the arrival of British settlers in 1820, who were in desperate need of land and livestock in order to make a living.

King Hintsa was fully aware of the magnitude of the existential threat; hence he avoided direct military engagement. He believed that as a supreme King of amaXhosa his role was to provide subtle support to amaXhosa who were in the frontline of the wars of resistance led by the descendants of Rharhabe. Therefore, it was important for his kingdom to remain intact in order to ensure stability and continuity. D'Urban's decision to launch a direct military attack as a result of the influence of the Wesleyan missionaries came as a surprise to King Hintsa.

D'Urban's decision to invade his kingdom placed him in an extraordinarily difficult position because he did not realise that it was missionaries like Rev Ayliff, whom he accommodated in his kingdom, who cultivated the fires of the invasion. King Hintsa was fully aware of the military capability and the real intentions of the British colonial establishment. The way he responded to the potentially insurmountable challenge was going to determine whether his nation survived or not. A few years earlier he had witnessed what happened to amaNgwane of Matiwane at the battle of Mbholompo in 1828. What was paramount to him was to ensure the survival of his nation.

Militarily, he was aware that the open terrain around Gcuwa was not suitable for the bush warfare waged by amaXhosa in the rugged fortresses of the Amathole Mountains. King Hintsa had no viable military strategy for direct engagement with the massive invasion. He knew that taking a direct stand against such a well-resourced army would be a futile exercise. The King realized that the most viable option available to him was to approach the British authorities to explore the possibility of negotiations whilst buying enough time for his people to escape and to conceal the cattle. At the same time he was not blind to the fact that anything could happen to him, considering the deep-seated abhorrence the British colonialists displayed towards African people, especially their royal leaders. He took the bold decision to walk into the jaws of the invading army, fully aware of the implications to his life. Decades earlier, the British army had butchered Prince Chungwa of amaGqunukhwebe on his sickbed during the ethnic cleansing of the Zuurveld.

The bold decision to walk into the British military instead of running to the neighbouring kingdoms to seek protection and support may have been perceived as an act of naivety. In actual fact, it was a well-calculated act of self-sacrifice and demonstration of selfless leadership, because he knew that final responsibility lay with him. Upon his arrival at the British camp, the king was immediately taken as a prisoner. He was neither rattled nor surprised as he continued to maintain his noble dignity in the face of imminent death. He cooperated and continued to carry himself in a manner befitting a king.

D'Urban and his senior commanders were surprised and intimidated by the noble disposition displayed by the supreme aristocrat of amaXhosa. The absence of fear from him was astonishing as he maintained his composure and a strong sense of moral high ground despite the arrogant display of the military might of the British. According to Mostert (1992), *"Xhosa were unusually sharp and astute judges of human nature"* (pg 765). The ability to avoid displaying fear, over-reaction and emotions in the presence of imminent death was an important psychological element meant to conceal one's vulnerability in order to keep the enemy guessing.

One of the compelling factors which influenced the king's decision to surrender was the realization that the British had managed to isolate him from the neighbouring kingdoms. According to Henderson Soga (1930) abaThembu and the Basotho started making raids into King Hintsa's kingdom, confiscating cattle and taking advantage of his vulnerability. Also, George Theal (1912) claimed that Sir Benjamin D'Urban confirmed in his letter to Henry Fynn written on 06 May 1835, that King Faku of amaMpondo and Prince Fadana of abaThembu pledged to remain neutral in the British war against King Hintsa. At the core of King Hintsa's concern was the possibility of total annihilation and the disintegration of amaXhosa.

After the arrival of massive British forces, led by Governor Benjamin D'Urban and Colonel Harry Smith, in the Kingdom of amaGcaleka, it was very clear that their intention was to obliterate amaXhosa and to confiscate the livestock in order to finance the war against the sons of Prince Ngqika; Princes Maqoma, Sandile and Tyali, who stood their ground in the mountains of Amathole. Peires (1981) observed that, *"Hintsa was not prepared to save his life by betraying his nation... he sent secret messages warning them that he was a prisoner. Commanded to raise a ransom of 25 000 cattle and 500 horses for his release, he sent a secret message ordering that the cattle be driven further on"* (pg 111). Whilst King Hintsa continued sending secret messages to his people to hide the cows, D'Urban and Smith could not figure out what the king was doing except leading them to different areas in search of cows whilst his people were fleeing with their livestock.

In the meantime, they exerted pressure on him to stop the sons of the late King Ngqika from continuing with the war. In this way, he was being given an opportunity to be a collaborator in the way they did to King Ngqika, whom they later deserted, only for him to die as a miserable leader, rejected by his own people. As a reaction to their king being held hostage, amaGcaleka started to target amaMfengu, whom they perceived as collaborators under the influence of John Ayliff.

D'Urban hastened the relocation of amaMfengu to the designated land as a buffer between amaXhosa and the white settlers. On 14 May 1835, about 16 000 amaMfengu with around 22 000 cattle were settled in Ngqushwa, on the shores of the Nxuba River and Indian Ocean (Mostert, 1992). AmaMfengu pledged their allegiance to the British and commemorated their vows annually on 14th May (Bikitsha, 2019).

On 10 May 1835, D'Urban declared a hollow victory and claimed the area between Keiskamma and Kei River as the Province of Queen Adelaide, with the intention to permanently expel amaXhosa from the area. Qonce was identified as the headquarters of the envisaged Queen Adelaide Province under Harry Smith.

In the meantime, D'Urban continued to subject King Hintsa to captivity pending the ransom of thousands of cattle and horses. After King Hintsa realized that his people had managed to save the cattle from the reach of the British invaders, he started working out the possibilities for an escape. On 12 May 1835, whilst King Hintsa was near the banks of Nqabarha River, he attempted to escape. Harry Smith pursued him aggressively. The King managed to escape on foot and submerged under water showing only his head. Smith commanded Captain George Southey to shoot him. Southey shot him at close range, in the presence of Paddy Balfour, blowing his skull open and scattering his brains. He then took the King's brass for himself, while others came and grabbed whatever they could get from the King. George and his brother William cut off the ears. The king's head was decapitated. Assistant Surgeon Ford tried to extract his teeth. They left his mutilated body behind.

The manner in which he was killed and his body mutilated crystallized the extent of the resentment held against any form of authority of amaXhosa and all Africans who were perceived to be a threat to British interests. They probably hoped that the humiliation which the Supreme Authority of amaXhosa had been subjected to would result in their total disintegration.

It appeared that it was in the tradition of the British military officers to mutilate the bodies of the enemy in the battlefield. Thomas Stubbs (1820-1877), a seasoned colonial settler who participated in some of the African European Cape colonial wars, provided a more or less similar, chilling account in his published reminiscences. According to him, during the War of Mlanjeni (1850-1853), Taylor, one of the British officers, brought the head of an African man to the camp. He boiled it until all the meat was off. During the boiling process the smell was unbearable. *"The old fellow had the skull in his shop until he died"* (pg 176).

Similarly, Captain W.R. King who fought in the War of Mlanjeni, in his accounts of the war, admitted to having collected the head of an African combatant and taking it back to Scotland after the war. These horrifying accounts are indicative of the fact that the cutting off of King Hintsa's head was not an isolated incident, but a common practice at the time, where African were treated like savages whose lives and bodies were not accorded respect.

Later on, Harry Smith and Governor D'Urban fabricated a story claiming that King Hintsa was shot for refusing to surrender and charging at the British soldiers with an assegai. In their report, they omitted the crucial facts about how the King had pleaded for mercy for his life, the barbaric mutilation of his body and how they stole royal regalia from the king's lifeless body. D'Urban's fabricated version of what occurred on that fateful day was reported in the conservative Graham's Town Journal of 12 June, 1845: *"He defied all attempts to secure him. On being once more called upon to surrender, the indomitable chief raised an assegai, upon which Mr Southey for the third time fired, the ball entered his brain, and he ceased to live. Thus fell Hintsa, chief of the Amakosas Kaffirs, a victim to the savage duplicity and perfidy which were the leading features of his own character, and of his race"* (pg. 4). The journal portrayed

King Hintsa as a cunning victim of his own actions and thus exonerated the British military officers of the cold-blooded murder committed in pursuance of the British interests in Southern Africa. This was far from the truth because in terms of what actually happened, King Hintsa was killed whilst he was begging for mercy.

The version reported in the conservative Graham's Town Journal is similar to the accounts given by George Cory (1919), who went further to claim the king was armed with a spear and that is why Southey shot him. This narrative created a distorted impression that Southey shot King Hintsa in self-defence and therefore exonerated him from the reality that he executed a defenceless, wounded man.

The brutal murder of King Hintsa and mutilation of his body was the highest point of the war of 1834 to 1835. The ultimate political objective of the colonial conquest was not limited to the possession of the land; it was to ensure that Africans remained permanently dehumanized in order to create a lasting psyche of inferiority even for future generations. They knew that physical conquest alone would not guarantee the security of coming generations of Europeans in Africa. Conquering the mind, the soul and the spirit by creating a permanent imprint of European superiority was the ultimate objective.

The British officers informed Prince Sarhili, the son of King Hintsa, and Bhuru the King's brother, of the tragic death of the king. To the shock of the British military commanders both Sarhili and Bhuru showed no visible emotion. According to Mostert (1992) it was in the nature of amaXhosa that under such trying circumstances they would prefer to keep the enemy guessing. This feature stood out as one of the defining characters of the African people, which was later demonstrated by the incredible boldness of Steve Biko in the face of adversity, the extraordinary fearlessness of Griffiths and Victoria Mxenge and the astonishing courage of the Cradock four, Matthew Goniwe, Fort Calata, Sparrow Mkhonto and Sicelo Mhlauli.

Professor Archibald Campbell Jordan, the father of Pallo Jordan, made a similar reference in his book *Ingqumbo Yeminyanya/ The Wrath of the Ancestors*, which was published in 1940. In this novel, Jordan portrayed a strong character who had a reputation for an uncanny ability to conceal his emotions in the face of tragedy in order to maintain an aura of inner strength and dignity. Such observations bear testimony to the fact it was in the natural disposition of African people in general to have the ability to absorb pain for the purpose of achieving bigger goals.

After learning about the agonising end and humiliation of Zanzolo, Prince Maqoma and other members of the royal family could not comprehend how the supreme royal aristocrat of amaXhosa could be subjected to such diabolical treatment. In their attempt to avenge the blood of the most senior aristocrat, they intensified their military campaigns in the Keiskamma region and widened the scope of the armed raids to the villages and farms of settlers.

D'Urban and Smith were compelled to abandon their military adventures in Gcalekaland in order to acquire much-needed reinforcements in the colony. On 1st June 1835, they reassembled a large force comprised of British regulars and settlers, Boers, Khoe and amaMfengu to resume the military onslaught in the Amathole Mountains. They utilised everything in their arsenal with the intention of finishing Maqoma and his brothers off. To their frustration and desperation, in spite of the relentless carpet bombardment and ruthless execution of scorched earth military tactics, the army continued to suffer an increasing number of casualties from the targeted deadly ambushes launched from the thick bushes, narrow gorges and steep ridges. The British military commanders had no answer to Maqoma's mastery of bush warfare executed through deadly ambushes in close combat positions as a counter-offensive to the British-led army. They had their backs to the wall as they found themselves trapped in an unbearable cauldron, facing a much more determined and well-prepared enemy than they had encountered before crossing the Nciba River. This time amaXhosa were more united and with a greater resolve to avenge the blood of Zanzolo. Having to face an elusive lethal enemy in the rugged terrain of the Amathole Mountain fortress was, for the British, an impossible military campaign.

Towards the end of June 1835, Jongumsobomvu increased the tempo of his counteroffensive strategies upon realization that his adversaries were exhausted and desperate to end the war. His combatants launched a vicious surprise attack targeting an isolated British patrol of 30 soldiers who were lured into a vulnerable position in one of the bushy slopes of the Amathole Mountains. At first, they tormented them from a distance until the soldiers had emptied their ammunition out of desperation to break away from the deadly encirclement. Thereafter, Jongumsobomvu and his regiments moved in to engage the patrol in a man-to-man brutal encounter. The agonising combat was terrifying for the desperate soldiers as they fought hopelessly in a situation in which they knew that the writing was on the wall; their end was inevitable under such a ferocious attack, launched from different directions, in close proximity. The British patrol was completely wiped out in a single engagement (Mostert, 1992).

The obliteration of an entire British patrol was the highest military loss after the spilling of the blood of Zanzolo on the waters of Nqabarha River about a month earlier. The viciousness of the assault was a manifestation of his people's anger. Jongumsobomvu intensified his synchronised blitz and pushed the British-led army back from the fortress of the Amathole Mountains. The potency and the precision of the relentless onslaughts were a military phenomenon the colonial military leaders had never witnessed before in the Cape colonial wars. The sleeping giant had been awakened!

What became more unbearable to D'Urban and Smith was the realization that whilst the protracted and costly war was raging on in the Amathole Mountains, the white farms and settler villages were subjected to perpetual lethal raids, which went as far as Gqeberha and Graaff-Reinet in the triangle of resistance.

The devastating destruction of settler farms and military villages was Jongumsobovu's strategy of reciprocating the British-led scorched-earth tactic, which had been carried out in the villages of African people. Jongumsobomvu's strategy of deploying his combatants in small, highly mobile groups throughout the colony was a master plan that made a huge difference in the war, because he had numbers on his side and was more familiar with the rugged terrain. D'Urban, Smith, Somerset and Cox found themselves overwhelmed and overstretched beyond their capacity, as they had no answer for the tit-for-tat strategy which put the entire region on fire. They watched the destruction of farms and villages and confiscation of livestock helplessly, as desperate white settlers retreated to Makhanda for protecttion. The soldiers were trapped in the forts, whilst the centre of the army was subjected to a series of deadly ambushes in the cauldron of the Amathole Mountains.

As amaXhosa combatants were gaining the upper hand, they launched bolder and more direct onslaughts. On 19 July, Fort Cox and other forts came under heavy attack. The troops were besieged in the forts by the amaXhosa combatants in order to cut supply lines and demobilise the colonial military machinery. Even the simple act of trying to get water from a nearby river was met with lethal attacks from men who were concealed in the bushes.

It dawned on D'Urban and Smith that their demonstration of overwhelming military firepower was rendered useless by the manner in which Maqoma marshalled his combatants of amaXhosa who mastered the military art of adaptability, agile mobility and effective execution of bush ambushes. The British-led army was in a weakened state as supplies were running out; their uniforms and shoes were in poor condition; the horses were sick; and general morale was low, whilst amaXhosa increased the tempo because they were fighting in familiar terrain, with unlimited access to resources. The British-led military campaign in the Amathole region was paralysed.

D'Urban, the colonial governor, and Smith, the top military commander, had no choice but to retreat in the face of the advancing enemy who continued to inflict an increasing number of casualties. Much as they resented being outsmarted by Maqoma, there was nothing they could do and had run out of options. The ambitious military strategies to attain decisive victory and expel amaXhosa across the Nciba River, collapsed. Such plans were hollow ambitions because they underestimated the capability of their opponent.

The British had committed a military blunder by allowing Prince Maqoma to dictate the terms of military engagement by deciding where and how the war would be fought. They were lured into the impenetrable fortress of the Amathole Mountains, chasing shadows, whilst their troops were exposed, vulnerable to targeted deadly ambushes.

In a face-saving exercise to conceal the humiliating defeat, they devised an honourable exit strategy by staging superficial peace talks with the royal leaders of amaXhosa. In August 1835, Cox sent one of the captured warriors to Maqoma for peace negotiations. In September 1835, Jongumsobomvu, together with his brother Prince Tyhali, Prince Mhala of amaNdlambe, Prince Nqeno of amaMbalu and Prince Bhotomane of imiDange, participated in the so-called peace proceedings as a pragmatic strategy in order to recuperate and re-establish their communities (Mostert, 1992; Stapleton, 2016). In conclusion, the War of Hintsa of 1834-35 marked the decisive first defeat of the British army in Southern Africa by much more organized battle hardened combatants of amaXhosa led by Prince Maqoma the brilliant military strategist.

7. The Aftermath of the War of Hintsa of 1834 – 1835

In the aftermath of the war, General Harry Smith targeted Rev James Read as a scapegoat in order to hide their defeat by amaXhosa despite having murdered King Hintsa, burnt houses, destroyed crops and expropriated the livestock in the Qoboqobo region. He labelled Read as a traitor who was instrumental in the arms trade with amaXhosa, although he knew that the arms trade was the business of white settlers. By contrast, Dr John Philip argued that D'Urban and Smith had provoked the war and responded excessively.

The phrase used by D'Urban, defining amaXhosa as "irreclaimable savages" during the declaration of Queen Adelaide Province between Keiskamma and Nciba Rivers, was quoted by Dr Philip in the reports sent to London, which criticized D'Urban's controversial handling of the war (Mostert, 1992).

Dr Phililp also lambasted the Wesleyan missionaries who sided with D'Urban in portraying amaXhosa as savages who were responsible for the war. Subsequently, Dr Philip and Fowell Buxton influenced the establishment of a Parliamentary Committee to investigate the war, which had started in December 1834. Dr Philip wrote a scathing letter to the Committee condemning D'Urban's portrayal of amaXhosa as savages. He disputed D'Urban's claim that the assault by amaXhosa was unprovoked, thus denying the many warnings he gave to the Governor about the combative nature of the frontier policies and the destructive impact of the armed commandos deep in the territories of amaXhosa. He further argued that amaXhosa were driven by colonial policies to a point of exasperation. He highlighted the fact that during the war amaXhosa combatants exercised restraint and discipline by not killing women and children, unlike the British soldiers who attacked everyone and destroyed everything in sight. His letters were corroborated by Reverend John Ross of the Glasgow Missionary Society. All of them condemned the barbaric acts of the British-led army, which carried out massacres in their desperate efforts to expel amaXhosa across the Kei River.

Based on submissions sent to the Colonial Office of Lord Glenelg in London by D'Urban, Philip, and Stockenström, the British government concluded that there was no justification for the killing of King Hintsa and the implementation of the scorched earth policy on the villages of amaXhosa. D'Urban's unilateral declaration of Queen Adelaide Province was repudiated. According to Mostert (1992) Glenelg's report sowed the seeds of racial antagonism towards amaXhosa. The white settlers were bitter about the absence of compensation for the huge losses they suffered during the war, as they felt that amaXhosa were exonerated from paying any price for the war. The extent of the deep-seated bitterness of the white settlers from the huge losses suffered in the war of 1834 to 1835 reinforced the seed of racial divisions in South Africa (Mostert, 1992).

Upon receiving the Glenelg dispatch in April 1836, D'Urban and Smith were discharged. They both felt that instead of receiving rewards and accolades for their military adventures, they were unfairly condemned. The instruction to abandon Adelaide Province and the expulsion of amaXhosa shattered them to the core.

One of the significant lasting legacies of the war, which shaped the demographic landscape and the history of South Africa, was the decision of the Boers to abandon the Cape Colony and moving to the northern part of the country. They were tired of fighting disastrous British wars that did not benefit them in any way. During the war, they suffered huge losses of life and resources and received no compensation. After the war of 1834 to1835, they were neither paid for their military services nor compensated for their losses. The scale of the invasion of the Cape Colony and the colossal destruction of farms convinced the Dutch farmers that there was no future in the colony. They realized that they had to participate in British wars against amaXhosa, whilst their own interests were not given priority. The exodus of the Boer settlers from the Cape to the north was a huge spectacle as they abandoned their farms in search of total emancipation from the tentacles of British control. The exodus became known as the *Great Trek*. In the process, the British colonial establishment lost skilled military assets.

To the British military establishment and the white settlers, the adaptability displayed by amaXhosa, the ability to inflict lethal casualties and engaged in sustained wars became a source of frustration and deep-seated resentment. Most importantly, the military defeat created a state of permanent fear among the British settlers that as long as amaXhosa possessed the capability to strike back and to inflict pain, the completion of total conquest through military domination would remain a mirage. Consequently, as the wars dragged on, with intermittent intervals of peace which allowed each side to recover and to regroup, the colonial establishment in the Cape colony became increasingly despondent.

The series of catastrophic raids that were carried out by about 12 000 warriors of amaXhosa was a shattering experience to the white settlers, considering the devastating impact of the widespread attacks, the destruction of farms and the confiscation of livestock. The colonial army could not protect them since it was trapped in the war of the Amathole Mountains. The white settlers were extremely bitter that they were never compensated for the countless losses they suffered during the war. George Cory (1919) estimated that the white settlers lost 450 farms. The war came as a huge disappointment to the prospective British settlers who arrived in the Cape and travelled to Makhanda from 1820 onwards because they had been assured by the British government of a life of prosperity in the newly acquired colony.

Prince Maqoma emerged victorious after the war by proving himself to be a skilled mobilizer, capable military commander and a fearless warrior who led his combatants from the front. There was much at stake for Maqoma that compelled him to raise the bar: His nation of amaJingqi was expelled from the rich Kat River area in 1829; he was a regent for the young Prince Sandile; King Hintsa's life had been brutally taken away and amaXhosa faced the prospect of permanent expulsion from the Keiskamma region and neighbouring areas. *"Maqoma distinguished himself as a prudent and innovative tactician. Faced with an overwhelmingly superior enemy, he responded sensibly by utilizing the amaThole to conceal his cattle and subjects. Avoiding open battles, which would favour the Europeans, Maqoma used this mountainous and forested area to further develop his favourite tactic, the ambush"* (Stapleton, 2016: 118). Maqoma neutralized and repulsed the British-led army despite the fact that they possessed superior firepower and well-trained, seasoned soldiers. No wonder Rev Henry Calderwood described Maqoma as a fine soldier, gifted with brain power, determination and fearlessness (Stapleton, 2016).

The controversial actions of Wesleyan missionaries such as Reverend John Ayliff negatively impacted the reputation of the missionaries in the colony. Their influence and legitimacy were severely dented despite the self-sacrificing efforts of other missionaries such as Reverend James Read, Dr John Philip and Reverend John Ross, who condemned the despicable treatment of amaXhosa by the British establishment in the colony. The missionaries who stood for justice and fairness were ostracised and humiliated by the colonial authorities and the white settlers as indicated by the ill-treatment of Reverend Read, who was labelled a traitor.

Following Lord Glenelg's commissioning of an inquiry into the grotesque death of Zanzolo on 29 August 1836, General Smith abdicated his position to Andries Stockenström and resorted to alcoholism. The inquiry strained Smith to breaking point. In 1840 Smith was saved from his self-destructive actions by being deployed to India, thus giving him the opportunity to redeem his shattered military career. Smith returned to the Cape colony in 1847 as governor after he had been promoted to the position of an army General in India. He faced Maqoma for the second time in the defining war of Mlanjeni from 1850 to 1853, which is explored in the following Chapter.

In another development, D'Urban swallowed his pride and renounced the province of Adelaide between Keiskamma and Nciba River as instructed. Stockenström was ostracised by the white settlers, isolated and subjected to persistent harassment by the close cabal of D'Urban and associates. He resigned and went back to England. The influence of Dr John

Philip declined in London after Fowell Buxton lost his seat in Parliament. In 1838, Lord Glenelg sacked D'Urban and replaced him with George Napier, the one-armed Major General. D'Urban chose to remain in Cape Town as a private citizen until his departure for Canada in 1846. He died in Canada in 1849 and was buried in Montreal.

Chapter Three

African Victorious Wars of Resistance

"However, unlike Maqoma, most nineteenth-century African leaders thoroughly failed to recognise the special and permanent nature of colonial conquest until it was too late" (Stapleton, 2016: 287-8).

1. Sandile's Decisive Victory in the Battle of Mkhubiso

In March 1844, Sir Peregrine Maitland (1772-1854), the decorated Peninsular and Waterloo war veteran, replaced the one-armed Major General George Thomas Napier (1784-1855), another Peninsular War veteran, as the governor of the Cape Colony. Maitland was a versatile, multi-talented man, a distinguished soldier in the battlefield, a gifted cricketer, and a seasoned administrator. He came across as a refined personification of the British Empire, bestowed with the enormous responsibility of neutralising the military sting of amaXhosa whose persistent resilience remained a thorn in the flesh of the Empire.

Maitland hit the ground running by pursuing an aggressive policy of divide and rule in order to weaken amaXhosa by building an alliance with the formidable battle hardened amaGqunukhwebe. This was an interesting alliance considering the fact that in the war of 1811 to 1812, Prince Chungwa of amaGqunukhwebe was killed during the ethnic cleansing of the Zuurveld. Maitland revived the controversial system of armed commandos whose draconian actions triggered the previous war of 1834-35. To rub salt in the wound, Maitland implemented a policy which exempted amaXhosa residing in the missions from the rule of traditional authorities. Missionaries such as Reverend John Bennie exploited the situation by accusing Prince Maqoma of being an anti-missionary leader (Stapleton, 2016). Maitland's antagonistic policies cultivated fertile ground for another potential war.

The question was whether he had a better plan than D'Urban and Smith in the event of an all-out war, as he continued pushing amaXhosa to the brink. He did not seem to have learnt any lessons from the abrasive policies of D'Urban, whose reign of pursuance of conquest at all costs came to a crushing and disastrous end. The common shortcoming of most of the arrogant British governors was the blatant demonstration of superior power by underestimating the capabilities of amaXhosa whilst they did not have a clear backup plan. It remained to be seen whether Maitland had any secret weapon in his arsenal to neutralise amaXhosa in the event of a full-scale war.

At this stage, Prince Maqoma, the eldest son of Prince Ngqika by birth, who acted as a regent after the death of this father, had relinquished power to King Sandile in 1842, the designated heir to the throne of amaRharhabe. Prince Bhotomane was the reigning head of imiDange; Prince Mhala was still leading amaNdlambe; amaNtinde were under Prince Tshatshu and Prince Phatho was the leader of amaGqunukhwebe. All these royal leaders resented the humiliating policies of the colonial authorities. They tried to restrain their people for some time, because they knew the price of war and what it took to sustain armed conflict.

Image 3.1: King Sandile "Aa! Mgolombane". Source: Weldon (1993)

Eventually, in March 1846 tensions exploded, after Maitland declared war against King Sandile, following the ambush of a British patrol commando sent to arrest Tsili of imiDange, who was accused of stealing an axe in Fort Beaufort. Sandile found himself in a position similar to the situation faced by his brother Maqoma in the previous war. This was going to be the first war under his reign as the senior aristocrat of amaRharhabe between Nciba and Xelexwa River. The huge expectations placed him under tremendous pressure to lead and protect his people from the endless threats of British encroachment. King Sandile had to dig deep in order to mount a formidable resistance against the massive army of Maitland. At first he responded to the declaration of war by ordering systematic coordinated raids into the colony to repossess cattle confiscated by the commandos since the implementation of Maitland's policies in 1844. During the series of battles in different parts of the colony, the British were able to withstand the onslaught of amaXhosa through the assistance of amaMfengu.

On 21 March 1846, Maitland mobilized a combined well-resourced colonial army under the command of Lieutenant General John Hare (Mostert, 1992). The force comprised the British regular infantry and cavalry, settler volunteers, Khoe mounted riflemen and amaMfengu auxiliaries. The army was assembled in Makhanda and headed towards the Keiskamma region in order to displace Prince Sandile. The British-led army was a huge spectacle of a long military procession of 125 wagons, loaded with ammunition and supplies to sustain the army over a considerable period of time. The convoy of wagons was pulled by 1750 oxen, 14 oxen to each wagon.

Maitland and Hare's military plan was to establish a strategic base at the heart of the mountains of Amathole as a launching pad to direct a series of operations to dismantle the strongholds of amaXhosa. They were convinced that the only way to break the backbone of the resistance was to create a state of permanent military presence through the execution of bold and direct sustained onslaught. Maitland believed that it was his moment to end the seemingly endless wars, and he was convinced that the inexperienced senior royal head of amaRharhabe did not possess the military prowess of his elder brother. That is why he took a bold position to amass such a huge army to be stationed under the nose of King Sandile. This time there were no liberal voices to condemn the draconian colonial policies as the missionaries were in decline, despised by amaXhosa and hated by colonialists (Mostert, 1992).

On 17 April 1846, Hare and Somerset directed the wagons to move from Mkhubiso towards the base of the Amathole mountains. During this time, Prince Sandile was monitoring the movement of the British troops through the deployment of his informers, positioned in strategic locations of the forested mountains. As the five-kilometre cavalcade of massive wagons meandered through the forested steep mountains with rugged gorges, Sandile realized that the maintenance of the long single line formation of wagons would provide him with a strategic military advantage to launch simultaneous surprise attacks on both sides of the line. The destruction of the wagons loaded with massive supplies would dismantle the British military plans from the onset. Sandile deployed his armed acrobatic combatants on both sides of the narrow path. The lengthy convoy was not aware that it was marching into the jaws of the vigilant enemy. When the British-led army was halfway towards its destination, a loud command was given to the warriors of amaXhosa. At first, the thrust of the brutal ambush targeted the centre of the convoy in order to isolate the head from the tail and thus weaken any form of organised resistance. The wagon ambush occurred just below Fort Cox on the lower valley from the river towards the mountains of Amathole. The ferocious onslaught was well executed as it successfully cut the convoy, leaving the rest of the entourage vulnerable and disorganised. The speed and accuracy of the overwhelming assault was a catastrophic disaster for the convoy as amaXhosa warriors released the oxen from the wagons, took possession of the supplies, burnt the wagons and chased away the survivors.

The invading army lost valuable supplies including uniforms, tents and cooking utensils. It was reported that 22 soldiers, numerous settlers and amaMfengu and Khoe riflemen were killed as well. Considering the gravity of the attack, the actual figures may be significantly higher than what was reported. To the British military commanders this was a shattering and unanticipated defeat. The war that was planned to last for some time was finished in less than a day. Mostert observed that *"It was by far the worst humiliation the*

British army had yet suffered in its campaigns in South Africa..." (pg 877). Hare and Somerset were compelled to retreat to Block Drift. AmaXhosa pursued the retreating army and launched a series of raids deep into the European-occupied territories, confiscating livestock and destroyed farms and military settlements.

The victorious battle of Mkhubiso legitimised and cemented the authority of King Sandile as he demonstrated his leadership, ability and confidence in the battlefield. The sterling execution of the bush warfare and the decisive defeat of the well-resourced British army remained one of his defining legacies in the history of wars of resistance in Southern African in the nineteenth century. The significance of the decisive victory was the successful dismantling of Maitland's strategic plan to establish a permanent British military presence in the fortresses of the Amathole Mountains.

Unfortunately, the significance of this famous battle in the history of Cape wars of resistance has either been glossed over or distorted in order to water down the courageous stories of African triumph in the face of European encroachment in Southern Africa. The second line on the official tourist sign on the R63 road from Dimbaza to Xesi (Middledrift) at the junction to Qoboqobo, says "Burnshill Wagon Disaster" (as shown in the image below). The usage of the word *disaster* was largely influenced by the dominant Euro-centred narratives on how these wars of resistance had been characterised in order to portray the highly glorified history of European conquest of Southern Africa and downplay the victories achieved by Africans during the wars. The deliberate usage of such misleading definitions was part of a well-orchestrated, systematic distortion of history, centred on the dichotomy of European superiority and African inferiority. The fact that Africans with limited resources were able to defeat well-resourced professional European armies was unthinkable and unacceptable even to those who had the privilege to document that history. The institutionalised structural systems of knowledge production of history were designed in such a way that Africans were deprived of the opportunity to read about the triumphs of their forebears during the era of African wars of resistance.

Image 3.2: Battle of Mkhubiso. Source: Klaas, JJ. 2023.

During that time, Ngqushwa had been resettled by amaMfengu who were drafted into British military units. After the decisive military victory of Mkhubiso, Sandile, with the support of Mhala, Siyolo, and Phatho, targeted Ngqushwa and the Nxuba River area as the next battlegrounds in order to cut the colonial supply line from Makhanda to the hinterland. On 21 May 1846, a convoy of 43 wagons from Makhanda to Ngqushwa was attacked on the Fish River by amaXhosa combatants. Prince Stokwe of amaMbalu and Prince Mhala of amaNdlambe joined the armed attacks in the Nxuba River region. The British army retreated, whilst their wagons were emptied, stripped and burnt. Prince Mqhayi was the only one who collaborated with the British army by providing them with sensitive information (Mostert, 1992).

In May 1848, amaXhosa invaded Fort Peddie. Whilst the British soldiers barricaded themselves inside the fort, amaMfengu were fighting amaXhosa. It was a terrific encounter, and eventually the amaXhosa were pushed back with the assistance of the artillery in the fort.

In June 1846, Maitland assembled an army of 14 000 men, which was the largest British-led army in Southern Africa at the time, in order to avenge the defeat of the army at Mkhubiso. The serious shortage of vital supplies and the potency of the resistance of amaXhosa, coupled with targeted ferocious attacks, made it extremely difficult for the army to make any impact. The British colonial army, in its entirety, was overwhelmed by the incredible determination, enduring resilience and brilliant execution of the well-coordinated simultaneous attacks launched from different directions by amaXhosa.

Governor Peregrine Maitland and Lieutenant General John Hare never recovered from the disastrous defeat of Mkhubiso, despite follow-up military campaigns that were pursued with the hope of avenging the humiliation. The strain of the defeat was unbearable for John Hare in particular. He resigned from the army and returned to Great Britain. A few days later, whilst on his sea voyage, he collapsed and died. In 1847, Maitland was fired as governor after he made a false declaration of victory out of desperation to be seen as having done something. The dismissal of Sir Peregrine Maitland at 70 years of age marked an unpleasant end to an illustrious career. He returned to Great Britain and died in 1854.

The highly decorated war veteran was replaced by Sir Henry Pottinger, who at the time was suffering from a kidney illness (Mostert, 1992). Pottinger attempted to appease the resentful white settlers by embarking on aimless military campaigns. *The Xhosa were far more pragmatic than the British. They recognised when enough was enough and were ever conscious of the greater importance of preserving life and existence, of holding their society together*" (Mostert, pg 934). AmaXhosa resorted to passive resistance by avoiding any form of military engagement and retreating to their stronghold areas. Pottinger was replaced by Lieutenant General Sir Harry Smith, the hero of Aliwal.

2. The Writing was on the Wall

Smith had left the Cape colony as a dejected, miserable Colonel, and returned as a highly celebrated Lieutenant General, the distinguished war veteran of North America, Spain, Cape Colony and Aliwal in India. On his second posting to the Cape Colony, Smith still harboured bitterness about what he perceived as unfair treatment following the unceremonious departure of King Hintsa for which he was complicit. He was determined to continue from where he left off in pursuance of D'Urban's failed policies of total expulsion of amaXhosa between Keiskamma region and Nciba River. At the time, the colonial authorities and the white settlers were still very bitter about the huge losses they had suffered in the wars of 1834–35 and 1846-47. They welcomed the return of Smith, whom they saw as a leader sharing similar antagonistic sentiments towards amaXhosa. The stage was set for the possibility of unprecedented military campaigns driven by the desire to avenge previous defeats, to recover losses and eventually push amaXhosa across the Nciba River.

Smith accelerated the construction of military forts and posts in order to consolidate his power and exert his authority. He granted the missionaries greater leverage as part of the extended colonial machinery in the entrenchment of a stronger domination over amaXhosa. More territories of amaXhosa were confiscated to make way for white settlers who were desperate for the land and the livestock of amaXhosa in order to make a living. He worked towards the total destruction of the power and the influence of the African royal leadership to coerce the African people into cheap labour for the white settlers. He was determined to ensure that amaXhosa would never rise up again.

As Smith continued to entrench his power and authority, the Cape Colony witnessed the rise of Mlanjeni, the militant son of Kala, who was a patriotic subject of amaNdlambe under Prince Mqhayi at the time (Soga, 1930). According to Nomalungisa Maxengana (1989) Mlanjeni was a descendant of the Umkye tribe. The courageous patriot engineered the events leading to what became known as the War of Mlanjeni of 1850-53. He spent his early life working as a labourer for the white settlers in the Cape Colony settlements. He became exposed to the ways and practices of the European missionaries in the colony. He learnt their mannerisms, the messages of Christianity and probably how such messages were communicated to the African people. In the process he learnt and partook of the established practices of Christianity.

As he immersed himself deeper into the spiritual fundamentals of the Christianity, Mlanjeni was transformed and emerged as a liberator of amaXhosa. According to Mostert (1992), Mlanjeni appealed to amaXhosa to abolish witchcraft and the killing of witches. He perceived the brutal killing of people on allegations of witchcraft as a national self-defeating exercise. He believed that they should rather focus their attention on the bigger threats posed by European encroachment and the resultant rapid shrinking of the land of amaXhosa. Mlanjeni's rise as an influential prophet was also triggered by the effects of the grinding drought of 1850, fragmented royal leadership and the growing colonial dominance (Stapleton, 2016).

As one of the senior counsellors of King Sandile, he resented the continued humiliation of amaXhosa and the gradual erosion of the authority of royal leaders. According to Maxengana (1989) Mlanjeni admired King Sandile's stand against the British establishment. After the war of 1846-47, Sandile occupied a special place in the hearts of amaXhosa. *"His passionate nationalism was interpreted as insubordinate, his diplomacy as treachery; his dreams of Xhosa nationhood as rebellion against Queen Victoria, his maintenance of Xhosa customs and traditions as a relapse into barbarism"* (Maxengana pg 25). Consequently, Mlanjeni embarked on a solitary mission in the mobilization and the reawakening process of amaXhosa to open their eyes to the bigger threat. As a result, he was welcomed as a prophet in the form of the resurrected Makhanda ka Nxele who led amaXhosa in the battle of Makhanda a few decades earlier (Mostert, 1992). There were expectations for him to follow in the footsteps of Nxele in leading amaXhosa to another war of resistance.

During this time, the colonial authorities became unsettled by what they perceived as the provocative political rhetoric aimed at undermining the colonial establishment. According to Mostert (1992), Lieutenant Governor George Mackinnon requested Prince Mhala, the British loyalist, to bring Mlanjeni to him. Mlanjeni defied Prince Mhala. Mackinnon retaliated by destroying Mlanjeni's house after he ran away. Mlanjeni intensified his mobilization of amaXhosa, calling them to take up arms against the British colonial authorities. During this time, he stayed in the bush, surrounded by spies who monitored the movement of the British.

The return of Smith in 1847 heightened the tensions. The royal leadership in the region despised him as the man who had spilled the blood of King Hintsa. His physical manhandling of Jongumsobomvu in Gqeberha was a disdainful public spectacle that demonstrated his hatred of the royal leadership (Mostert, 1992). To rub salt in the wound, Smith would subject the leadership of amaXhosa to constant public humiliation, to the point where he would demand that the royal leaders kneel before him during public gatherings. Maqoma was always the voice of reason who restrained other leaders from reacting to Smith's contemptuous treatment with the assurance they must wait for the right moment to strike a deadly blow from which he would never recover. That moment was not far off.

Maqoma had the incredible gift of reading the personality of his enemy, while displaying a deceptively malleable disposition. Smith fell into this trap, believing that amaXhosa had been completely broken and that the leadership had succumbed to his abrasive and authoritarian display of power. On one occasion, Smith summoned all the royal leaders as usual, but King Sandile boycotted the meeting. In retaliation, Smith made a public declaration that he had dethroned King Sandile. Such an announcement enraged amaXhosa, who perceived it as a declaration of war. It reopened the wounds of the brutal murder of King Hintsa fifteen years earlier. The humiliation of Sandile was a final straw in a situation that was already strained.

To the surprise of Smith, who thought amaXhosa dreaded any prospects of war because they feared his power, the white settlers started to desert their farms together with their livestock and wagons, retreating towards Makhanda and Gqeberha. According to Mostert (1992) the white settlers who chose to remain on their farms built laagers as security barriers, and started storing food and ammunition.

Smith underestimated the gravity and the impact of his disdainful actions towards King Sandile. The draconian policies of the colonial authorities such as Henry Calderwood, the missionary turned magistrate, who was notorious for subjecting amaXhosa to public floggings in the Tyhume valley, were some of the factors which created fertile ground for popular insurrection (Mostert, 1992).

Smith was compelled by the unexpected prospect of imminent war to mobilise his troops. At the time, Lieutenant Colonel William Eyre was stationed with his army in Qonce; the second army was at Fort Cox under Lieutenant Governor George Mackinnon, whilst General Somerset was positioned at Fort Hare. On 16 December 1850, Smith issued a bounty of 500 pounds for the arrest of King Sandile. The issuing of the bounty for a king to be arrested by his subjects was an act of perceived madness, which poured petrol on the fire. Smith was acting as if he were in Europe, because the concept of bounties was not part of the culture and tradition of amaXhosa. If he had failed to capture Mlanjeni, how was he expecting the people to capture a revered royal aristocrat? For that matter, amaXhosa were fully aware of the presence of British informers in their territories and the double standards of some of the missionaries, so there was no chance they would participate in the humiliation and betrayal of their king. The baffling actions of Smith were probably a reflection of his lack of understanding of the gravity of the highly volatile situation which was about to explode in front of him. Little did he know that his contemptuous actions would mark the beginning of the longest, bloodiest war ever fought between Africans and Europeans in Southern Africa in the nineteenth century.

In terms of the balance of forces in the colony, Prince Phatho of amaGqunukhwebe, who was located between East London and Qonce, decided not to partake in the war because of fears of subjecting his people to British firepower, in an open, and therefore vulnerable, area. Also, in the war of 1846 to 1847, amaRharhabe took a considerable number of his livestock. His non-participation in the war proved to be a vital turning point. Firstly, it was the weakest link on the side of the Africans, which made them unable to encircle the colonial forces and win the entire war. Secondly, Phatho's non-participation allowed the colonial establishment to deliver much-needed vital supplies from East London to Qonce at a critical period, when the British could have lost the war completely. Had Phatho participated in the war, amaXhosa would have succeeded in besieging Qonce, Fort Cox and Fort Hare, completely cutting British supply lines and placing Smith in a trap.

One of the reasons why Emperor Menelik II was victorious against the Italians in the famous battle of Adwa in 1892 was because he was able to rally all the Ethiopians as a united force against a common enemy. Although it was only Phatho who did not participate in the war, in the end all the Africans were treated as barbaric savages by the colonial establishment. In the long term his non-participation in the war did not help him or his people. The lack of unity among Africans was always a source of vulnerability which was exploited by the colonialists.

Prince Siyolo, the nephew of Mhala, occupied the strategic area between Nxuba River and Qonce, whilst Prince Stokwe of amaMbalu was positioned between Nxuba River and Makhanda. Both Siyolo and Stokwe were going to play an important role in cutting the supply line between Gqeberha and Makhanda. During the war, both these leaders were involved in the direct onslaught on the British soldiers stationed in

Line Drift. Prince Bhotomane occupied the vast plains beneath the mountains of Mathole (Mostert, 1992). King Sarhili of amaGcaleka remained as the strategic fall-back buffer and provided logistical support from a distance, although he did not openly declare his support for the war. Prince Maphasa, the son of Bawana of abaThembu, was positioned between Whittlesea and Queenstown. He resented the encroachment of the colonialists; hence he made an open declaration of his support for the war against Harry Smith (Soga, 1930).

This time amaMfengu were the only African group which fought in solidarity with the Europeans against the Africans since their exodus from Gcalekaland to Ngqushwa in May 1835. They found themselves in a precarious position. On the one hand, they were compelled to partake in the British wars against their own African people to repay the debt of the land of Ngqushwa. On the other, they were fully aware that they were not British allies in the true sense of the word and that they were treated as disposable commodities that were often placed on the front line in order to absorb the impact of contact in the battle. When casualties of war were counted, the number of amaMfengu who fell in the battle were excluded because their lives did not matter, as indicated by the accounts of King (1855) and McKay (1871), the British officers who fought in the War of Mlanjeni. At the time, The Graham's Town Journal of 18 April 1853 reported that the population of amaMfengu who participated in the war as British allies stood at 2 900 people. At times amaMfengu were placed as bait in strategic positions in order to lure the African combatants from their concealed positions. King (1855) acknowledged that amaMfengu played a considerable part in plundering and conducting mass killing of the survivors at the height of the war.

Based on the accounts of the diary of Reverend Robert John Mullins (1833–1913), the Anglican Missionary in the Cape Colony at the time, which were published by Nichols, Charton, and Knowling in 1998, during the War of Mlanjeni, amaMfengu were commanded by Reuben, the second son of Reverend John Ayliff. Reuben later became the Mayor of Makhanda between 1869 and 1872. Interestingly, Stubbs, in his reminiscences of the raging Afro-European Cape colonial wars at the outbreak of the War of Mlanjeni, which were published by Maxwel and McGeogh in 1978, reported that Jonathan, one of the sons of Ayliff, also commanded amaMfengu during the war. Since their father John was instrumental in engineering the exodus of amaMfengu to Ngqushwa, it appeared that they were also used in the pursuance of British conquest.

3. Imela Yagobel' Esandleni *"Knife Turned Against the Handler"*

In isiXhosa the literal translation of *Imela yagob'elesandleni* is jack-knifing of a pocket knife into one's hand. The deeper figurative meaning is what you use to hurt others has turned against you. At the outbreak of the War of Mlanjeni, the British colonial establishment lost the support of the Khoe, who were important allies because they were always dependable and lethal in the battlefield. Colonel Graham's expulsion of amaXhosa from the Zuurveld was made possible by the crucial role of the Khoe, who were reported to have located the hiding place of Prince Chungwa of amaGqunukhwebe, since they were more familiar with the terrain. The Khoe contribution had been a vital element that enabled the colonial armies to sustain the war.

Despite their significant contributions and immense sacrifices, the white settlers had an ambivalent attitude towards the Khoe people. On the one hand, they were in desperate need of their services and on the other hand, they resented the fact that they excelled at almost everything. Their ambivalent situation is best described by Mostert (1992): *"The Khoe believed that they were fighting on behalf of the British settlers who hated and despised them more deeply even than the Boers ever had"* (pg 1046). They were treated as commodities whose bodies were seen as instruments to serve the white settler colonial interests. Since the Khoe people excelled especially as sharpshooters on the battlefields, the British settlers resented the unpleasant reality that those they perceived to be sub-humans were actually superior to them.

According to Meintjes (1971): *"They had rendered good service in the previous war, only to be treated so shabbily that they were inflamed with resentment"* (pg 207). The Khoe may have been conquered, displaced, dehumanized and commodified, but they were not stupid. They endured the continued ill-treatment, despite having served and protected their colonial masters in several wars, and waited for an opportune time to strike back hard. The events leading to the outbreak of the War of Mlanjeni emerged at the perfect moment of the Khoe people's insurrection against their colonial masters. The opportune moment the Khoe had been waiting for to strike back is best captured in this quote from William Shakespeare, *"There is a tide in the affairs of men, which, taken at the flood, leads on to fortune; omitted, all the voyage of their life is bound in shallows and in miseries"* (Julius Caesar, Act IV.ii.269). The Khoe people were fully aware that the continued appeasement of their colonial masters never made any difference to their material status, and their living conditions deteriorated over time. Prince Maqoma's mobilization of the war presented itself as a golden opportunity for the Khoe to strike at their ungrateful colonial masters.

The eviction of the Khoe from the Kat River in June 1850 was still fresh in their memories. At the outbreak of the war, they had an influential leader, Hermanus Matroos, known as Ngxukumeshe, who was the son of a Gqunukhwebe father and Khoe mother (Stapleton, 2016). He was a strong tall man of solid frame. He had *"long black curly hair, a face with widely-spaced eyes and a thin ridged nose...had slightly reddish tint..."* (Dekker, 2016). He was multilingual, as he spoke isiXhosa, Dutch and English. He started his early life as a fisherman and seaman. According to Dekker (2016), in his 30s he wanted to explore something new. He left the coast and ventured into the interior towards the Fish River, the land of his father. Since he was multilingual, he was recruited by the British to be an interpreter in the diplomatic engagements with amaXhosa royals. He later became the military leader of the Khoe and the British gave him land in the Kat River.

In the winter of June 1850, Smith ordered the destruction of the Khoe settlements in Kat River. The land was then given to white settlers and amaMfengu. The leaders of the Khoe, Matroos, Andries Botha and Willem Uithaalder, were very bitter. Matroos convinced the Khoe not to partake in the war on the side of the British because it became clear to them that despite years of submission to the British rule, their interests did not matter to the colonial authorities. They were neither honoured nor rewarded for their participation and sacrifices in the previous wars. Instead, they were despised and resented, especially by the white settlers. *"Khoe and mixed-race people began to resist the emergence of a coercive, racial capitalism in which they were becoming a landless working class"* (Stapleton, 2016: 199). They were aggrieved to find themselves landless after having served the colonial establishment for decades. Eventually, Matroos and his people took a bold decision to desert the British establishment and fight alongside Maqoma. Meintjies (1971) noted that Ngxukumeshe led about 900 Khoe combatants who joined Maqoma in the war against the Europeans.

The insurrection of the Khoe against the British colonial establishment came as a huge shock to Smith and Somerset, as well as to the white settlers and soldiers. They had been a crucial element of the colonial military machinery. McKay expressed his resentment and shock in his war diary. *"I cannot believe that any sane man who has ever studied the first page of England's history or geography, would be so insane as to help in the slightest form any attempt at rebellion by the few inhabitants of the Kat River, against the reigning government of England"* (McKay, 1871: 57). What McKay failed to understand were the deep-seated grievances of the Khoe. Similarly, the Graham's Town Journal of 11 January 1853 lamented the insurrection of the Khoe at a very critical time *"People who have been raised by the British from the lowest state of human degradation, and who have repaid the debt by the blackest ingratitude..."* pg (2). The focus was more on the insurrection and not on their grievances and the manner in which they had been treated: as if their lives, emotions and aspirations did not matter.

At the time of the insurrection, there were about 900 Khoe stationed in the Kat River region. According to the Cape Frontier Times, Graham's Town, May 10, 1853, about 300 Khoe participated in the insurrection. Theal (1904) observed that *"The rebellion of a large number of Hottentots made this the most expensive and destructive of all the wars yet waged in South Africa"* (pg 95). The timing of the Khoe insurrection happened at a critical point, providing Prince Maqoma with the formidable ally he needed for the consolidation of his forces in anticipation of a long period of war. At the outbreak of the war the Khoe controlled the critical region between Fort Hare and Fort Beaufort.

This time the Boers, who were still in the Cape colony, were also reluctant to participate on the side of the British, because of the appalling treatment they experienced from the colonial establishment after their participation in the previous war. The British settlers resented the fact that the Khoe and the Boers were excellent sharpshooters and well-suited to fight in the most challenging terrain of dense forest, dangerous gorges and impenetrable ravines.

4. Prince Maqoma's Finest Moment

The War of Mlanjeni meant many things to Prince Maqoma. It was a make-or-break opportunity for him after he lost influence and a considerable number of followers due to his decision not to participate in the previous war. It was a war fought after he relinquished power to King Sandile. Dowsley (1932) described Prince Maqoma as the greatest politician and military strategist in the Cape Colony at the time. McKay, who fought in the war of Mlanjeni, described Maqoma in these words: *"Red demon of war burst his fetters and the savage determination of the K... was formed to annihilate the white man..."* (McKay, 1871: 45). While Mlanjeni was rallying people to a war, Jongumsobomvu found himself burdened with the enormous responsibility of leading amaXhosa into war after Smith declared a bounty on his highly-revered brother, King Sandile, in his own land.

The belligerent policies of Smith, who perceived conciliation as a sign of weakness, convinced Maqoma that it was a matter of time before the outbreak of another war. Maqoma had a heavy weight upon his shoulders, namely the unbearable strain and agony of having witnessed how Africans and their leaders were periodically subjected to dispossession, displacement and dehumanization. He witnessed the disdainful treatment of Africans stripped of their dignity, reduced to the degrading state of being wretched savages of the earth. Africans continued to be demeaned as people with no history, no culture and no identity up to the twentieth century; therefore the history of what actually happened was distorted.

Jongumsobomvu was celebrated by amaXhosa not only as a royal leader but for his amazing gift of decisive leadership both in the military field and in the political and traditional sphere. He had great oratorical skills, which were vital in time of war. Maqoma established himself as the skilful mastermind who marshalled African people, instilled pride and confidence in them, and pulverized his enemy.

In March 1849, Prince Maqoma visited King Sarhili in his Kingdom of Gcalekaland and stayed there for about three months, working on the strategies in preparation for an imminent war (Stapleton, 2016). He probably knew that in the event of a war, he would require a continued supply of well-trained men in order to sustain it.

Upon his return, he mended his strained relationship with King Sandile in order to unite amaXhosa against colonial dominance under the highly pompous Smith. He obtained the support of the Khoe, who took a stand against the colonial establishment, the assurance of support from Prince Mapasa of abaThembu as well the support of various royal leaders in the colony. This placed him in a strong position to engage in sustained war because of the alliances and the support he managed to get.

Maqoma took advantage of the fertile ground which had been prepared by Mlanjeni in revolutionising amaXhosa into war. The lessons he learnt from the two previous great wars included the importance for African people to arm themselves and to be more united if they had to make a lasting impact on the wars of resistance. He embarked on clandestine mass mobilization of people and the amassing of muskets and horses from the white traders. He also started training his people in how to master armed ambushes (Stapleton, 2016). Maqoma made sure that amaXhosa had collected ammunition and guns to be able to engage the colonial army over a sustained period.

It is estimated that Africans amassed about 3000 arms, six million rounds of ball cartridges, and about half a million assegais through transactions with white traders (King, 1855). Maqoma was fully aware that they faced the prospect of a tough opponent with a professional army of infantry, superior artillery, cavalry and mounted soldiers, who could have easily wiped out amaXhosa in one day, especially in open terrain.

The drive behind his massive mobilization campaign for the war can be attributed to several incidents that had occurred in his life pertaining to the actions of the colonial authorities. Maqoma was still very bitter about his unceremonious expulsion from the Kat River in April 1829, in which Henry Somerset and Andries Stockenström launched an unprovoked attack on him and his people. He was still hoping to recover his stolen land, which was populated by white settlers and the Khoe (Stapleton, 2016). The expulsion of amaJingqi from the Kat River in 1829, was a common occurrence during the colonial era, where the armed colonial commandos would raid identified villages of amaXhosa unannounced, and clear them for the white settlers who were desperate for rich land, a good water supply, and the livestock of the African people.

He had not forgotten the public humiliation he was subjected to by Smith on 14 December 1847 in Gqeberha. On that fateful day, Smith violently knocked Maqoma down, placed his shoe on his neck and wielded his sword on his face (Stapleton, 2016). Maqoma was deeply incensed by Smith's barbaric actions. The awful incident remained ingrained in Maqoma's mind on the day Smith made a spectacle of his deep-seated hatred for the African people. He was resolute that the imminent war was going to be his finest hour to avenge the public humiliation, as Smith was going to receive the bitter taste of his own medicine.

5. King Sandile Drew First Blood in the Battle of Boma Pass

Whilst Lieutenant Colonel Eyre was positioned in Qonce and General Henry Somerset in Edikeni[4], Lieutenant Governor George Mackinnon commanded the first military attack against King Sandile with a force of 580 soldiers (King, 1855). He departed from Fort Cox, near Mkhubiso, in the early hours of 24 December 1850, leading his troops to the heart of the fortress of amaRharhabe in Qoboqobo, leaving Governor Harry Smith in a place of central command in Fort Cox to direct the military operations. His army was fully equipped with enough ammunition and supplies to engage the enemy over an extended period of time. From Fort Cox, he navigated through forested mountains with dense bushes, narrow winding routes, thick impenetrable ravines and deep gorges.

The purpose of the military exercise was to humiliate and to harass amaXhosa, and no resistance was expected from them, since Sandile was a fugitive and not in a position to organise and rally his people to war. Since Jongumsobomvu did not participate in the previous war of 1846 to 1847, they expected similar inaction from him. They assumed that he was probably happy that Sandile was on the run, after he had been compelled to grudgingly relinquish power to him. The colonial commanders assumed that they were going to pursue and completely displace Sandile with minimal resistance from

---

4   Ediken was known as Alice during the colonial era. In 1852, the town was named after Princess Alice the daughter of Queen Victoria (1819 -1901). Ediken is a small town of great historical significance on the banks of the legendary Tyhume River separating the town from the University of Fort Hare built on the grounds of a military fort named after Major General John Hare. Before it was named Alice, the original African name was Ediken referring to a pond (Pollock (1954).

amaXhosa. The misreading of amaXhosa's seemingly docile demeanour proved to be a catastrophic miscalculation, with disastrous consequences for the British military commanders and their political leadership.

Sandile learnt from his older brother Maqoma how to execute bush warfare ambushes by targeting vulnerable positions of the advancing enemy. As Sandile did to Lieutenant General John Hare in the previous war, he was watching the movement of the British-led army from Mkhubiso to the jaws of Boma Pass, where he was waiting patiently to launch his surprise assault. He continually received messages from his informers about the movements of the enemy and the extent of the arsenal in their possession. His army was strategically positioned on both sides of the Boma Pass rugged gorge to attack from the higher ground and block the enemy troops on the flanks, front and rear of the gorge.

After the British troops arrived at the fortress of the Boma Pass gorge, where part of the current Sandile Dam is built, they received the shock of their lives after witnessing amaXhosa warriors in their thousands amassed on opposite sides of the winding gorge. The agile warriors of amaXhosa subjected the British-led army to a surprise ferocious attack that was intensified relentlessly. They first rolled down massive stones from the upper steep position of the gorge in order to disorganise and confuse the army. When the army was in state of disarray, they started firing down on them and throwing their spears at the troops on the long narrow path of the gorge (Mostert, 1992).

There are contradictory accounts with regard to the actual number of casualties incurred by the British soldiers at the agonising battle of Boma Pass. King (1855) claimed that eleven British soldiers perished in the war and two officers were badly wounded, whilst Mckay (1871) reported that fifteen soldiers were killed in the battle and their bodies were badly mutilated. Considering the nature and location of the attack, the number of casualties and those who died from their wounds a few days later, the figures were probably significantly higher.

According to King (1855) it was the African police of the colony who lured the soldiers to the ambush because they were never attacked; they simply disappeared with the ammunition, never to be seen again.

The battle of Boma Pass obliterated Mackinnon's column. They army suffered heavy casualties and a significant number of soldiers were wounded, while others were captured and tortured. It is reported that the same King Sandile, whom they went out to harass and humiliate, was leading his forces from the front. According to Mostert, *"Harry Smith and George Mackinnon had been outmatched, outwitted and outgeneraled by the strategies of Maqoma and the national defiance of a lame young Xhosa Chief whom no one had considered would be willing to show himself on a battlefield"* (Mostert, 1992: 1040). The tables had quickly turned on the pompous colonial military leadership because they had no clue about the type of enemy they had just encountered in the battlefield.

Boma Pass marked itself as a site of historical significance in the annals of wars of resistance at kwaRharhabe. Sandile's victorious obliteration of Mackinnon at Boma Pass marked the beginning of the long agonising War of Mlanjeni. What made the amaXhosa British wars different from other military encounters in South Africa in the nineteenth century, they were not battles fought in few days, these were long agonising hauls of brutal engagements. The intensity and viciousness of the attack marked the ultimate explosion of the simmering tensions that had been fermenting due to the draconian policies and the unethical conduct of Governor Harry Smith, the highly celebrated hero of Aliwal. Sandile's military strategy to launch a deadly surprise attack in awkward places, where the British firepower had limitations, was the defining hallmark of the determination to take the bull by its horns at strategic positions. From there simultaneous and relentless attacks were launched, targeting white settlers on the farms, settlements and towns.

6. The Agonisng Siege of General Harry Smith in Fort Cox

Whilst Mackinnon and his army were fighting the battle of their lives in the gorges of Boma Pass, Sandile dispatched another group of his warriors to Fort Cox in order to take the battle right into the face of the colonial Governor, Harry Smith. The ability of Sandile and Maqoma to command simultaneous extensive blitzes in different strategic locations took Smith and his military commanders by surprise. Before Smith knew it, Sandile's men subjected the well-fortified Fort Cox to a blistering onslaught. Smith was shattered to the core, as he did not foresee the enemy resorting to such a decisive and direct attack to his centre of military command. He was paralysed after realizing that he did not have enough firepower to repel the pulverising offensive. *"He was besieged...cut from the world, unable to direct a war that he declared"* (Mostert, 1992: 1040). The acclaimed British war veteran was dismayed, mortified and demobilized by the quick turn of events. His military plans crumbled in a short space of time. The folly of his ill-informed polices and the pejorative manner in which he discharged his mandated authority over amaXhosa led to an unforeseen and disastrous disintegration of his power (Mostert 1992). AmaXhosa maintained the targeted siege of Fort Cox over a considerable period of time.

Since Fort Hare was the closest available fort, Smith depended on General Henry Somerset to rescue him from the excruciating encirclement. Somerset was more familiar with the terrain, as he was involved in the humiliating defeat of the British at Mkhubiso. On 29 December 1850, General Harry Somerset assembled his army of 200 soldiers from Fort Hare and headed to Fort Cox to liberate Smith from the harrowing encounter (Theal, 1904). The British officers, soldiers and white settlers had a low regard for Somerset. He was portrayed as a corrupt and immoral man, whose personal interests mattered more than serving the British Empire. McKay, who joined the war in the spring of 1851, had this to say about him; *"He always kept a tribe of bastard Hottentots about him — some passable looking wenches among the number — who he rationed.*

Whether these women were the wives or daughters of his orderlies, or his own personal attendants, I will not take upon myself to say" (McKay 1871: 40-41). Dekker (2016) also described Somerset as a man with a lavish lifestyle, lazy, indecisive and always surrounded by young Khoe women.

Prince Sandile obtained information from his informers, who were mostly women, that Somerset was leading an army towards Fort Cox. At the outbreak of the war, Maqoma was positioned in the area around Fort Hare, Fort Beaufort and Fort Armstrong, whilst his brother Sandile commanded his troops between Fort Cox, Fort White and Fort Hill.

Maqoma was assigned to counter Somerset's advances at Fort Cox, a task he relished as he quickly assembled foot soldiers with spears and mounted riflemen and placed them in strategic positions along the anticipated route of his enemy. *"They swarmed out of every valley along the way, and across every ridge, densely massed, and with the dispositions arranged with evident skill and prompt, shrewd observations by Maqoma. The Xhosa appeared to be held in large reserves, able to be summoned when required. This alone enhanced the impression all the British had of overwhelming numbers issuing suddenly from some point whenever the situation appeared to require Xhosa reinforcement"* (Mostert, 1992: 1061). During all this time, Somerset was oblivious to the extent to which Maqoma had amassed his warriors on the route to Fort Cox.

Eventually on the outskirts of Fort Cox, at the foot of the range of the Amathole Mountains, his army came under heavy attack from Maqoma's regiments (McKay, 1871 & Mostert, 1992). The intensity of the vicious onslaught brought Somerset's advancing army to a standstill. He was compelled to retreat in the face of the rapid waves of the relentless pulverising blitz. The tempo and the potency of the deadly offensive were so overwhelming that the army never managed to position the artillery to repel the enemy. In the process of retreat, Somerset's army suffered heavy casualties. Twenty-two soldiers fell in the ruthless battle and 17 of them were seriously wounded as they retreated back to Fort Hare (Cape

Frontier Times April 15, 1853 & Mostert, 1992). However, according to Cory (1930) 22 soldiers died whilst 20 of them were wounded in the battle *"…150 of the 91ˢᵗ Regiment and 70 of the C.M.R with a three-pounder gun, – a force which Col. Somerset, in his ignorance of the true state of affairs, considered more than sufficient to overawe any opposition"* (pg 321). Had a further reinforcement not arrived from Fort Hare, they would have been completely wiped out (Mostert, 1992). According to MacKay (1871) the total number of casualties was 24 soldiers, including two officers; and 17 wounded. However, King (1855) claimed that 20 soldiers and two officers were killed and many were wounded. Whatever the case may be, the figure excluded the number of amaMfengu auxiliaries who were often placed on the frontline to absorb the brunt of the contact.

It took about four hours of close brutal combat for Somerset's men to start retreating from Fort Cox to Fort Hare. This was one of the worst military encounters the British troops suffered during the War of Mlanjeni. *"This too was a decisive field victory rather than an ambush, as Boma Pass had been. It was a triumph of generalship in the open, something that the Xhosa otherwise consciously sought to avoid. In the personal sense it represented humiliation of Maqoma's two old enemies, Henry Somerset and Harry Smith, in the most forceful possible manner"* (Mostert, 1992:1063). This was one of the defining moments Maqoma had been preparing for since the expulsion from the Kat River region two decades earlier. The bone-crushing brutality drove the British troops to a point of desperation, as they faced the prospect of total annihilation. The arrival of reinforcements from Fort Hare did not stop the offensive of Maqoma's men; instead, it provided a reasonable ground for resistance whilst continuing to retreat to Fort Hare.

General Somerset's failure to rescue Smith from Fort Cox, as well as the casualties he suffered in the disastrous defeat, was a military calamity for Smith. He was under tremendous strain, as he had to juggle multiple harrowing events in an attempt to get out of the quagmire he had created. Fighting an elusive enemy, who created a sense of being everywhere, managing the unfolding crisis of the Khoe's rebellion, dealing with the aftermath of the humiliating defeat of Boma Pass and the latest setbacks was just too overwhelming for Smith. He found himself in a terrifying position he had never encountered in his entire military career. The war he had declared had exploded into an uncontrollable fireball, with a series of disastrous costly defeats.

Maqoma's obliteration of Somerset laid bare his glaring shortcomings as he had no mental capacity and material capability to withstand the onslaught. *"He plainly lacked the will, ingenuity and impulse that such an emergency and that such a responsibility required..."* (Mostert, 1992: 1070). The failure of Somerset to rescue him made Smith realize that something extraordinary had to be done before he ran out of supplies. He worked out an escape plan informed by careful observation of the movement of the enemy forces that had besieged the fort.

On the night of 31 December 1850, Smith made a daring escape from Fort Cox, disguised as one of the Khoe Cape Mounted Riflemen who accompanied him (Mostert, 1992). According to the Cape Frontier Times, Graham's Town, April 5, 1853, Smith escaped, escorted by 300 Khoe men after he had been held for six weeks. However, Theal (1904) claimed that when Smith escaped, he was escorted by 250 Khoe Cape mounted riflemen. McKay (1871) reported that, *"Sir Harry fled from the fort, accompanied by the Cape Mounted Rifles, it was with a misgiving heart, for he really thought that he never would reach King Williamstown, but, as the old adage goes, it was 'die dog or eat the hatchet '"* (McKay 1871: 37). During the escape, they had to fight their way from the fort until they reached Qonce . From the well-secured confines of Fort Harding and Fort Hill at Qonce, he issued a declaration appealing to the white settlers to assist the colonial troops in the expulsion and extermination of amaXhosa from the fortresses of the Amathole Mountains (King, 1855). By calling for the genocide of amaXhosa, he re-ignited the ethnic cleansing policy executed by Colonel Graham four decades earlier.

The agonising wait for reinforcement after his arrival in Qonce pushed Smith to breaking-point. What made matters worse was the refusal of white settlers to participate in the war because of lack of confidence in the controversial leadership of both Smith and Somerset, which was characterised by poor decision making, excessive overreaction and shallow understanding of amaXhosa. Smith was under immense pressure from Britain to finish the war as a matter of urgency before it could drain more resources from the Empire. That was an impossible task, as amaXhosa were more resolute and united than before as they continued to widen their ferocious attacks in small groups as far as Gqeberha (former Port Elizabeth) and Komani (Queenstown).

After Smith's escape from Fort Cox, Fort Hare became the next target. On 21 January 1851, a massive offensive was launched at Fort Hare. AmaMfengu were placed on the frontline to defend the fort, whilst the British soldiers and settlers fired their guns and artillery from inside the fort. Sandile's forces were compelled to retreat after facing a barrage of relentless artillery.

Despite the fact that Smith, Somerset and Mackinnon had a well-trained, sizeable army, superior firepower and enormous resources, they were outsmarted, defeated and humiliated by men with limited resources. Maqoma and Sandile drew a line in the sand, sending a clear message that the war was not going to be a walk in the park. The outcomes of the war were to be decided through sweat and blood in the battlefield.

On the one hand, the British military commanders thought that heavy reliance on superior firepower was going to be an easy solution to attain decisive victory through total annihilation of the enemy. On the other hand, what mattered to Maqoma and Sandile was when and where to engage the enemy in order to inflict maximum impact from a position of strength. The decisive leadership and the brilliant execution of the military strategies by the sons of Prince Ngqika was what made the difference during the brutal battles of the war.

7. The Pulverizing Fireball of the War of Mlanjeni

King (1855) reported that on 25th December 1850, following the battle of Boma Pass, members of the 45th Regiment came under heavy attack in Debe Nek whilst escorting the wagons to Qonce . The pulverizing attack was so quick and impactful that they never had a chance to form a defensive line in order to withstand the African fighters. The entire group of fourteen soldiers and a sergeant were wiped out by combatants of amaXhosa. On the following day, their bodies were found in a terrible state by the soldiers of George Mackinnon who were the fortunate survivors from the heart-wrenching defeat at Boma Pass.

Theal (1904) lamented the tragedy of the white settler village, Woburn in Tyhume, which was completely obliterated. At the outbreak of the war in December 1850, the three villages of Woburn, Auckland and Juanasburg in the Tyhume Valley were occupied by military settlers and their families. Woburn had 16 soldiers; Auckland near Hogsback had 22 soldiers and 30 women and Juanasburg had eight soldiers. During the waves of direct onslaught, Woburn suffered 15 casualties; 22 British soldiers were killed in Auckland, whilst women and children were allowed to escape to Tyhume Mission, in line with the principles of engagement of amaXhosa in warfare. Juanasburg suffered three casualties, whilst five managed to escape in time to Alice. Theal (1904) observed that in the first three days of the war, about 84 British settlers were killed.

Coetzee (2000) bemoaned the total annihilation of white settler males in the unfortified villages of the Tyhume valley, which were built not far from the royal headquarters of Prince Tyhali. Maxengana (1989) observed that the obliteration of the villages and the bloodbath in Boma Pass were a clear indication of the collective determination of amaXhosa, who were led by the highly courageous great grandsons of the great senior Prince Rharhabe.

On the 3rd of January, 1851, King Sandile, on his white horse, led three columns in the invasion of Fort White. His warriors launched simultaneous attacks from three different directions with mounted fighters and men on foot (McKay, 1871). The fighting continued for some time with both sides exchanging fire. Eventually, amaRharhabe retreated after coming under the intensity of heavy firepower. According to McKay (1871) Prince Sandile lost 22 men, whilst the British suffered only injuries.

It was at Fort Armstrong that the Khoe combatants took a stand, turning against the colonial power. The knife that had been sharpened for decades to cut amaXhosa, since the ethnic cleansing of 1811-1812, had turned violently against its handlers, as amaXhosa would say *"Imela igobel' esandleni."* (The knife has jack-knifed against the handler). The Khoe launched a well-coordinated surprise attack that the defenders of the fort could not withstand. After the fall of the defensive line, the Khoe took occupation of it and did as they wished to the occupants. *"The Hottentots of the Kat River Mission, driving out the European occupants, in a most inclement night, to escape as best they might...across the mountains of Whittlesea, took possession of the Post... living in the most disgraceful licentiousness and depravity, offering indignities to the English women, plundering the neighbouring farms and revelling on the spoil"* (King, 1855: 283). The direct and bold attack conducted by the Khoe riflemen on Fort Armstrong was a shattering tragedy to their former masters in their hour of need. What exacerbated the situation was the fact that they did not see it coming and therefore they had no clue as to how to neutralise it. Such attacks happened at a time when the colonial establishment was in desperate need of the services of the Khoe people.

On 23rd February 1851, General Somerset subjected the fort to two hours of ferocious bombardment using all the ammunition at his disposal in a desperate attempt to break the resistance of the Khoe fighting men. The decision to barrage the fort must have had been taken after the failure to retake the bastion from the determined Khoe combatants. For Somerset to resort to collapsing such a strategic defensive military post in a critical location must have been a difficult decision. The Khoe took a stand and returned fire, taking positions from the surroundings. However, the continued devastating shelling of the fort finally collapsed it, leaving the Khoe vulnerable to the deadly British firepower. About 40 Khoe fell, whilst 160 of them surrendered and about 400 women and children were also captured. Somerset lost three men and 20 soldiers were wounded. No one knows what happened to the captured Khoe. Considering the resentment white settlers had against the Khoe, the captured Khoe were probably subjected to public hanging as a deterrent to those who continued fighting. In March 1851, the majority of the Khoe Cape Mounted Rifles deserted the British army to join amaXhosa (King, 1855).

As amaXhosa, the Khoe and abaThembu launched attacks targeting white settlers in farms as well as military posts and forts between Fort Beaufort and Komani, the settlers in Albany requested more reinforcements. Lieutenant Colonel Mackinnon, after the disastrous campaign of Boma Pass, was dispatched to rescue the settlers of Albany in Nxuba River.

On the 9th of September 1851, amaXhosa regiments had close man-to-man combat with the British soldiers of the freshly-arrived 2nd Queen's Royal Regiment in the thick bushes of the Nxuba River. McKay (1871) chronicled chilling accounts of the Nxuba River encounter in his war diary, which was published in 1871, describing it as the massacre of the 2nd Queen's Royal Regiment. On 1st September 1851, the 2nd Queen's Regiment, in white military jackets, proceeded to Qonce after landing in East London, under the command of Colonel Burns and Major Wilmot, joined by a second column under the Lt Col George Mackinnon. They proceeded towards Ngqushwa.

Around Committee's Heights, they saw amaXhosa combatants. On the 8th of September 1851, they marched from the ridge approaching the deep slope towards the Nxuba River. On the following day the army split into different groups, Colonel Mitchell to the right, Captain Addison to the left and Captain Oldham direct to the bushy ravine towards the Nxuba River. All along the combatants of amaXhosa were watching their movement and waiting to launch surprise offensive in different locations.

Suddenly, the 2nd Queen's Regiment came under heavy attack in the early hours of the morning from amaXhosa warriors of Prince Siyolo, who were positioned in various locations. They continued the exchange until the day cleared. In the process, Oldham moved in a dangerous direction with his men and found themselves completely encircled in a trap by the charging forces of African combatants. It was always the military strategy of amaXhosa to drive an impactful thrust into the centre of the charging British army, splitting it into different groups, then encircling each band and wiping it out. According to McKay, when Oldham's assistant approached him, he gave his ring and his watch to the soldier and asked him to keep them for his wife, Lady Oldham, and his mother and he succumbed to his injuries shortly thereafter. The rest of Oldham's men continued fighting until all 40 of them were killed. In addition to such a huge loss, about 80 soldiers of 2nd Queen's Royal Regiment were reported missing in action as they disappeared during the vicious battle in the bushy ravines of the Nxuba River (McKay, 1871).

What stood out for McKay (1871) was the extraordinary incident of one of the British soldiers named Buck who had thirteen wounds. What defined Buck as an extraordinary soldier was not the number of wounds he had absorbed but his remarkable courage and sober willingness to face death. "*The appearance of the man, covered over with blood from his many wounds, rendered him a horrid spectacle. The doctor approached him...but he respectfully declined the doctor's help, and told him to attend to others who were worse than himself*" (McKay, 1871.85). The act of declining help in order to save others was a remarkable demonstration of benevolent humanity. In isiXhosa "*walala ngenxeba*" – slept on his wounds, as the epitome of a courageous and selfless soldier. To everyone's surprise, Buck survived the horrendous trauma. Eventually he was released from the army and returned to Great Britain.

In retrospect, the huge losses suffered by the British army in the battle of Nxuba River were among many serious setbacks that shattered the illustrious military career of General Harry Smith beyond any prospects of recovery. The white settlers were embittered by the series of catastrophic losses, from the humiliating defeat at Boma Pass, to the annihilation of the military villages in the Tyhume valley, the Debe Nek tragedy and the carnage in the Nxuba River. They became convinced that Smith had no clear military strategy on how to withstand the pulverising fireball thrown at them in every direction by the raging African combatants. The Nxuba River bloodbath was an incomprehensible military loss that created a sense of psychological paralysis within the British army and desperation among the European settlers.

8. The Fall of Fordyce in the Ferocious War of Mount Misery

The Kat River Valley, wherein lies the town of Fort Beaufort, was a contested place between amaXhosa and the white settlers because of its abundant water-rich land. In 1855, Captain King described it as *"One of the finest and most fruitful districts in the whole colony. Surrounded by vast chains of fine mountains, this extensive valley spread its smiling uplands and fertile holms, picturesquely relieved by belts of valuable timber and watered by the winding Kat River"* (King, 1855:122). Prince Maqoma grew up hunting in this area. Later on King Nqgika granted the land to Prince Maqoma and this is where he established his nation of amaJingqi. During the governorship of Galbraith Lowry Cole (1772-1842) between 1828 and 1833, Maqoma and his people were violently expelled from this region by the forces of General Somerset and Stockenström in 1829. The incident marked a turning point in the life of Prince Maqoma, because he grew up under the wing of his father, who had a close relationship with the British establishment. Now he was being driven away from his land by his father's friends in the same year Prince Ngqika departed.

In April 1851, Maqoma took advantage of the paralysed colony by returning to the occupied Kat River region of his youth (Stapleton, 2016). During the first few months, his people, together with the resentful Khoe, pushed the white settler farmers and amaMfengu out of the region and confiscated their farms and livestock. Maqoma identified the mountain of Mthontsi in the Waterkloof region as his strategic stronghold from which he would wage war. The British troops named the mountain Mount Misery, because it marked the climax of the unimaginable suffering and gruesome death they endured during the harrowing war of Mlanjeni. *"Mthontsi was composed of some of the roughest and most impassable terrain in southern Africa...Jongumsobomvu knew all the secret trails and caves that could be used to elude an adversary and to hide small numbers of cattle as a reliable food supply...Mthontsi was thus an ideal military stronghold"* (Stapleton, 2016: 203-4). Jongumsobomvu made Mthontsi the legendary mountain his stronghold to wage and to sustain the agonising war

Mthontsi Mountain still bears the scars of the agonising encounter that ended the lives of thousands of combatants. Some of the key grounds of the brutal contact were Blinkwater, Fullers Hoek, Horse Shoe, the Kroome and Maqoma's cave (King, 1855; McKay, 1871). Saks (2005) provides a vivid portrayal of this historically significant scene. *"Sprawling series of high hills and plateaus, intersected by deep, heavily forested valleys, gorges and ravines. The Waterkloof itself is a deep, narrow valley, six kilometres long, bounded by the Kroome Heights to the south and to the north by a second series of majestic ridges falling away to a rolling plateau. Running roughly south-east and open at its western extremity, it comes to a head in high, grassy tableland fringed with bushes and gigantic trees. To the east, this tableland falls away into another deep, heavily-forested gorge, known as Fuller's Hoek. It was in this gorge, in a gigantic overarching cave of a type that proliferates in the area, that Maqoma had his headquarters. The plateau is linked to the Kroome by a narrow ridge and where this joins the plateau is a horseshoe-shaped flat, approximately a square kilometre in area and fringed by towering forests...abound in the surviving first-hand accounts of the fighting that took place there"* (Saks,2005:2-3). During the agonising one hundred years of wars of resistance, the Mountain Misery stood out as the towering and impenetrable fortress of defiance, courage and refuge, whose ground had absorbed the blood and bones of thousands of combatants during the longest and deadliest war ever fought between Africans and Europeans in the history of Southern Africa.

Mount Misery became the defining ground where Jongumsobomvu sharpened his military strategies, focusing on gaining leverage and ascendancy in the battle through the exploitation of the vulnerabilities of his enemy. Firstly, he was fully aware of the type of enemy he was fighting; its strengths and its weaknesses. Secondly, he knew how to adjust his strategies in order to engage the enemy through sustained targeted attacks. He placed informers in strategic areas to monitor the movement of the enemy troops. The informers enabled him to determine the position and the extent of the required assault. He thus emerged as one of the greatest military strategists of the nineteenth century in Southern Africa.

After Maqoma had established himself in Mthontsi, he raided farms as far as Gqeberha, Cradock and Komani in the triangle of the wars of resistance. The reoccupation of the Kat River region by Maqoma, the continued attacks on white settler farmers and confiscation of livestock, further eroded white settler confidence in General Smith. They had to fend for themselves in order to save their lives. The limitations of Smith and his military commanders were laid bare by his inability to protect them. About six months later, reinforcements arrived from Great Britain. The Kat River region became their priority area. By directing the reinforcements there, they played into Maqoma's military plans. Making his mountainous stronghold the centre of the war was a better strategy to relieve the rest of the Keiskamma region from the endless scorched earth military destruction, so that it could provide a continuous supply of fighters and resources to sustain the war and deplete the British army.

During the war of Mount Misery, Stapleton (2016) observed that Jongumsobomvu maintained about 200 mounted armed warriors on a rotational basis in order to sustain the war and to prevent incurring a higher number of casualties. He developed innovative ways to sustain the war by dictating where the battle was going to be fought, when to launch targeted surprise attacks, and how to destroy supply lines, whilst he kept a small herd to feed the light and agile army that was concealed in the bushes.

Between January and August 1851, the united Africans, except amaNdlambe of Prince Phatho, Mhala and Toyise, waged war everywhere in their respective areas, while the depleted British troops were trapped in their forts for several months, awaiting reinforcement from Britain. The occupied territories around Makhanda, Fort Beaufort, Gqeberha and Graaff-Reinet were retaken as the settlers fled to the nearest forts and fortified towns.

In June 1850, the reputable 74th Highlanders, under the command of the highly respected Lieutenant Colonel Thomas Fordyce from Great Britain, landed in Cape Colony and headed towards Mount Misery. The 74th Highlanders were the darlings of the British army after their heroic military successes in India. They were the refined military machinery of the British Empire, bestowed with the mission to break the backbone of resistance of amaXhosa. Fordyce possessed an illustrious military career, renowned for strict discipline and remarkable dedication, an eminent veteran who took his work very seriously. He was a highly acclaimed officer, who preferred to command his regiment independently in the battlefield.

His arrival was a breath of fresh air to the demoralized and exhausted soldiers in the battlefield, at a time when the white settlers had lost confidence in the leadership of Governor Harry Smith, General Henry Somerset and Lieutenant Colonel George Mackinnon. Colonel Fordyce had a clear mandate to bring the costly war to an end in the shortest possible period.

On 6 September 1851, Lt Col Fordyce led 613 infantrymen in preparation to dislodge Maqoma from Mount Misery (McKay, 1871). The encounter was the first major assault directed by Fordyce against Maqoma. They ascended to a ridge towards the heights of Fuller's Hoek, marching in a line along the narrow path. They arrived in a grassy valley, saw some grazing oxen, and chased and slaughtered them. That night they marched towards the Horse Shoe, viewed as *"the most impregnable and dangerous part of the enemy's position"* (McKay, 1871: 64).

In the early hours of 7 September 1851, Fordyce's column saw Maqoma's men taking positions from a distance, encircling them from the height of the valley. The British soldiers were surprised by the "beating of a gong, the sounds of which reverberated through the mountain" (McKay, 1871: 64). Maqoma's men must have been singing a war song to inspire the forces for the battle, as a way of welcoming Fordyce and his 74th Highlanders to the battlefield. In the process, Jongumsobomvu appeared prominently on horseback, wearing colourful European clothing, leading his forces of about 300 fighting mounted men (King, 1855; McKay, 1871). His brother, King Sandile, did the same when his warriors attacked the British army in the Battle of Boma Pass near Gwiligwili. *"His horse was soon shot; another was brought to him, which he bravely mounted"* (McKay, 1871: 66). The two sides started exchanging heavy gunfire. Maqoma counter-attacked using a deadly multipronged attack from the thick bushes along the narrow path and continued closing the gap until they were engaged in close deadly combat. As Fordyce's troops continued firing and advancing in their structured formations, Maqoma returned the ferocious fire and intensified the attack on the approaching formation.

According to Stapleton (2016), Maqoma would position his warriors in the thickness of the forest along a narrow path and leave one man at the entrance of the forest to blow the horn once all the British forces had entered the forest. Maqoma's men would attack the enemy troops in the thick bushes using spears, whilst the white soldiers were unable to use their rifles.

Fordyce ordered his men to retreat in order to draw Maqoma's men out of the bushes and to conduct the battle in open terrain, where the British troops could maximise their firepower. As they retreated they found themselves surrounded and overpowered to the point of man-to-man combat. The encounter was brutal! According to McKay, *"Assegais came whirling among us, as well as shot; one sergeant, named Eveleigh, having been struck in the back with an assegai, did not get it drawn out until we reached the bottom"* (McKay, 1871: 68). In the process of the engagement, a soldier named Hartong was captured and subjected to excruciating torture for some days. Fordyce's 74th Highlanders were overwhelmed to a point where each man had to fight for his own survival. The structured formation fell into disarray as they ran from Maqoma's charging forces. The battle was so intense that the British army were compelled to leave the dead soldiers behind in order to save their own lives.

Captain King, who was present in Mount Misery during the battles of spring 1851, appeared to have been overwhelmed. *"The underwood swarmed with K..., they were perched in the trees, firing upon us from above, and rushed from the bush below in hundreds, yelling in the most diabolical and ferocious manner, hissing through their white teeth; their bloody faces, brawny limbs, and enormous size, giving them a most formidable appearance"* (King, 1855:90). During these encounters, Maqoma skilfully drew the British forces into the thick forests and attacked from selected strategic positions of strength, using shock and awe; an element of surprise and intensity usually followed by close man-to-man combat.

McKay (1871) acknowledged that on the night after the encounter with Maqoma, the agonising groans of the wounded soldiers were an unbearable experience which kept others awake the whole night. According to King (1855) a few days after the dreadful encounter, some of them visited the hospital to offer support to the wounded soldiers. *"On entering the crowded hospital, the groans of the wounded men were heartrending and their sufferings most acute, the heat of the climate and the loathsome flies and vermin (which no care could keep away from the smallest wound) adding to their misery"* (King, 1855:155). King lamented the gruesome incident of Gordon, one of the officers who endured excruciating pains from a shattered limb, only to die after three days, as a lonely miserable man in the wilderness of a foreign land. Leaving home to fight a war in the Cape colony was one thing, but to be subjected to unbearable pains of shattered bones and later die thousands of miles away from home must have been an unimaginable end. One wonders if families of the wretched soldiers were compensated or their names inscribed into a memoriam of remembrance as recognition for the sacrifices they made for the empire, whose prestige was built on the sweat and blood of poor men, some of whom probably joined the army to make a difference for their families.

Although Mostert (1992) claimed that the British forces lost 13 soldiers and 14 of them were wounded, according to McKay (1871) they lost 20 men from the deadly onslaught. To Fordyce and his soldiers, the unexpected overwhelming engagement and the viciousness and intensity of the attack was a baptism of fire. The shocking encounter marked the beginning of what was going to be a long and agonising campaign in Mount Misery. *"For the British soldiers Mount Misery became a Calvary of especially cruel distinction"* (Mostert, 1992:1117). McKay believed that had they continued fighting as Colonel Fordyce intended, they would have been wiped out by Maqoma's forces. Fortunately, Colonel Fordyce was persuaded by Colonel Sutton to retreat, as the writing was on the wall on that day. Considering the fact that the empire placed its hope on Colonel Fordyce to attain victory in the shortest possible period, the senior officer was under immense pressure. After the first encounter, Fordyce was compelled to rest his men for a month in order to recuperate.

What made the situation more difficult was the fact that a number of the wounded soldiers died a few days later, thus stretching the capacity of Fordyce's regiment. *"The gallant brigade, literally in rags, marched steadily through our camp for Fort Beaufort in the storm of wind and rain, many with bare feet, and their thin and scanty clothes so tattered as to be hardly decent. They had suffered very much in their exposed position, diarrhoea and dysentery"* (King, 1855:141). The first few months of the military engagements occurred in the spring of 1851, which proved to be devastating for the British forces, as they were trapped in a protracted bush war whilst they continued to suffer more casualties than any other wars fought in Southern Africa. According to Mostert (1992) Mount Misery was a death chamber for the British soldiers, who were subjected to extreme weather conditions and endless suffering. It was such an agonising hell that whenever they launched an attack against Maqoma's forces, only half of the men who entered the battlefield would survive unharmed.

The role of the skilled Khoe soldiers on the side of Maqoma cannot be underestimated in inflicting the devastating pain to the British army. *"The Waterkloof was where the rebel Khoe made their greatest impact. Their contribution made it an even more dangerous and difficult campaign than it would otherwise have been. They aimed for the officers, and gave this war a disconcertingly long list of officer casualties, a list that distressed Queen Elizabeth"* (Mostert, 1992:1120). The military strategy to target senior officers using Khoe sharpshooters was meant to demoralize and paralyse the British army. Fighting an elusive enemy in the impenetrable montane forest was not child's play. This was an enemy that dictated the rules of military engagement by deciding when and where to strike during battle.

The relentless onslaught in the Waterkloof began to take a toll on the soldiers as the top commanders continued asking for more reinforcements. The terrain was challenging and it demanded a lot from the soldiers. They ascended steep winding ridges, navigated deep, narrow, dangerous gorges and had to crawl on extremely dangerous precipices. What must have been more frustrating was the fact that they were a standing professional army, used to fight conventional wars in Europe. Despite being in possession of superior firepower, including artillery, well trained infantry, agile cavalry and deadly mounted soldiers, while accompanied by wagons with supplies of ammunition and food, they faced an elusive and highly mobile enemy who continued to dictate the rules of the military engagement, deciding when to engage or disengage through deadly ambushes. King (1855) acknowledged the superior advantages of the African army, since they only carried guns and assegais and were not held back by huge bags of supplies. They were able to navigate the difficult territories, unlike the British soldiers loaded with rations and ammunition.

As exhaustion and sickness took its toll, a number of soldiers were withdrawn and sent back to Great Britain. One of them was Major Fordyce, the brother of Lieutenant Colonel Fordyce, who was compelled to return home due to severe illness.

On 12 October 1851, upon learning that amaXhosa were amassing their forces in the Waterkloof, where men secretly travelled through the bushes at night, General Somerset assembled a force of 1 500 soldiers, organised into two columns under Lt. Col John Mitchel and Lt. Col Thomas Fordyce backed up by artillery (King, 1855; Stapleton, 2016). Since Prince Maqoma had deployed informers to intercept and monitor the plans and activities of the British army, he knew in advance about the attack and placed his forces at strategic points to launch counter simultaneous surprise attacks. At the point of contact with the advancing enemy troops, Maqoma unleashed his spirited regiments on the enemy, with impactful pace and intensity. The British soldiers were overwhelmed and compelled to retreat. General Somerset was infuriated. He went on punishing his desperate men by subjecting them to an uninterrupted four weeks of a hopeless and deadly campaign.

As the sapping war of attrition dragged on, it dawn to the British soldiers and their commanders that the military campaign was becoming a grinding haul with no end in sight. *"By the beginning of November the soldiers were drained both mentally and physically. Their uniforms were in tatters and many were suffering from dysentery and fever"* (Stapleton, 2016: 206). The drained British army was subjected to unbearable hardships that pushed some to breaking point. They were fighting a doomed calamitous war. Consequently, there were instances of suicide where some soldiers exposed themselves to the enemy firing line, as they could not stand the cauldron of Mount Misery.

On 15 October 1851, the army was organised into three columns, the 91st Regiment in front, Fordyce's 74th in the centre and the 12th Regiment in the rear, whilst General Somerset oversaw the artillery. The formations proceeded to Mount Misery where Maqoma's forces awaited them. According to Mckay (1871) Prince Maqoma often preferred to launch a surprise from the rear of the British forces in order to catch them off guard. This time his strategy worked very well because the 12th Regiment, deployed at the rear, became disorganised, leaving its position and becoming enmeshed with the 74th Regiment. When Maqoma's forces attacked from behind, the 12th Regiment was caught off guard. The 74th Regiment was compelled to leave its assigned position to engage the attacking forces from behind (McKay, 1871). During the confusion Fordyce's 74th Highlanders had to take the lead in in the direct bone crushing engagement with the charging forces of amaXhosa. At the point of the brutal confrontation Maqoma's combatants retreated drawing the 74th Regiment into dangerous positions in the process. Within no time, Maqoma's forces subjected Fordyce's regiments to a merciless assault. Women also took part in the combat, taking on the British soldiers using knobkerries (McKay, 1871). The Khoe sharpshooters also continued targeting officers of the British army. During the encounter two British soldiers were killed and several others were injured.

Several attempts were made on the 23rd, 27th and 29th and 31st of October 1851, which had no significant impact in neutralising Maqoma. The British soldiers were frustrated. *"They had retreated deeper into the jungle as the troops advanced, and their swarthy appearance rendered it impossible to distinguish them from the surrounding trees and brush wood; but when the troops began to retire from the bush, the enemy, emerging from their lair, sent volley after volley at the retiring skirmishers. Such a system of warfare was very discouraging to officers and men"* (McKay, 1871: 99). What was frustrating to the British soldiers was the complex nature of the peculiar enemy executing unfamiliar military tactics in a dangerous bush warfare. To them it was a horrifying encounter fighting an elusive deadly enemy in one of the roughest terrains in the world. During the series of multipronged offensives in Mount Misery, they went on to destroy villages, confiscate livestock and lay waste to crops in their desperate attempts to weaken Maqoma and his forces.

In the early hours of 06 November 1851, General Somerset commanded a colossal military operation comprised of the cavalry, infantry and artillery in three columns with the sole objective of finishing off his adversaries. The columns were led by General Somerset, Lt. Col. Fordyce of the 74th Highlanders, Lt. Col. Michell and Lt. Col. Sutton using different directions, heading to the Kroome and Fuller's Hoek (King, 1855). They planned to launch simultaneous early morning surprise attacks. *"The mountain was enveloped in clouds so dense that we could not see more than twenty yards before us, until about six, when a gentle breeze cleared the summit of the ridge and left the clouds floating like a vast sea below our feet, completely shutting out the lower world..."* (King, 1855: 144). The dense cloud on the mountains was probably a symbolic indication of the tragedy ahead.

In the early morning of 28 January 1991, on my way from Cumakala (Stutterheim) to Qonce, there were strange dark low-lying clouds covering the area between Kwazindenge and Zeleni villages of the Amathole Mountain range. Later that day we learnt about the shocking news of the execution of Lieutenant General Charles Sebe by the firing squad of the then Ciskei Defence Force in the village of Ezeleni. In the African context, the strange weather conditions at times do communicate certain messages linked to the events of the day. King's observation in reference to the low floating dense clouds was of great significance.

Maqoma must had been informed in time about the approaching British army, because although Somerset meant this to be a surprise attack, by the time they arrived at the points of contact, the combined forces of amaXhosa and the Khoe were ready for them in their entrenched positions. On contact both sides executed overwhelming high-tempo offensives in order to annihilate each other as the protracted war was taking a toll on the weary and exhausted combatants. Witnessing their comrades violently killed in the battlefield and stepping on top of their bodies and the bones were gruesome encounters they experienced on an almost daily basis.

Around nine in the morning, Fordyce's regiments had a direct engagement with the forces of Maqoma. It was a bone-crushing brutal confrontation. At the time Fordyce was not aware that he was a marked man since Maqoma instructed his Khoe sharpshooters to target senior commanding officers in order to demoralise the British army. Fordyce commanded his regiment from an elevated position above the fighting troops. When his officers could not hear him calling them to move to the left, he went down the hill to the centre, where brutal fighting was taking place. The Khoe sharp shooters noticed Fordyce as he descended, making himself a clear target. During the war at Mount Misery, part of Maqoma's military strategy was to position his snipers behind the combatants on elevated ground in order to have a clear view of their targets. *"He continued shouting and waving his hat to No. 2 company to keep to their left...Just as he was placing his cap on his head, after waving it to his men, he was struck with a ball upon the breast... He staggered and fell... he calmly requested to be carried to a shady place out of the scorching heat...Dr. Frazer was soon in attendance, but alas! the bullet had done its work... the spirit of one of the best, kindest, and bravest men that the British army could boast of, passed away..."* (McKay, 1871: 111-112). Immediately after the fall of Fordyce, Colonel Yarborough took the command and exhorted his troops to action.

Other senior officers were killed in the process. Lieutenant Carey was killed while calling his fighters to action, followed by Sergeant Diamond next to him. Lieutenant Gordon was shot and both legs were shattered. He died a few days later. Sergeant Kearney also succumbed to his injuries. *"Besides our deeply lamented officers, the casualties among our brave fellows were very heavy; Sergeants Cairnie and Diamond and two rank and file were killed; a Lance corporal and one private mortally wounded and a Corporal and five men severely, two of who afterwards underwent amputation"* (King 1855: 147). General Somerset attempted a retaliatory offensive to avenge the death of Fordyce and other senior officers, only to suffer more casualties. The military campaign became an unbearable exercise as the British army was pushed to breaking-point. The more they tried to dig in, the more fatalities they incurred. Eventually, Somerset had no choice but to withdraw his army from the agonising battle. To the shock of his officers, Somerset declared a false military victory in order to be seen as having done something to avenge the tragic fall of the highly decorated Lieutenant Colonel Thomas Fordyce of the 74th Highlanders.

On the day, the fall of Fordyce was a devastating blow, which left the British army paralysed for a while. Fordyce's esteemed 74th Highlanders slowly disintegrated in the long term because there was no officer who could replace a man of Fordyce's calibre at the time. This was exactly what Prince Maqoma wanted to achieve. *"At three in the afternoon the clouds again settled on the ridge and the fog became so heavy that all further operations were at an end and the enemy having evacuated all his positions, and being nowhere visible, we were withdrawn from our tiresome duty"* (King, 1855:149). It was as if the universe intervened because so much blood had been spilled and many souls had departed unceremoniously. It rained heavily that evening, clearing the blood of the fallen men. Army operations were suspended for a couple of weeks to recover from the shock of the fall of one of the finest British commanders.

Governor Harry Smith admitted in his correspondence to Earl Grey in Britain that he was fighting a dreadful war against a terrifying opponent. *"Sir Harry Smith, in his dispatch of the 18th of December 1851, to Earl Grey, gives a very just estimate of the character of the enemy with whom we had thus to contend ...in their mode of guerrilla warfare, most formidable enemies, as much so as I ever encountered..."* (King, 1855: 145). Smith's observations testified to the fact that the wars of resistance in the Cape colony were defining extraordinary events of historical significance that shaped the developments in South African in the nineteenth century. The shocking death of Fordyce was followed by the calamity of the sinking of the Birkenhead on 26 February 1852. According to McKay (1871) nine officers and 349 men perished with the ship. However, most historical accounts state that the ship perished with 445 people.

Maqoma's military strategy, of targeting high-ranking officers during the combat, worked well to slow down the pace of ferocious battles. The serious attacks and bombardment by the British army failed dismally as they continued to absorb heavy casualties, including high-ranking military commanders. The fact that the war, which started a year earlier, had drained such massive resources and taken such a heavy toll on the soldiers, was an unforeseeable albatross hovering over Smith, Somerset and Mackinnon. After they had thrown everything at their disposal at Maqoma without making much progress, they felt that they had hit a brick wall. *"The effects of the hardships, privations, and constant exposure to the extreme of the heat and cold, began to tell among our ranks"* (King, 1855: 96). As a result, Smith and his military commanders were less than enthusiastic in attempting another attack on Mount Misery.

In December 1851, Smith assembled a larger force of 8 660 soldiers and artillery and organised them into columns led by General Somerset, Colonel George Mackinnon, and Captain Tylden. This time Maqoma made a strategic retreat in order to deny Smith any sort of victory in the battlefield. Maqoma knew that Smith was desperate for a military victory as his illustrious military career was in jeopardy. The strategy worked and Smith was enraged. What worsened the situation was the growing realization that the soldiers were exhausted and bitter about being led by incompetent and corrupt leaders, especially George Mackinnon and Henry Somerset (Mostert, 1992). There were allegations that the latter made money by hiring out wagons to the colonial government during the war in order to finance his extravagant life of having children with Khoe women (Mostert, 1920).

In the same month, Major General Somerset led about 5 000 soldiers across the Nciba River to harass King Sarhili, whom he saw as an easy target after his failure to defeat Maqoma. He was looking for livestock in order to sustain the war. The unprovoked attack and pillaging continued until 11 January. He confiscated 30 000 cattle, killed everyone they came across, and brought back a group of amaFengu as if they were commodities. King (1855) acknowledged that there was nothing honourable about the abuse of military power by attacking defenceless people in their villages.

General Somerset attempted another desperate military storming of the Waterkloof, which left his senior officers Lt. Col. Yarborough, Captain Bramley and Ensign Herbert severely wounded and many soldiers dead. After the December military campaign, things took a turn for the worse. On 1st March 1852, Smith received the news of the sinking of the Birkenhead, which carried reinforcements of soldiers and supplies. At the same time, he received a letter of dismissal as governor, because of the protracted war, which was draining the resources of the British Empire (Mostert, 1992 & Stapleton 2016). Smith's sacking marked the end of one of the most illustrious military careers in the history of the British Empire. His second return to the colony as governor had emboldened him and inflated his ego.

On 9th March 1852, Smith made what turned out to be his last desperate attempt to salvage victory at Mount Misery by mobilizing three columns accompanied by six artillery pieces. The right column was commanded by Lt. Col. Eyre and resourced with four artillery pieces and a Rocket troop, the 43rd Light Infantry; the 73rd Regiment and two companies of the 74th Highlanders and amaMfengu. The column was to depart from the Blinkwater Post, launch the attack at Fuller's Hoek and then proceed to Maqoma's cave (King, 1855). Lt. Col. Michell led the centre column, with two artillery pieces, the 6th Regiment, four companies of the 45th, the 60th Rifles and amaMfengu. Its role was to ascend the Kroome and launch the attack from the bushy kloof connecting Fuller's Hoek with Waterkloof. The left column, headed by Lt. Col. Napier, had two artillery pieces, four companies of the 74th Highlanders, the 91st Regiment, 150 Cape Mounted Rifles, 200 amaMfengu and Burghers. The column was to depart from Bushneck and ascend to the valley of the Waterkloof. The intention of the three-way formation was to attack from strategic positions and push Africans to the centre with no way of escape.

AmaMfengu were present in all the columns because they were being used as a buffer between the British army and the Africans in order to absorb the first blows of the attack. Also, they were deployed to finish off the survivors and the wounded, to look after the pillaged livestock and to do as they wished to women and children. Despite their role, the number of amaMfengu who died or were wounded in battle is often omitted from the narratives of the war, which implies that despite their submission and sacrifices, their lives did not matter to their masters.

In the early hours of 9th March 1852, the three columns launched synchronised attacks from different positions. The combined forces of amaXhosa and Hottentots stood their ground by firing back. This time the British troops were supplied with Minie rifles[5] with a longer range of 900 yards (King, 1855). The three columns kept moving for four consecutive days in Blinkwater, Fuller's Hoek, Kroome and Waterkloof. They captured horses and cattle that were left behind, and destroyed villages. According to King, the military operation was successful as Napier attacked Maqoma's Den, which was considered to be an impregnable stronghold. Women were reportedly captured. Michell and Napier continued with their assault in Waterkloof and Kroome. General Smith also participated in the war by directing attacks from Waterkloof. The combined forces continued with the pillaging, destruction and indiscriminate killings.

---

5   The British Minie Rifles were developed in 1849 and represented a new innovation which allowed for the rapid loading of the muzzle. At the outbreal of the War of Mlanjeni the British soliders were supplied with these rifles in order to maximise their firing power.

After the campaign, Smith travelled to Cape Town. On 7th April 1852, Smith was replaced by Lieutenant General George Cathcart. General Somerset was also fired after 30 years of military service in the Cape Colony.

On 18 April 1852, Smith finally left the colony, a broken and humiliated general, defeated by his arch enemy Maqoma (Mostert, 1992; Stapleton, 2016). *"With ironic symbolism, Jongumsobomvu's foot rested on the throat of Sir Harry who had been 'a dog and so behaved like a dog.' Maqoma's humiliation in Port Elizabeth had been avenged"* (Stapleton, 2016. 209). He was crushed. Eight years after returning to Britain, he died of a heart attack, aged 73. In September 1852, Lieutenant Colonel George Mackinnon and General Henry Somerset also returned to Britain after losing the war.

Cathcart was instructed to either end the war or find a pragmatic exit strategy without admitting defeat. He developed a three-pronged approach, including the building of military posts in Mount Misery in order to create a permanent presence, the intensification of the scorched earth destruction and cutting of the supply line from Qoboqobo to Mthontsi The strategy was designed to subject Maqoma to a state of long-term siege.

In July 1852, Cathcart commenced the building of military posts in Mount Misery. In August 1852, almost a year after he assumed leadership, he led the invasion of King Sarhili's kingdom in search of cattle to finance the war (Mostert, 1992; Stapleton, 2016). In September 1852, he assembled 3 000 British soldiers, including amaMfengu. He organised the army into fifteen columns that invaded Maqoma's stronghold from different directions.

On 12 September 1852, the British troops prepared for what they planned as the final attack on Waterkloof. On the 14th of September they marched from Kroome to Yellowwood River. The other three columns followed on the next day. On their way, they passed through bones and skulls of the dead combatants. *"On the morning of the 26th September 1852...we again climbed the Kroome Pass... As we ascended, the evidences of the fight became more frequent; rolling skulls, dislodged by those in front, came bounding down between our legs; the bones lay thick among the loose stones in the sluits and gulleys, and the bush on either side showed many a bleaching skeleton. A fine specimen of a Kaffir head, I took the liberty of putting into my saddlebag and afterwards brought home with me to Scotland, where it has been much admired by phrenologists for its fine development"* (King, 1855: 271). They carried on searching for African people and killing them on sight. King reported that in January 1853, the Waterkloof was finally cleared, after a protracted and deadly war.

Considering the fact that the war had been going on for two years, with periodic breaks in between, the white settlers resented the enormous loss of life and resources incurred. They were determined to make sure that Cathcart obtained victory in the end and punished Prince Maqoma. As far as Maqoma was concerned, the war had accomplished its objective by getting rid of General Smith and restoring the dignity of King Sandile. The two years of unabated armed conflict had taken a toll on his men and the people. The installation of military posts around Mount Misery was a serious setback for Maqoma, because it meant that the supply line of men and cattle that had sustained the war through his rotational system of combatants was cut off. He realized that there was no point in engaging Cathcart's advancing army since he was low on resources. Consequently, Maqoma made a tactical retreat by evacuating his people from Mount Misery to the Amathole Mountains. Some historians believe that in the final stages of the war the British army may have committed a massacre by killing the fleeing women and children because Maqoma denied them victory in the battlefield (Mostert, 1992; Stapleton, 2016).

On 2nd March 1853, Cathcart appointed Charles Brownlee to mediate between him and King Sandile in order to end the war. He was concerned that Maqoma's retreat may have been a ploy to amass resources in order to resume the war. It was therefore imperative to formalise the cessation of hostilities. Such a pragmatic approach was probably a face-saving exercise, since both suffered enormously during the war. Cathcart, just like Smith, claimed a fallacious victory for the war of Mlanjeni.

9. The Significance of the War of Mlanjeni

The British newspaper, The Advertiser, whose opinion was published in the Cape Frontier Times, Graham's Town, March 22, 1853, observed that there were between eight and nine thousand British soldiers who participated in the War of Mlanjeni, which lasted for two years and three months. The newspaper argued that Africans demonstrated extraordinary bravery against the British army and stood their ground to avoid total extermination.

Most historical sources estimated that the agonising war of Mlanjeni resulted in the death of 1 400 Europeans and an estimated 16 000 Africans. However, considering the relentless attacks on farms, villages and forts over a considerable period of time, the number of Europeans who died was significantly higher than the figures provided by most historians of European descent. Considering the unprecedented higher number of casualties absorbed by the British army as well the deadly targeted attacks on the villages and farms of the European settlers, the estimation of 1 400 is not a true reflection of the number of the European casualties. Therefore, based on the numerous accounts of the intense relentless battles and the unprecedented huge loss of life by both sides over a two year period, about 18 000 people comprised of Africans and Europeans died in the War of Mlanjeni.

The British Empire spent three million pounds on the war. The Graham's Town Journal of 30 April 1853 reported that the British government and the colonial settlers lost money and property worth 4, 506 403 Pounds from the three wars of 1834 to 1835, 1846 to 1847 and 1850 to 1853.

This was the first war fought along racial lines, if one discounts the collaboration of amaMfengu with the British colonial establishment. The united Africans fought it with vigour and tenacity because their existence and that of future generations was entirely dependent on it. Although what triggered the war was the fight for the dignity of King Sandile, the revered royal aristocrat, the rapid encroachment of Europeans into African people's territories had to be stopped.

The Khoe soldiers and their families deserted their colonial masters in large numbers for the first time in the history of the colony after it dawned on them that the very same people they defended and served for decades, actually resented them. Had it not been for the bravery and commitment of the Khoe, Colonel Graham would not have succeeded in expelling amaXhosa from the Zuurveld. They led from the front because they knew the terrain very well.

In the history of the Southern African wars of resistance in the nineteenth century, the defining War of Mlanjeni will always be remembered as the longest and deadliest one fought between Africans and the Europeans. It lasted for two years and three months, whilst the Anglo-Boer War of 1899 to 1902 lasted for two years and eight months. According to Mostert (1992) the war of Mlanjeni remained the greatest single conflict between Africans and Europeans south of the Sahara in the nineteenth century, greater in its recorded losses to the combatants than the Zulu wars, which occurred twenty-five years later. *"For the Xhosa, those things that composed their picture of oppression and suppression, of deprival and hardship, melted together into a single image: the white face"* (Mostert: 1083). The Africans realised that Europeans came to Africa to pursue their own interests. Prince Maqoma's remarkable military brilliance, coupled with his courageous combatants of amaXhosa, abaThembu and the trained Khoe riflemen, elevated the war to unexpected levels of resistance.

The insurrection of the Khoe, the catastrophic collapse of the colony, the thousands of casualties, the fall of Fordyce, the dismissal of Smith, Somerset and Mackinnon, the sinking of the Birkenhead with 445 officers and the collapse of the government of Prime Minister Russell in Britain in February 1852, stood out as the hallmarks of the impact and the significance of the War of Mlanjeni. As a direct consequence of the war, the British Empire was stretched beyond its limits and compelled to surrender its jurisdiction beyond the Orange River. In January 1852, it signed an agreement with Andries Pretorius, recognizing the independence of the Transvaal (Mostert, 1992).

The war had far-reaching implications for South Africa as the fissure of racial divide between Africans and Europeans deepened and widened. The seeds of a dichotomised society became deeply rooted in determining the unequal ownership of the land, the systematic institutionalisation of structural inequalities and the Eurocentric production of knowledge in order to erase the history, culture, language and identity of African people. The replacement of the original African names of rivers, mountains, regions and villages with Europeans ones signified the psychological presence and imprint of Europe in Africa.

In the aftermath of the war, Reverend Robert John Mullins, in his diaries, which were published by Nicholls, Charton and Knowling in 1998 observed that the pace of the British encroachment deep into the territories of amaXhosa was accelerated. The white settlers were allocated more land with the protection of the colonial military machinery. The Khoe who fought alongside amaXhosa were left in an unfortunate situation. They clashed with King Sandile because they were not comfortable being subservient to him. They crossed the Kei River to join King Sarhili's kingdom. Unfortunately, tensions developed between them and King Sarhili and they returned to the colony and re-joined the white settlers. They became targets of harassment. The public hanging of Khoe people by white settlers was a clear sign of the flames of resentment against Africans who dared to challenge the mighty British Empire.

Since Maqoma sustained the war through livestock and crops, the Europeans were determined to destroy the productive capability of Africans by depriving them of ownership of livestock and the land. Gradually Africans were displaced from the rich productive lands and concentrated into small reserves. Crifton Crais (1992) observed that after the War of Mlanjeni, the British authorities continued with a scorched earth policy, destroying homes and crops and confiscating the remaining cattle. The Africans were hunted down like animals and were forced to launch guerrilla attacks by targeting the settlements and farms of the white settlers.

On 4th December 1854, Sir George Grey replaced Cathcart as the Governor of the Cape Colony. Grey was a strategist who came to continue the war at a different level. He was a smooth operator who silently targeted the royal leaders, especially those who played a significant role in the war. Whilst everyone thought the war was over, each leader would receive a surprise visit of armed commandos to arrest him. On 19 December 1857, Prince Maqoma was arrested and charged for alleged trespass and insubordination. He was put in heavy chains and shipped to Robben Island. On arrival in Cape Town, huge crowds of white settlers gathered at the harbour to celebrate the arrest of Prince Maqoma. Next, Grey pursued the following princes; Mhala, Stokwe, Xhoxho and Phatho, despite the fact that the latter did not even participate in the war of Mlanjeni and saved Harry Smith by keeping the Qonce – East London route open for transportation of supplies.

Robben Island became a notorious centre for incarceration of courageous and influential African leaders. Nxele, the religious leader who had led the battle of Makhanda in 1819, died on the island. Prince Siyolo of amaNdlambe, who fought the British force around Fish River during the War of Mlanjeni from 1850 to 1853, was also incarcerated on Robben Island. Prince Delima was also incarcerated on the island in 1853 (Stapleton, 2016).

The conditions on the island were horrific. Prisoners were housed in dilapidated, leaking shacks, exposed to the biting night rains and winds and forbidden from even walking around the island. In April 1869, Governor Wodehouse ordered the release of the prisoners. However, it is not clear what prompted this sudden decision. Maqoma, Katyi and Xhoxha were released after having served 11 years, whilst Siyolo had served 16 years. Maqoma was 71 years old when he was released (Stapleton, 2016).

Upon his release after 11 years, Prince Maqoma was shocked to see how his place of birth had changed. His people, amaJingqi, were broken and scattered. The coastal territories of East London and Makhanda and inland areas of Kat River, Kubusi River and Kei Drift were occupied by white settlers with fenced farms. AmaXhosa were landless and impoverished labourers. Maqoma's eldest son, Kona, who collaborated with the colonialist settlers at Qonce and the second son, Namba, were placed in Stutterheim.

Prince Maqoma was rearrested in November 1871 by Governor Sir Philip Wodehouse and banished to Robben Island for life. The colonial establishment feared that Jongumsobomvu would reignite amaXhosa to take up arms against the white settlers who had occupied the land, considering his popularity, reverence for his royal status and his great skills in mobilising people. *"A member of the well-known Bowker family, which had fought in the Cape-Xhosa Wars, urged the government to continue Maqoma's imprisonment"* (Stapleton, 2016: 264). After about two years on the island, his condition deteriorated and he died on 9th September 1873 under mysterious circumstances. *"Not satisfied with stealing Maqoma's land, people and cattle, the Europeans also wanted his soul. It was a tragic end"* (Stapleton, 2016: 265). The fall of Prince Maqoma marked the end of one of the greatest eras of courage, bravery and resilience in the African wars of resistance.

There are conflicting reports up to the present day about how Prince Maqoma died on Robben Island. In 1978, Charity Sonani, the crippled seer, located Maqoma's grave on Robben Island in the presence of Prince Lent Maqoma. After opening the grave, Prince Maqoma was found in iron shackles with broken bones. It is believed that he was murdered by the prison guards. The decision of the British establishment to subject a man of his age to the unbearable conditions on Robben Island was tantamount to a death sentence, because they knew that he was not going to last long under such inhuman conditions.

In retrospect, Prince Maqoma was a visionary leader far ahead of his time. He understood the magnitude of the insurmountable complex challenges they faced at the time, yet he played his part to the best of his abilities until the end. His lonely death on Robben Island was the sacrifice he paid for his people. *"Unlike Maqoma, most nineteenth-century African leaders thoroughly failed to recognise the special and permanent nature of colonial conquest until it was too late"* (Stapleton, 2016: 87-8). Stapleton (2016) defines Prince Maqoma as a courageous leader who immortalised his name in history by devising innovative means to withstand the firepower of the enemy.

Jongumsobomvu emerged as the towering military genius gifted with remarkable leadership qualities. He ignited his people to engage in the relentless wars fought in the triangle between Gqeberha, Graaff-Rienet and Gcuwa. *"Of all the nineteenth-century African rulers who resisted European expansion in South Africa, and perhaps the entire continent, Maqoma was the most successful."* (Stapleton, 2016: 283). What made Jongumsobovu to stand out was his ingrained belief and unshakable conviction that he was as capable as the Europeans despite the fact that they were in possession of well-resourced professional army. In essence, the fall of Prince Maqoma marked the end of an era where amaXhosa attained three consecutive military victories over the British army in 1834-35, 1846-47 and 1850-53.

Some of his defining military tactics that enabled him to sustain deadly protracted wars are as follows:

8.1   Avoided Waging Wars in Open Terrains

Prince Maqoma took time to develop deeper insight about the strengths and vulnerabilities of the British army as well how to manage the ego of its abrasive military commanders whilst waiting for the opportune time to strike when they least expected. From the lessons of the disastrous defeat of amaXhosa in what became known as the Battle of Grahamstown on 22 April 1819, Maqoma often avoided facing the mighty British firepower in open terrain by choosing mountainous areas with thick forests to lure the colonial troops and execute counter deadly ambushes. He knew that the traditional British military formation and the suitable discharge of artillery were not suitable in rugged terrains. His familiarity with the environment and the agility of his mobile combatants often placed him in a stronger position to gain an upper hand in the battlefield hence the British forces incurred heavy casualties in wars of 1834-35, 1846-47 and 1850-53.

8.2 Operated Small Mobile Combatants

In the Battle of Grahamstown, amaXhosa incurred highest casualties compared to other wars of resistance because they were easily mowed down by the British artillery since they were concentrated in thousands in one area. From that catastrophic experience, the military commanders of amaXhosa including Maqoma organised their combatants in small highly mobile groups positioned in different locations in order to overstretch the British army and create a sense of omnipresent. The strategy was used effectively both in the War of Hintsa in 1834-35 and the War of Mlanjeni in 1850-53, where multipronged offensive campaigns were launched simultaneously in Qonce, Makhanda, Gqeberha, Qoqoboqo and Edikeni whilst the thrust of the bigger force conducted operations in the heartland of Mount Misery. The British military commanders and the vigilant settlers had no answer for such a devastating military strategy. Consequently General Smith was subjected to crushing defeats by Prince Maqoma in both wars. The second defeat of General Harry Smith, in the War of Mlanjeni marked the end of his remarkable military career.

8.3 Execution of Pre-emptive Targeted Ambushes

The rugged terrains of Amathole montane forests with thick impenetrable bushes, steep ridges and rough gorges was suitable for bush warfare. Maqoma and his brother Sandile in particular, executed pre-emptive surprise ambushes on the British army whilst navigating to the designated battleground. The surprise targeted ambushes functioned as disruptive military manoervres that prevented the British army from launching offensives from suitable positions. The strategy was effective, frustrating and lethal to the advancing enemy. In most cases the British army was often caught off-guard in exposed positions to the concealed warriors. In the War of Axe in 1846-47, King Sandile executed the astonishing ambush with precision and intensity against the huge army of 125 wagons led by Lieutenant General John Hare. It was so effective that the war that was meant to last for few months ended in one day.

8.4   Rotation of Warriors to Sustain the War

Prince Maqoma and other military leader realized fighting overwhelming battles using large numbers was counter effective because the British army was well resourced and experienced in waging wars over a considerable period of time until the enemy is vanquished. AmaXhosa did not have the luxury of wagons to carry supplies in order to support the warriors on long haul battles. Maqoma devised the system of rotating his combatants in order to maintain sustained military engagements. The system of rotation is what enabled him to engage the British army in the War of Mlanjeni which turned to be the longest military confrontation fought between Africans and Europeans in the nineteenth century.

8.5   Strategic Deployment of Women as Informers

One of the reasons why Prince Sandile was able to plan the successful execution of the deadly ambush in the War of Axe in 1846-47 was the information he obtained from women informers pertaining to the movement of the massive British army from Makhanda to Qoboqobo. He was informed that Lieutenant General John Hare maintained a long military procession of 125 wagons, loaded with ammunition and supplies to sustain the army over a considerable period of time throughout the journey. Such vital information informed

Sandile to plan the ambush in such a way that armed mobile combatants concealed on both sides of the approaching military convoy launched simultaneous surprise attacks by cutting the convoy in the middle and encircled various groups of the British army in order to attain quick decisive annihilation of the enemy.

8.6   Ability to Dictate Military Engagement

One of Maqoma's greatest legacy in the history of wars of resistance in Southern Africa was his brilliant mind to determine when and where to wage effective military campaigns against the British army. To be able to do that, it took great sacrifice, meticulous planning, inner insight on the strength and vulnerabilities of the enemy as well as decisive leadership to mobilize and to energize his people. His ability to dictate military engagements kept the British army on continuous reactive offensive whilst he maintained a certain degree of ascendency because of his proactive strategies. It was Maqoma who decided to wage the War of Mlanjeni in the precipitous mountains of Mount Misery. Consequently, the British army found itself sucked in to the trap of an agonising costly military campaign chasing after Maqoma's forces.

The War of Mlanjeni was followed by the catastrophic arrival of the highly lethal European cattle lung sickness that decimated about 80% of the livestock of amaXhosa, which is explored in the following Chapter. The War of Ngcayechibi of 1877 -1879, known as the Ninth Frontier War, broke out almost three decades after the agonising War of Mlanjeni.

It started from a beer-drinking brawl at a gathering hosted by Ngcayechibi, who was classified at the time as part of the Mfengu community, on 3rd August 1877. Ngcayechibi hosted an event to honour his son Kewuti who had got married. In attendance were two Princes of amaGcaleka, Mxoli and Fihla. Towards the end of the event, the beer was finished, and people started leaving. Mxoli demanded more beer although he had been told it was finished. Mxoli struck the man who told him that the beer was finished. A fight ensued.

AmaGcaleka were defeated, and chased away. A few days later, amaGcaleka retaliated.

Spicer (1978) observed that the War of Ngcayechibi was a general reaction of amaGcaleka to what they felt to be the continued restriction of their independence as a result of the expansion of white settlers to their territories. On one hand, this was a continuation of the wars of resistance against the British conquest of the Cape colony. On the other hand, the British colonial establishment resented the Kingdoms of amaXhosa's sense of independence, because they perceived them as an impediment to accessing the cheap labour of AmaXhosa.

The colonial authorities assisted amaMfengu against amaGcaleka. The British colonial army joined the internal conflict as a pretext to supporting amaMfengu, in order to justify the invasion of Gcalekaland. The followers of King Sandile, known as amaRharhabe, joined the war to support amaGcaleka of King Sarhili. In February 1878, amaGcaleka were overwhelmed by the combined forces whilst amaRharhabe continued engaging the British forces. King Sandile became the target of the British forces assisted by amaMfengu. On 28th May 1878, King Sandile was fatally wounded during military engagements with the British-led forces. Finally, in 1879, the ongoing hostilities between the colonial forces and amaXhosa warriors ended following the defeat of the latter. The fall of King Sandile in the War of Ngcayechibi signified the last stand of resistance of amaXhosa in the triangle of one hundred years wars that started in 1779.

Table 3.1: A Table of the One Hundred Years Wars

The Wars of Resistance	Battlegrounds	Groups Involved	The Significance
FIRST WAR OF RESISTANCE: 1779–1781	The war was fought between the Nukakama/ Sundays River and Nxuba/Fish River	Commandant Adriaan Van Jaarsveld scattered tobacco in front of the group of amaXhosa as a gift. After the group of amaXhosa lowered their guards to collect the tobacco, Van Jaarsveld and his group opened fire, mowing them down. This led to a series of clashes between the Boers and amaXhosa, which went on until 1781.	This was the first d contested major contact between amaXhosa and the Boers. The Boers attempted to take the Zuurveld region from amaXhosa. They were trying to do what they did to the San and Khoe during a series of wars of resistance and conquest that lasted over 150 years.

The Wars of Resistance	Battlegrounds	Groups Involved	The Significance
SECOND WAR OF RESISTANCE: 1789–93	The war occurred in the Zuurveld region located between Fish River and Sundays River.	The war broke out between Boers and amaXhosa and it emanated from the frustrations to evict the latter from the Zuurveld region. The Boers, with the support of Prince Ndlambe, again failed to expel the section of amaXhosa known as amaGqunukhwebe of Prince Chungwa from the region.	This was a clash where Prince Ndlambe aligned himself with the Boers, led by Barend Lindeque. This was Ndlambe's attempt to use the Boers in order to eliminate Prince Chungwa of amaGqunukhwebe in the contestation of the Zuurveld region. The strategy was a serious miscalculation since the Boers had similar interests. In the following war, Ndlambe joined amaGqunukhwebe against the Boers.

The Wars of Resistance	Battlegrounds	Groups Involved	The Significance
THIRD WAR OF RESISTANCE: 1799 – 1803	The main battlegrounds were around Graaff-Reinet, Gqeberha and Makhanda.	This time the San and Khoe took a stand against the Boers in Graaff-Reinet and later joined amaXhosa in the war of resistance against expulsion from the Zuurveld.	The San and Khoe fought for emancipation from the Boers by attacking white settler farms. The Boers were overwhelmed by the combined African forces. The battles went on until 1803. The Boers failed for the third time to expel Africans from the Zuurveld because of strong resistance.

The Wars of Resistance	Battlegrounds	Groups Involved	The Significance
FOURTH WAR OF RESISTANCE: 1811–1812	The nature of the war was largely determined by the three British columns which targeted the coastal belt from Gqeberha to Nxuba River, Makhanda and Kat River region.	Governor John Cradock instructed Colonel John Graham to expel amaXhosa from the Zuurveld. Graham launched a surprise attack using three columns. Chungwa was killed whilst Ndlambe stood his ground through sterling resistance in the first close bush warfare combat with the British army. Eventually he retreated across the Fish River following the killing of women and children by the British forces. He resorted to guerrilla raids which made it impossible for the white settlers to occupy the coveted Zuurveld.	The war marked the first contested armed contact between amaXhosa and the British army; the first implementation of the British colonial policy of ethnic cleansing of amaXhosa from the Zuurveld; the first time King Ngqika officially collaborated with the Europeans in order to eliminate Prince Ndlambe and the first time 20 000 amaXhosa were displaced from the Zuurveld.

The Wars of Resistance	Battlegrounds	Groups Involved	The Significance
WAR OF GRAHAMS-TOWN IN 1819	The centre of the battle was in Makhanda.	This was an opportunistic retaliatory war instigated by the British to avenge the defeat of King Ngqika by a united amaXhosa army in the Battle of Amalinde in October 1818. Subsequently, Prince Mdushane and Makhanda kaNxele led amaXhosa to the Battle of Grahamstown on 22 April 1819. They were repelled by the combined forces of the British, Boer and Khoe regiments. AmaXhosa resorted to relentless raids of the occupied Zuurveld.	Although amaXhosa suffered considerable casualties, the European settlers paid a heavy price as villages and farms were destroyed and livestock confiscated through targeted systematic raids. Following the defeat of Grahamstown, amaXhosa retaliated by launching a series guerrilla war attacks deep in the Zuurveld region. With the assistance of King Ngqika , the British finally settled their people in the Zuurveld in 1820 and established Grahamstown as a key strategic town. This is the only war the British attained decisive victory over amaXhosa.

The Wars of Resistance	Battlegrounds	Groups Involved	The Significance
THE WAR OF HINTSA: 1834 – 1835	The centre of the major battles occurred in the Fish river region and in the mountainous forests of Qoboqobo (Keiskammahoek).	Following the expulsion of amaXhosa from the Zuurveld in 1811–12, the rich Kat River region in 1829 and Tyhume valley in 1833, the boiling tensions exploded into a full–scale war between amaXhosa and the British army. D'Urban's frustration about failing to attain victory over the united amaXhosa led by the military strategist Prince Maqoma, led to the first crossing of the Kei River, targeting the less battle–hardened King Hintsa. Rev Ayliff was instrumental in encouraging the invasion after persuading amaMfengu to be British allies who were later relocated to Peddie as a buffer state and to provide cheap labour for white settlers.	The significance of the war was the execution of King Hintsa, the staged exodus of amaMfengu from Gcuwa to Ngqushwa, the exodus of the Boers from the Cape to the north, the heavy losses suffered by white settlers, failure to defeat and expel amaXhosa from the Keiskamma region after Maqoma led a united amaXhosa army, following the death of his father King Ngqika in 1829, the British collaborator. This was the first war amaXhosa defeated the British which resulted in the recall of D'Urban and Smith. The huge material losses, higher number of casualties and successful resistance of amaXhosa became a major catalyst for the Great Trek of the Boers from the Cape to the northern part of the country.

The Wars of Resistance	Battlegrounds	Groups Involved	The Significance
THE WAR OF AXE: 1846–1847	The war occurred around Mkhubiso in the region of Qoboqobo, the natural fortress and stronghold of amaXhosa.	Major General John Hare led a well-resourced British army with the intention to occupy the strongholds of amaXhosa over six months in order to expel amaXhosa permanently from their stronghold of Qoboqobo and Tyhume valley. Prince Sandile strategically placed his army on the mountains of Mkhubiso. The British army walked into an ambush in which 125 wagons, with six months' supplies of ammunition, were obliterated.	This was the first war in which King Sandile led amaRharhabe against the British army. He attained decisive victory and protected his people from eviction across the Kei River. Major General Hare resigned. He died from a heart attack on his way back to the United Kingdom. The war showed the incredible adaptation of amaXhosa on how to neutralise the firepower of the British army. This was the worst defeat the British army had ever suffered in Southern Africa.

The Wars of Resistance	Battlegrounds	Groups Involved	The Significance
WAR OF MLANJENI: 1850–1853	The major battlegrounds were in Qoboqobo, Middledrift, Tyhume, Kat River and Fish River region.	Major General Harry Smith started the war in an effort to dethrone King Sandile. This was a serious miscalculation, as Smith underestimated the strength of amaXhosa. Mackinnon faced heavy defeat in Boom Pass in Qoboqobo where Sandile Dam is built; several military villages were wiped out; Khoe deserted the British and joined amaXhosa in the war; abaThembu also joined to support Maqoma.	The war stood out as the longest and deadliest conflict ever between Africans and Europeans in Sub–Saharan Africa in the nineteenth century. It was characterised by the Khoe insurrection against the British, the heaviest African–European casualties, British surrender of territory beyond Orange and Vaal River to the Boers. The British army suffered a third defeat in the face of the united Africans.
WAR OF NGCAYECHIBI: 1877–1879	It started as a conflict between amaGcaleka and amaMfengu. Later on it was exploited by the colonial regime in order punish amaXhosa.	AmaXhosa, amaMfengu and the British colonial forces.	This was the last war of the one hundred years of resistance, whose major highlight was the fall of King Sandile the son of King Ngqika.

Chapter Four

The Hidden Narrative in the Celebration of Nongqawuse

The promotion of the distorted narrative of Nongqawuse became a convenient historical exercise to exonerate the British authorities who engineered the cattle lung disease as a successful biological weapon of cattle mass destruction. Jongi Klaas (Reflections at the time of writing the book)

1. Critical Review of Perspectives and Circumstances around Nongqawuse

This chapter seeks to critically re-examine the constructed British led narrative of the Nongqawuse phenomenon in the wider context of the wars of resistance between amaXhosa people and the British colonial establishment in the nineteenth century. The critical re-interrogation of Nongqawuse is located in the broader context of the sequential interconnected events that occurred prior and during the Nongqawuse period. Such chronologically intertwined historical events which led to the cattle killing are the fundamental basis to understand the authenticity of the highly celebrated Nongqawuse narrative. The significance of the sequence of the interrelated events is the critical missing gap in the construction and deeper analysis of Nongqawuse phenomenon. The deconstruction of the skewed narrative where historical events of great significance had been presented in highly compartmentalised and isolated forms in pursuance of specific interests to the detriment amaXhosa. In essence, this is an attempt to establish whether the calamity of such magnitude occurred as a reaction to the prophecy or culling of infected cattle. Also, to establish whether the systematic manifestation of the crafted narrative of Nongqawuse was a euphemism for the biological weapon of cattle mass destruction.

Andrew Offenburger, who published a comprehensive article titled *The Xhosa Cattle Killing Movement in History and Literature* from the History Campus of Yale University in 2009, acknowledged that although Nongqawuse lived about 160 years ago, historians are still trying to understand the causes, the meaning and the symbolism of the Nongqawuse phenomenon. According to Offenburger (2009) the period between 1857 and 1947 was characterized by the dominant historical narratives of white settler historians such as George McCall Theal (1837-1919), George Edward Cory (1862-1935) and John Maclean (1810-1874). They believed that the killing of cattle was driven by a self-destructive movement of national suicide and savagery, in order to wage a war against the British establishment. Although African intellectuals of the time such as William Wellington Gqoba (1840 - 1888) questioned the distorted discourse around Nongqawuse through *Isigidimi* samaXhosa[1] newspaper, they were largely marginalized by the white settler historians who controlled the forms of knowledge production at the time.

Offenburger (2009) also made critical observations about issues that arose around the Nongqawuse incident, such as the role of missionaries, who for years had *"infused Xhosa cosmology with the symbols and teachings of Christianity"* (2009.02). Even so, there is very little mentioned about the role of missionaries during the time of lung sickness and cattle killing. Missionaries such as Charles Brownlee were often portrayed as saviours in the aftermath of the decimation of cattle.

Offenburger argues that the play *The Girl Who Killed to Save (Nongqawuse the Liberator)* (1936) that was written by

---

1   Isigidimi samaXhosa was a newspaper written in isiXhosa. It was founded by Reverend James Stewart in 1870 in Lovedale. The newspaper was published monthly and remained active until 1888. John Tengo Jabavu and William Gqoba were active journalists of the newspaper. In 2012, Unathi Kondile re-established the newspaper.

Herbert Isaac Ernest Dhlomo (1903-1956), the highly gifted African creative writer, was a representation of the new mission-trained African intellectuals. To a great extent their interpretation of Nongqawuse was largely influenced by their Christian perspectives anchored on the Western school of thought. For instance, Dhlomo's play portrayed Nongqawuse as a liberator of amaXhosa. He concluded that the miserable destitution of amaXhosa in the aftermath of the harrowing cattle killing actually brought them closer to knowing God. In this regard, *"Dhlomo thus relied on religious Darwinism to credit the Cattle-Killing for 'waking up' the Xhosa to Christianity"* (Offenburger 2009:03). Dhlomo's assertion was an overt extension of the influential discourse of the British centred narrative on Nongqawuse. The interpretation of Nongqawuse by Dhlomo reflected the powerful influence of missionary schools in the production of African intellectuals shaped by dogmatic religious perspectives.

Coming to back to the positions of Theal, Cory and Maclean, it is of paramount importance to ask first what informed them in the development of such a controversial narrative and whose interests did they serve in the process? It was unfortunate that the historians that came after them never went further to test the reliability of the skewed compartmentalised narrative. What made the narrative to fly was the fact that it was reinforced by the African intellectuals of the nineteenth century and those that followed at the beginning of the twentieth century. On the same note, it is not always easy to challenge what has been accepted as the true historical account of what happened. It takes extraordinary efforts and great sacrifice to develop courage and perseverance to convey what may not be accepted in the community of leading thinkers on the same subject.

One of the shortcomings of the British led narrative are inconsistences in the controversial portrayal of amaXhosa as intellectually challenged victims of self-inflicted calamity. This is contrary to the rich history of adaptability of amaXhosa, the enduring complexity of their culture and their remarkable natural disposition. The fact that they waged one hundred wars with the world super power at the time cannot be reconciled with the Theal, Cory and Maclean's underlying assumptions which implied that amaXhosa committed the horrific cattle mass extermination to their detriment. In as much as Theal, Cory and Maclean appeared to believe that Nongqawuse happened on a grand scale, they deliberately ignored the devastating impact of cattle lung sickness. The closer interrogation of their thoughts and position on Nongqawuse reflect serious shortcomings of imbalanced highly subjective narrative that had been crafted to pursue a particular agenda in the interests of White settlers.

On the same note, Mary Waters the granddaughter of Reverend H. T. Waters, a missionary attached to King Sarhili at the time of Cattle-Killing, published *U-Nongqawuse* in 1924. According to her the killing of cattle marked the end of the period of darkness centred on savagery and gave rise to the Western civilization, portraying Grey and the missionaries as the saviours of amaXhosa. The blatant portrayal of amaXhosa in a disdainful way by Waters was not different from that of the white settlers and the colonial authorities which assumed that Africa was a dark continent in pre-colonial period.

The pioneers of African intellectualism Reverend Tiyo Soga (1829-1871) and Dr Mpilo Walter Benson Rubusana (1858 - 1936), the products of the missionary institutions, their perspectives were not different from that of the British leading producers of knowledge on the subject. They perceived Nongqawuse tragedy as a blessing in disguise that brought divine redemption to amaXhosa. Dr Mpilo Walter Benson Rubusana's interpretation of Nongqawuse in particular, centred on the premise that Nongqawuse came as a messenger who appealed to amaXhosa to turn away from practising witchcraft, and to purify themselves and get ready for a new dawn. In his book *Zemk' inkomo Magwalandini*, he provides a narrative similar to Mary Waters.

In essence, Soga, Rubusana, Dhlomo and Waters reinforced the narrative of Theal, Cory and Maclean, using religion as a convincing convenient narrow explanation of the apparent tragedy. The underlying assumption was that amaXhosa lost the land, livestock and the foundations of nationhood and gained spiritual redemption. This was not far from the British led narrative which implied that amaXhosa were not spiritually conscious about the existence of the Creator in pre-colonial period.

The ability of the majority of African intellectuals at the time to transcend the white-settler-dominated narrative was suffocated by their socialization and schooling in Euro-centric mission schools. The essence of their interpretative analysis remained trapped in the parameters of a dogmatic religious school of thought, centred on the highly politicized view of African inferiority and European superiority. Consequently, the form of education they received from the mission schools at the time was built on well-orchestrated philosophical foundations that were inextricably linked to the perpetuation of European forms of civilization and the marginalization of the African value systems. They were made to believe that they were fortunate and better off. Therefore they had an enormous responsibility to save their own people from savagery and barbarism; hence to them, Nongqawuse was a divine redemption in the form of a catastrophic tragedy, meant to awaken and enlighten amaXhosa. African intellectuals of William Gqoba's calibre were marginalized, as they represented a contrary view. The dominant narrative failed to examine the intertwined events of the time in the bigger context of the wars of resistance and the British encroachment in South Africa.

The position of Soga, Rubusana, Dhlomo, Waters, Theal, Cory and Maclean is centred on the premise that Nongqawuse as a tragic phenomenon that triggered the redemption which assumes that the mass extermination of their livestock was an inevitable calamity in order to gain spiritual ascendancy. Such a view is very problematic as it overlooks the fact that amaXhosa had often exercised moral high ground and reverence for the higher spiritual being. For instance, they often ensured that women and children of the European settlers were not killed during the brutal wars of resistance. It was not because they were afraid to do so but it was a demonstration of their spiritual maturity and deeper understanding that lives of women and children are sacrosanct and therefore should be respected and protected in order to ensure continuity of humanity. Therefore, it cannot be argued that amaXhosa actually gained spiritual redemption after cattle killing as if they were not spiritual people.

What has come out clearly so far is the realization that the volumes of knowledge of the Nongqawuse narrative were predominantly pioneered and perpetuated by historians of the British descent supported by the religious scholars of missionary schools. They often presented Nongqawuse as a catastrophic phenomenon of amaXhosa self-inflicted tragedy that led to the demise of their power and disintegration. Such a narrative was completely detached from major events that occurred prior the period of mass cattle killing. They went further to say amaXhosa were saved from total extermination by the benevolent British colonial establishment and the philanthropic missionaries.

Although historians such as Majeke (1952), Jaffe (1952), Mutwa (1966) and Peires (1989) attempted to highlight other significant events that occurred at the time before and during the Nongqawuse period, they still maintained that Nongqawuse was the main cause of the mass killing of cattle. Although they had a general acknowledgment that lung sickness decimated the majority of cattle in King Sarhili's Kingdom, they were accomodative to the dominant narrative that what broke the power of amaXhosa was Nongqawuse.

King Sarhili, the son of King Hintsa, was the most senior royal leader of amaXhosa who was reported to have encouraged his people to slaughter their cattle after the majority of herds were decimated by the deadly lung cattle sickness. The other leaders of the African people in the Cape, such as King Faku of amaMpondo, Prince Sandile of amaRharhabe, as well senior Princes of amaXhosa and royal leaders of abaThembu objected to the killing of cattle. Probably their regions were not yet affected by lung sickness.

Peires (1989) provides an interesting insight into the political context around the leadership crisis created by King Sarhili's state of mind. This view proposes that, considering the king's fragile state, he was susceptible to the flawed prophecy of Nongqawuse. According to him, King Sarhili was shaken by the loss of his sons, the brutal death of Bomela, his closest advisor, and the devastating impact of the lung sickness which wiped out his cattle. Also, about two decades earlier, his father King Hintsa died an agonising death at the hands of British soldiers, whilst the young Sarhili was a captive in a British camp. Such tragedies left permanent psychological scars in his life and impacted his mental state, and made him an easy target of false prophecies. Even if that perspective holds water, it is highly likely that, considering the far-reaching impact of the lung sickness, King Sarhili was not left with much of a choice except to kill the infected cattle in order to save the few uninfected ones. This would have been a perfectly logical solution to the problems caused by this deadly and highly contagious disease.

In the context of Nongqawuse, Peires (1989) acknowledges that not all amaXhosa agreed to kill their cattle. *"This is a generalisation considering the fact even within Sarhili's area there were Chiefs like Ngubo who were strongly opposed to it, let alone the fact across the Kie at KwaNdlambe and kwaNgqika it was viewed with mixed reaction"* (Peires 1989.128) Even within the inner circles of King Sarhili, leaders like Prince Ngubo were strongly opposed to the cattle killing linked to Nongqawuse prophecy. The people of amaNdlambe and Rharhabe did not kill their cattle, because of the opposition from leaders such as King Sandile, Prince Maqoma and Prince Makinana. King Faku of amaMpondo was also opposed to the cattle killing, because he believed that Mhlakaza was a false prophetess.

Furthermore, Peires (1989) recognised that Prince Kama of amaGqunukhwebe in British Kaffraria, together with Prince Mhala and his son Makinana of amaNdlambe, were strongly opposed to the cattle killing. King Sandile of amaRharhabe was sceptical about the validity of the prophecy. These observations are contrary to the generalisation perpetuated by the early settler historians that the majority of African people in the Cape Colony slaughtered their cattle in their thousands influenced by the false prophecy.

From early 1856, when the Nongqawuse phenomenon began in the Kingdom of Sarhili, amaXhosa experienced a gradual weakening of their political power and traditional institutions through the introduction and the installation of magistrates. The introduction of these colonial institutions was meant to undermine their power as well as their indigenous practices. At the same time, the lung sickness ravaging their herds was spreading at an alarming rate without much effort from the colonial authorities to arrest it because it served their interests. To make matters worse, the enduring drought at the time thwarted any prospects of potential harvests.

To amaXhosa, the cattle were an important symbol of wealth and they fulfilled various socio-economic and cultural functions in the traditional ceremonies of amaXhosa. The cattle were inextricably attached to the lives of amaXhosa. It is incomprehensible and inconsistent with their culture and traditions that they would have killed their cattle with no concrete reason. The cattle were like an umbilical cord connecting the living and the dead.

If cattle had such a special place in the lives of amaXhosa, there was no way the majority of amaXhosa could have easily bought into such an implausible prophecy. As most historians acknowledged, amaXhosa were intelligent, and they had the ability to read a situation and act appropriately. It is inconceivable that considering the complex challenges they had navigated and overcome, they would easily believe such a prophecy.

In essence, what the historians had ignored over the decades was the link between the contagious cattle lung sickness and the targeted killing of cattle. In an effort to arrest the rapid spread of the highly lethal and contagious lung sickness, amaXhosa killed the infected cattle in order to save the remaining ones. By the time they did that they had already lost the majority of their cattle. The impact of the highly contagious and lethal cattle lung sickness as the cause of the destruction of cattle had been largely ignored.

2. Sir George Grey Enters the Scene

It is of paramount importance to interrogate the role of Sir George Grey as the Governor of the Cape Colony, who arrived in the aftermath of the longest African European War of Mlanjeni. Mnguni (1952) believed that the decision of the British Empire to bring Grey to a colony, whose inhabitants had stretched its financial resources through the deadly protracted war, was not an ordinary one. Unlike his predecessors who were military men, Grey was a civilian administrator mandated to bring an end to the protracted costly wars of African resistance. What made him stand out from the others was how he broke the backbone of resistance of the Maori people in New Zealand between 1845 and 1853.

At the time, Great Britain, France, Turkey and Italy were involved in the Crimean War of 1853-1856 against Russia. The British government had no appetite for wars in the Cape Colony. Hence the deployment of Grey signalled the beginning of a new strategy in the quest for conquest of South Africa. Grey's era as the Cape colonial governor was characterised by the landing and the outbreak of the European deadly cattle lung sickness which was followed by the cattle killing. The outbreak of the contagious disease turned out to be a game changer with far-reaching implications in relation to the amaXhosa British wars.

Sir George Grey was born in Lisbon, Portugal on 14 April 1812 and died on 19 September 1898 in South Kensington in London. George was born just after his father Lieutenant Colonel George Grey died together with 4 800 British-Portuguese soldiers in the bloody Battle of Badajoz, fighting against the French occupation of Spain during the Peninsular War of 1807 to 1814. The timing and the tragic incident concerning his father automatically placed Grey at the core of the British machinery. The fact that he served as a soldier and a skilled colonial administrator made him the perfect leader in the expansion and the pursuance of the interests of the British Empire.

Grey was the Governor of the province of South Australia between 15 May 1841 and 25 October 1845. He proceeded to become Governor of New Zealand in 1845 until 1852, where he had vanquished the indigenous Maori people. Between 1854 and 1861, he became Governor of the Cape Colony and returned to New Zealand in 1861, where he remained Governor until 1868. In the period between 1877 and 1879 Grey became the Premier of New Zealand.

Grey stands out as one of the most highly influential colonial administrators. What made him unique was the fact that he went beyond the colonial duties to study the cultures of the natives' colonies in order to develop a more comprehensive understanding. He is recognised as a pioneer in the study of the Maori culture. The fact that he became a Governor of New Zealand in 1841, at age 29, and was knighted in 1848 at age 36, is indicative of his standing qualities and his contribution to the expansion, building and consolidation of the British Empire.

Grey excelled in the implementation of the colonial policies under the most challenging environments. *"To his mind, possibilities presented themselves, which others could not see. So long as he was the possessor of almost despotic authority, and he was thereby enabled to carry his plans to execution"* (Rees, 1892: 225). The fact that he took time to develop himself as a reputable specialist in the understanding of the complex culture of the Maori in New Zealand is a testimony to the depth and sophistication with which he pursued the interests of the British Empire.

Unlike his predecessors in the Cape Colony who were mostly one dimensional military men, Grey was multi-skilled, well-travelled and had a deeper understanding of the complex challenges facing the British dominions. *"There was Grey, the man of the highest and most honourable principles, and Grey, the egoist, convinced his own infallibility, trampling reputations to enhance his own unscrupulous, deceitful in his presentation of his policies to his masters in London, enraged by those who sought to obstruct his plans"* (Mostert,1992: 1236). He operated at a highly sophisticated level with an exceptional ability to harness odd social environments and manage delicate political spheres, involving people of various cultural backgrounds. His vigour in understanding the hidden nuances, the strengths and the vulnerabilities of the local cultures enabled him to use such insights as a secret weapon which often worked to his advantage. In the process, Grey's adaptability made him one of the most effective and celebrated colonial administrators in the history of British imperialism in the nineteenth century.

For the British establishment to consider a man of Grey's calibre was a political master-stroke. On 4th December 1854, Sir George Grey replaced Sir George Cathcart as the Governor of the Cape Colony at a time the British Empire was recovering from the devastation War of Mlanjen in 1850-1852 and at the same time engaged in the Crimean War of 1853-1856 which was followed by the Indian War of 1857. Cathcart, the military man, admitted that the volatile Cape Colony required an experienced administrator to restore stability and to normalise the relations between Africans and Europeans.

Grey faced tremendous pressure to hit the ground running in stabilising the fractured Cape colony. To his advantage, the Empire granted him superior powers and he was not treated as an ordinary governor, due his vast experience and the ability to stabilise volatile situations. Grey wasted no time in first developing a comprehensive understanding of the underlying complex challenges that characterized in the colony.

The presence of a community of European settlers in the colony was a strength Grey was keen to build on in order to consolidate the gains and the interests of the British establishment. He made sure that they were provided with resources to drive the economic prosperity of the colony. The stability and prosperity of the European settlers would, in the long term, reduce the heavy dependency on the resources of the Empire. In the process, his popularity among the

British settlers grew and they gained confidence in him, and supported the implementation of his policies.

Grey's turnaround plan involved making the Cape Colony a profitable British dominion in order to recover the huge losses of the wars and to create bearable economic conditions for the devastated British settlers. He was fully aware that such a colonial policy was not achievable as long as amaXhosa remained a dominant threat to the interests of the British Empire. The consolidation of the Cape Colony and the long-term security of the white settlers were not guaranteed while amaXhosa remained a resolute force. Something drastic had to be done.

Unlike his predecessor, who relied heavily on war machinery to break the backbone of amaXhosa, Grey realized that an effective strategy was required in order to dismantle the power of amaXhosa. Grey introduced a policy in which leaders of amaXhosa received salaries from the colonial government. Their powers were diluted and neutralised through the appointment of European magistrates. The leaders were to collaborate with the magistrates in the administration of justice and maintenance of stability as well as the protection of colonial interests.

As an experienced strategist, Grey embarked on a myriad of surreptitious activities aimed at breaking the leadership of amaXhosa as well as the systems which held them together as a powerful force. At the same time, he wanted to be remembered as a Governor who brought civilization, prosperity and stability to the Cape Colony. He spearheaded the establishment of villages, institutions of learning, hospitals and new tools of improving the agricultural output of the colony.

For purposes of aligning the development around Grey as the centre of power, one will recall that the outbreak of the lung sickness was reported in November 1854 in Mossel Bay whilst Grey became the Governor in December 1854. In mid-1855, the epizootic cattle lung sickness landed in the land of amaGcaleka and reached its peak in 1857 (Andreas, 2005). The highest mortality of 5000 cattle per month occurred mainly in the land inhabited by amaXhosa.

It was not surprising that the lung sickness spread from Cape Town and landed in the land of King Sarhili. The question is why the Kingdoms of amaMpondo, abaThembu and Basotho were not affected. Why did the lung sickness spread rapidly from Cape Town and travel as far as the Kingdom of Sarhili, yet the trading routes purported to be the cause of the rapid spread went beyond the land of King Sarhili? Such a strange sequence of events raises questions about the direction and the targeted victims of the lung sickness.

The hidden hand and the interests of the British colonial establishment as well as its association with the cattle lung sickness as a weapon of mass destruction is deduced from the comments and the attitude of senior officials and administrators. In this regard, Colonel John Maclean, the Chief Commissioner of the British Kaffraria said, *"The prevailing cattle sickness will probably so far reduce the number of cattle in British Kaffraria, that the advantages which the chief and councillors derived from this barbarous mode of administering justice (cattle fines) are likely, for some time, to be so far diminished, that the present moment presents a most favourable opportunity for introducing a new system for the administration of justice amongst the K... population"* (Stapleton, 1992: 228). Colonel John Maclean's statement was an expression of the colonial policy and desire to deliberately spread the lung sickness on a large scale as an underhanded biological weapon of destruction of the power of amaXhosa, which was centred on pastoral patronage. Stapleton (1992) argued that the British destruction of the pastoral patronage through the epizootic lung disease weakened the fundamental power of amaXhosa aristocracy. For a senior government British official to say that the lung sickness presented the "most favourable opportunity for introducing a new system" was an expression of the colonial policy to dismantle any form of indepedence of amaXhosa in order to accomplish the ultimate conquest.

Stapleton (1992), made a bold assertion that the lung sickness provided Governor Grey with an opportunity to accelerate the destruction of the royal power of amaXhosa, by wiping out their productive capabilities. The question is how did Grey accomplish that? There was no reason why they had to stop it from spreading to as far as the Kingdom of King Sarhili. At the time, the colonial establishment had to ensure that amaXhosa would never have the capability to subject the British soldiers and settlers to another shattering war.

On the same note, Hosea Jaffe in his book *Three Hundred Years*, published in 1952, argued that the cattle-killing was Grey's form of clandestine war. Based on his deeper understanding of traditional mythology, he used it to decimate the cattle which formed the backbone of amaXhosa's resistance against British Imperialism. Similarly, Dora Taylor in her book *The Role of the Missionaries in Conquest*, published in 1952 in the pseudonym name of Nosipho Majeke, asserted that missionaries were complicit in the execution of Grey's decimation campaign. The assertions made by Jaffe (1952) and Majeke (1952) are supported by Mutwa (1966) and Stapleton (2016), who believed that the portrayal of amaXhosa as victims of their own beliefs was a cover-up for Grey's hidden masterplan in the destruction of the productive capabilities of amaXhosa.

According to Phelan (2020) some scholars believe that Sir George Grey had a hidden hand in the cattle killing following the devastating impact of the lung sickness. However, historians such as Peires (1989) seemed convinced that there was no conspiracy involved the killing of cattle. The inaction of the colonial authorities to arrest the rapid spread of the highly lethal and contagious lung sickness made Sir George Grey a complicit player in the cattle mass killing. It was the same Grey who emerged quickly as a saviour in the aftermath of the lung sickness and Nongqawuse.

Crais (1992) observed the coincidence between the rapid spread of bovine pleuropneumonia, popularly known as lung sickness, and the implementation of Grey's colonial policies.

"This disease, for which Xhosa had no previous knowledge, struck their cattle at precisely the same time that Sir George Grey began introducing his radical policies of Western Xhosaland. The coincidence was of enormous importance!" (pg 204). This extraordinary coincidence is ignored by most historians because it contradicts the dominant narrative that claimed that amaXhosa were victims of their own actions, thus exonerating Grey from having clandestinely implemented the first biological extermination of cattle in Southern Africa. The observation made by Crais illustrates that Grey was complicit in the spread of the cattle sickness because it served his purpose of breaking the backbone of resistance of amaXhosa, through the total destruction of their productive capabilities.

Another interesting observation made by Crais (1992) is the fact that the devastating impact of the lung sickness influenced the pattern in which amaXhosa executed the cattle killing. According to him, *"Where the disease was not severe, people participated in the movement to a much smaller degree. In killing, and not specifically sacrificing their cattle, many Xhosa may have hoped to prevent further spread of the disease"* (pg 209). This observation explains the essence of the cattle-killing in which the dominant narrative of most historians had always omitted the influence of the lung-sickness as the direct precursor of cattle killing. In essence, what transpired from the observations of Crais are two fundamental factors: the coincidence between the rapid spread of lung sickness and the implementation of Grey's policies and how the extent of lung sickness influenced the pattern of cattle-killing. The centrality of the observations is the intertwined relationship between Grey's pursuance of colonial policies, unabated decimation of cattle of amaXhosa by lung sickness and the killing of cattle in an attempt to stop the spread of the disease. All these factors worked in favour of the British in the aftermath of the devastating War of Mlanjeni.

Dowsley (1932) acknowledged that Grey was fully aware that amaXhosa, being a pastoral community, were the hardest hit by the lung sickness. According to Dowsley (1932) *"The ravages of this lung sickness had consequences of far-reaching importance to the whole country, and even in the early stages, Grey, quick to appreciate every opportunity, saw that it would help him in the efforts to encourage Native on the public works"* (pg 10). This is another instance which provides critical insight into what was in the mind of Sir George Grey, as well as his intentions and ambitions upon the outbreak of the deadly lung sickness.

Mary Mandeville Goedhals (1979), in her Masters Thesis from Rhodes University submitted in 1979, acknowledged that by 1857 the intentions of Sir George Grey were accomplished, as the power of the royal leaders of the amaXhosa people was finally broken through the destruction of their productive capabilities. Writing from the Christian perspective, Goedhals observed that the broken Nguni people were so desperate that they were willing to accept the new Christian faith. At that time, amaXhosa were under unbearable socio-economic, political and security conditions as they lost fertile lands; their livestock was exterminated; and they were deprived of their livelihoods. Their communities were heavily infiltrated by colonial agents, European traders, missionaries and colonial officials who were imposed to wield authority over them. Their national pride was crushed to the core as the power to rule themselves was violently snatched from them and given to the colonial officials.

Goedhals (1979) observed that *"the situation was exacerbated by high prevalence of lung sickness among Xhosa cattle"* (pg 33). It is worth noting that she also acknowledged that amaXhosa were the hardest hit by lung sickness. Reading between the lines, it has become clear that the catastrophic effects of lung sickness coincided with Grey's implementation of the new colonial policies of conquest. One can safely argue that the arrival of the European lung sickness in the Cape Colony, which coincided with Grey's tenure as a colonial Governor, was not accidental.

Yet to the likes of Johaness Meintjes (1971) Grey was *"the greatest statesman of them all"* (pg 231) probably because of his ability to crush the backbone of African resistance. Meintjes deliberately avoided any form of comprehensive reference to the origins and the impact of the cattle lung sickness. Instead, he discussed in great detail the Nongqawuse cattle killing, defining it as a 'fantastic occurrence', which coincided with the reign of Grey as the Cape colonial governor. Attributing the destruction of the power of amaXhosa to the killing of cattle is misleading, because it was Grey who engineered the lung sickness that wiped out the cattle herds of amaXhosa.

It was reported that Mhlakaza, the uncle of Nongqawuse, worked as a private servant of Nathaniel Merriman, archdeacon of Makhanda in the period between 1850 and 1853 (Peires, 1989). THe fact that he later returned to his ancestral land before the outbreak of cattle killing is an important factor linked to the broader Grey-coordinated strategy.

Now that the colonial authorities had seized the land, they needed labour to drive commercial development. Since amaXhosa had depended on their cattle for their livelihood, something had to be done to impoverish them in order create a labour pool for the white settlers. The outbreak and the rapid spread of the lung sickness fed into the colonial policy, not only to dispossess and to displace but to complete the conquest by destroying the productive capability of amaXhosa. The systematic extermination of the cattle of amaXhosa was to provide an opportunity to subject them to total subjugation. Therefore, the sequential interconnectedness of these factors points to the conclusion that Sir George Grey and his machinery of the colonial establishment had a hand in the rapid spread of lung sickness and hatching of Nongqawuse as a form of retaliation for the loss of resources and European lives in the war of Mlanjeni. The lung sickness provided an opportunity to ensure that amaXhosa would never again have the capability to challenge the British Empire.

In retrospect, the significance of the lung sickness lies in the fact that it ushered in the beginning of a new era in the history of Southern Africa. The period between 1857 and 1947 was characterized by the gradual entrenchment of British domination, continued systematic dispossession of the land, as well as displacement and dehumanization of amaXhosa and African people in general. This was followed by Boer domination between 1948 and 1994.

What one has attempted to communicate are observations that the lethal cattle lung sickness was a direct precursor of the cattle killing, which largely occurred in the territory of King Sarhili. Had the lung sickness, which nearly wiped out the herds of King Sarhili, not occurred, the cattle-killing would not have happened. The mass killing of the cattle was not driven by the alleged claims of resurrection of the ancestors; it was an act of desperation with the hope of containing the rapid spread of the lethal diseases.

Spicer (1978) estimated that about 20 000 amaXhosa perished from the cattle tragedy and about 33 000 of them became destitute and sought relief from the British colony. In the aftermath of the cattle catastrophe, Sir George Grey finished amaXhosa off through military invasion and confiscated the strategic fertile lands to establish military settler villages. According to Spicer, it was during this time that 2400 German settlers were settled in areas now known as Queenstown, Sutterheim, Berlin and East London in 1857. Some of the land was given to amaMfengu who participated in the total annihilation of amaXhosa. The military invasion, annexation of the targeted rich lands, resettlement of European settlers and rewarding of amaMfengu was followed by direct colonial rule. The completion of conquest was done through the installation of magistrates and headmen, building of the British institutions, subjecting amaXhosa into providing cheap labour for the white settlers and Anglicization through the destruction of African traditional institutions. In essence, the destruction of the productive capabilities through a biological weapon of mass killing of livestock became the ultimate weapon used to break the backbone of resistance of amaXhosa.

In conclusion, cattle lung sickness happened to have affected amaXhosa most more than any other group at the time. It became a convenient tool of Sir George Grey to accomplish conquest as indicated by the comments of the colonial officials as well as his attitude towards it. One way or another Grey was complicit in the deliberate destruction of mass cattle of amaXhosa in pursuit of the British conquest of Southern Africa. Further, It is not a coincidence that the name of Sir George Grey has lived on more than a century after his departure through institutions such as Grey Hospitals in Qonce and Pietermaritzburg, Grey College in Bloemfontein, Grey High School in Gqeberha, Greytown in KwaZulu-Natal, Greyton in the Western Cape, as well as Grey River and Lady Grey in the Eastern Cape.

3. European Cattle Lung Sickness: The Biological Weapon of Conquest In 1854 -1857

This section, explores the extent of the European cattle lung sickness in the decimation of cattle, the productive capabilities of amaXhosa. Andreas (2005) observed that lung sickness was brought to the Cape Colony in 1854 by infected animals with epizootic disease from Europe. Apparently, the animals were part of inter-continental trade meant *"to improve colonial herds through an infusion of Dutch breeds renowned for their high milk yields"* Andreas 2005, 50). According to Andreas, this was the most destructive cattle disease, followed by the rinderpest in 1896. This was an acute disease transmitted through contact between healthy and infected herds. Further, the unfenced pastures, shared watering and overnight kraaling made it extremely difficult to contain the spread of the lung sickness. *"The epizootic in the Cape has become infamous through its contributory role in the rise of the `Xhosa cattle-killing movement..."* (Andreas, 2005. 51). Andreas concluded that there was a sequential correlation between cattle lung sickness and the mass cattle killing.

Although there is a general impression that the lung sickness entered Southern Africa in mid-1854, there is a lack of reliable evidence of how it actually entered the colony. The disease travelled from the southern coast eastward and to the interior through the major roads. *"Peires claimed that, 'Some accounts assume that it entered the subcontinent in 1854, but fail to acknowledge their source.' It seems likely that year, origin and point of entry were copied from an article written much later by the government veterinarian Hutcheon, who did not present a source"* (Andreas, 2005: 52). The secrecy and lack of credible information on the credible and consistent sources of information raises concerns about the absence of conclusive official records on the exact landing of the infected animals, why the sickness was not detected on arrival and why the infected herds were allowed to mix with the local herds and for what purpose. Considering the fact that Europe at the time was a source of epizootic diseases, under reasonable circumstances, precautionary measures would have been taken upon landing of the Dutch breed in the Cape Colony.

Andreas (2005) estimated that the disease may have been detected in the Cape colony in July 1854, and the huge outbreak occurred in November 1854. Furthermore, based on the evidential material, Andreas believes that the lung sickness entered either through Saldanha Bay, which was the epicentre of the early outbreak, or through Cape Town, the major colonial harbour, from where the carrier may have moved to the Zwartland. However, Andreas admitted that the *"The expansion of the epizootic into the Xhosa chiefdoms is more difficult to reconstruct"* (pg 55). The lack of official records on the chronological sequence on how cattle lung sickness landed in the Kingdoms of amaXhosa creates reasonable grounds to conclude on the existence of colonial clandestine activities. It is highly likely that the colonial authorities were complicit in the surreptitious transportation of the lung sickness, to target the predominant areas of amaXhosa settlement.

Andreas argued that *"The chronology of the spread of lung sickness thus casts doubt on the alleged temporal and spatial coincidence between the occurrence of the epizootic and the rise of the cattle killing movement, because the epizootic reached the Xhosa chiefdoms at least one year before the Xhosa began to kill cattle on a large scale in mid-1856"* (Andreas, 2005: 56). If the cattle killing occurred a year after the arrival of the epizootic cattle disease, it is important then to establish the extent and the impact of it during that period from arrival in mid-

1855 until the beginning of the cattle killing in 1856. Also, it is critical to establish what informed the decision to kill the cattle. Was it not an attempt to contain the spread by killing the infected cattle; which would explain why the disease did not spread to the land of amaMpondo and abaThembu?

According to Andreas (2005) the epizootic disease reached its peak in 1857. Between 1855 and 1857 the epizootic cattle disease killed between 800 000 and 900 000 cattle in the Cape Colony. In comparative terms, it is worthwhile to establish how many cattle may have been killed in the land of King Sarhili, the apparent epicentre of cattle killing. Andreas (2005) admits that, *"It is impossible to differentiate between cattle that died of the disease and those slaughtered in accordance with the prophecies..."* (pg 58). Peires, in his article published in 1987 in the *Journal of African History*, claimed that between April 1856 and May 1857, it is estimated that about 400 000 cattle were killed and about 40 000 amaXhosa died of starvation. These figures do not differentiate between the killing of healthy cattle based on prophecy and the infected ones. On one hand, Peires gives the impression that it was the cattle killing which broke the back of amaXhosa. On the other hand, Andreas (2005) recognised the sequential correlation between the effects of the contagious lung sickness and the cattle killing. However, this figures provided do not specify how many cattle died in the Kingdom of Sarhili. This leads to another question: how many cattle died from lung sickness in the Kingdom of Sarhili compared to those that were slaughtered during the cattle killing? Also, why has the Nongqawuse narrative often failed to provide a comparative impact of both in order to assess and determine which one actually killed more cattle? The dominant narrative has focused mostly on the cattle killing, associated with the self-destructive beliefs and remained speculative on the impact of cattle lung sickness. The question is: why did most historians play down the deadly impact of the epizootic in wiping out the cattle of amaXhosa?

The lung disease was so devastating that an average of 5000 cattle died per month. The question is why it started in

Mossel Bay and not in Cape Town, which was the seat of the Cape colonial authority. From Mossel Bay, it travelled rapidly to Uitenhage in March 1854, Fort Beaufort in April 1854, Qonce in March 1855 and finally to Gcuwa in King Sarhili's kingdom in January 1856 (Peires, 1989). If this was detected in Mossel Bay in 1854, why did the colonial authorities allow it to spread? Also, it is interesting to note that once it arrived in Gcuwa, in the Kingdom of King Sarhili, it did not proceed further. In all probability, it stopped because it reached the intended target. The fact that it went as far as the Kingdom of King Sarhili, the target of the repeated invasions of the British colonial forces, was not an accident but a deliberate and systematic strategy to annihilate amaXhosa, who were at the forefront of the wars of resistance.

From the sequence of its spread across the Cape, interestingly in Makhanda where there was higher concentration of British white settlers, is not mentioned, which implies that it was not greatly affected. The question is: why not?

Andreas (2005) argues that although it is estimated that amaXhosa lost about 100 000 cattle from lung sickness, such a figure could not have been verified with absolute certainty because amaXhosa had no means of providing such data. Yet he contradicts himself by claiming that it was the cattle killing movement, rather than lung sickness, which killed more cattle.

The estimation of the Grahamstown Journal was that in 1855, amaXhosa lost an average of 5000 cattle per month. According to Andreas, Governor Sir George Grey estimated that amaXhosa lost about 130 000 cattle in 1856 alone. The number of cattle that died could be higher, considering the fact that the peak of the lung sickness occurred in 1857 (Andreas, 2005).

The mortality rate in the land inhabited by amaXhosa *"was extraordinarily high, most likely because the concentration of animals in a small area would have resulted in an extreme intensity of infection"* (Andreas, 2005. 69). The royal leaders of amaXhosa reported that they suffered a mortality rate of between 80 and 95% of their cattle. According to Andreas, by 1855, King Sandile was left with about 120 cattle in his possession. *"The cattle-killing movement started and in the end resulted in a devastation of Xhosa society that lung sickness on its own could have never caused"* (pg 68). Interestingly, he does not provide concrete scientific justification of his assertion in terms of how he determined the comparative impact of lung sickness and cattle killing in the territories occupied by amaXhosa at the time. What sort of data or link analysis informed him to arrive at that controversial conclusion? Also, Rees (1892) claimed that there were about 200 000 amaXhosa at the time, of whom about 50 000 died from starvation contrary to Grey's estimation of 130 000 (Andreas, 2005).

Andreas (2005) went into great detail in providing statistics and the factors that led to the rapid spread of the lung sickness. However, his narrative fell short in terms of explaining exactly how the infected Dutch breed landed in Cape Colony and whether any attempts were made by the British colonial authorities to contain the alarming spread of the deadly contagious disease. Why did it spread only as far as the Kingdom of King Sarhili, whilst the land of amaMpondo and abaThembu appeared to have survived the deadly cattle lung sickness? By Andreas's own admission, it is not clear how it entered the land of amaXhosa and stopped from spreading further to the neighbouring kingdoms.

Interestingly, the cattle lung sickness of 1854-1857 did not get as much coverage from the historians compared to the story of Nongqawuse. The question is why? Was it because it was less significant than Nongqawuse or were there other sinister reasons? It remains an important exercise to establish the magnitude of the lung sickness as well as the extent to which it wiped out the livestock over a period of three years.

In terms of the observations and reactions of the leaders of amaXhosa in the face of the deadly outbreak of lung sickness, Stapleton (1992) stated that Prince Maqoma was alarmed when a lung sickness epizootic which started in the Cape Colony started to destroy herds of amaXhosa cattle at an alarming rate. Prince Maqoma had reasonable grounds to be alarmed by such an alien catastrophe, coming so soon after General Harry Smith and General Henry Somerset failed to defeat him in the War of Mlanjeni. He may have suspected that there was something sinister about the European highly contagious and lethal cattle disease coming from Cape Town, the seat of the colonial establishment. It probably dawned on him that the wounds of the harrowing war of Mlanjeni were still raw given that General George Cathcart, who was deployed to replace General Smith and to finish off the war, also failed to attain victory. Therefore, Prince Maqoma was justifiable to be concerned by what he may have considered as an underhanded continuation of the war.

In the light of that, one argues the promotion of the distorted narrative of Nongqawuse became a convenient historical exercise to exonerate the British authorities who engineered the lung disease as a successful biological weapon of mass cattle destruction. A narrative was developed and perpetuated that through Nongqawuse, amaXhosa became victims of their own actions. Why was it also necessary to ensure that the grave of Nongqawuse remained preserved whilst we do not know with certainty where Prince Maqoma may have been buried?

Stapleton (1992) and Phelan (2020) concluded that the lung sickness epidemic, which decimated the cattle of amaXhosa, was the greatest factor which contributed to the killing of the sick cattle in order to cut the rapid spread of the highly lethal and contagious disease. Therefore, it was a logical act to kill the infected cattle rather than to allow them to suffer whilst infecting other cattle in the process. According to Phelan (2020) given the heavy dependency of amaXhosa on their cattle, the catastrophic lung sickness had a huge psychological impact, making amaXhosa more willing to kill their cattle rather than allowing them to suffer.

On the same note, Andreas (2005) wrote a detailed chronological account of the lung sickness in which he demonstrated through colonial records how it wiped out about 80% of the cattle of amaXhosa between 1855 and 1857. Also,

Peires (1989), made an interesting observation that wherever the lung sickness ravaged the area of amaXhosa, it was often followed by cattle killing. Such an observation implied that lung sickness precipitated the cattle killing carnage. Again, it is highly likely therefore that people may have decided to kill the infected cattle as an attempt to prevent the total extermination of their livestock. Therefore, the cattle killing tragedy was an act of desperation precipitated by the inability to stop the contagious and lethal cattle lung sickness.

Davenport (1988) concurred with Peires (1989) on the correlation between cattle killing and lung sickness and went further to attribute the mass slaughter to what he called *"a millenarian movement"* driven by mass hysteria. The repeated references to a hysteria-driven millenarian movement assume that besides Nongqawuse, there was an existing nameless millenarian movement in the land of amaXhosa, which was a driving force in the implementation of the prophecy. Although Davenport observed the correlation between cattle killing and Nongqawuse, he later implied that the latter was the outcome of an hysterical millenarian group. Having noted that, Offenburger (2009) goes as far as acknowledging that lung sickness destroyed the majority of the herds of amaXhosa.

At this stage of the critical interrogation it is of paramount importance to reflect on the significance of major devastating events that occurred at the time in the context of resistance of amaXhosa against the British expansion in South Africa. Just before the outbreak of the contagious lung sickness, the British settlers were still bitter about the heavy losses suffered during the War of Mlanjeni as well as the surrender of the dominions beyond Orange River. They blamed it all on the stubbornness of amaXhosa. What shocked both the white settlers and the colonial authorities was that, compared to the previous seven wars of resistance of 1779-1781, 1789-193, 1799-1803, 1811-1812, 1818-1819, 1834-1835 and 1846-1847, the War of Mlanjeni stood out as one in which the Europeans suffered highest casualties at the hands of the united forces of amaXhosa, abaThembu and the Khoe.

What was most concerning to the colonial establishment was how amaXhosa perfected the art of deadly bush warfare. The fact that in the War of Resistance of 1834-1835, Sir Benjamin D'Urban and General Harry Smith were frustrated by their failure to attain victory despite having mobilized a strong army with well-trained infantry, agile cavalry and deadly artillery, was a contributing factor to the quest for British conquest. The brutal killing of King Hintsa although he had never declared war against the colonial government, was an act of desperation. The recall of D'Urban and Smith further deepened the roots of resentment and bitterness towards the indomitable amaXhosa. The humiliating defeat of Lieutenant General John Hare in the following war of 1846 and 1847, despite having led a large army supported by 125 wagons, created uncertainty and desperation on prospects of the future of European settlers in South Africa. In the following War of Mlanjeni in 1850-1853, the Europeans suffered about 1400 casualties according to conservative figures, although the numbers were significantly higher than that.

To the despair of the British, Africans continued to improve their military strategies by inflicting more casualties through well-coordinated attacks, launched from the dense bushes. They developed an innovative strategy of rotating the fighters in order to sustain the battle and deploying spies in strategic locations in order to study the techniques and monitor the movement of the European troops. The continued inability of the British-led army to attain decisive victory in the face of an elusive and agile enemy remained a source of deep concern. Against such a background of uncertainty, resentment and hopelessness, something drastic had to be done to either come up with a permanent solution or surrender the Cape Colony. Some sort of lasting victory had to be attained at all costs. Therefore, the landing and the outbreak of the highly contagious and deadly cattle lung sickness towards the end of 1854 was not an accidental phenomenon. It was a well-planned continuation of the war of conquest in the form of the biological weapon to destroy the productive capabilities of amaXhosa.

The fact that amaXhosa were the most affected ones by the cattle lung sickness was a deliberate strategy to neutralise what was regarded as the main threat to the attainment of conquest. The significance and the impact of the defining wars between 1852 and 1853 was the most precarious period of uncertainty and desperation for the British Empire in the history of colonialism in South Africa. The British military machinery suffered three consecutive defeats, several military generals and governors were fired, Boers deserted the Cape Colony in what became known as the Great Trek, amaXhosa gained ascendance in the wars of resistance and the British Empire was compelled to surrender dominions beyond the Orange River. The several attempts to attain domination and conquest faced the brick wall as the disastrous wars became more costly in terms of resource and the huge loss of life. Therefore, an alternative strategy became imperative as the European settlers had their backs on the wall.

This section has crystallised the extent and the impact of the cattle lung sickness as the major cause of the extermination of the cattle of amaXhosa. Yet the catastrophic impact of the cattle disease was ignored and isolated in order to pursue a specific narrative that amaXhosa wiped out their own cattle. Davenport (1988), Peires (1989) and Andreas (2005) acknowledged the existence of sequential correlation between lung sickness and cattle killing which reinforced the findings that amaXhosa killed the infected cattle to control the spread of the contagious and deadly disease. In essence, the lung sickness accomplished what the British colonial wars failed to attain since the beginning of the nineteenth century.

4. Conclusion

In conclusion, at the core of the relentless wars the British versus amaXhosa, was the realization that the ownership of fertile land and thousands of cattle were the foundations of productive capabilities was what enabled the latter to sustain protracted wars. It made sense therefore to the British colonial establishment to find an alternative strategy on how to destroy the fundamental pillars of the backbone of resistance of amaXhosa.

In the aftermath of the War of Mlanjeni that drained the resources, caused huge loss of life and the failure of the British military leaders to attain victory, it made the arrival of Sir George Grey as a governor an imperative deployment. Grey was fully aware that military confrontation was not a solution. He had to find an alternative strategy in order to break the stalemate of decades of deadly wars in the Cape colony.

The assertion that the cattle lung sickness was a biological weapon of mass cattle annihilation is anchored on the critical interconnected events of historical significance; the costly War of Mlanjeni from 1850 to 1853, the governorship of Sir George Grey between 1854 and 1861, the outbreak of the European cattle lung sickness between 1854 and 1857 and the cattle culling between 1856 and 1857. It is of paramount importance to understand that the chronological sequence of the developments occurred in the broader context of the British pursuit of total conquest in South Africa. The sequence of the inextricable interconnected events and how each had an impact to another one makes it difficult to position cattle killing as an isolated event. What one has attempted to illustrate here is that the landing and the spread of the highly contagious and lethal cattle lung was the surreptitious continuation of the war of British conquest. The only difference was that the war took the form of a biological weapon of mass cattle destruction targeting the communities of amaXhosa.

In conclusion, this chapter explored the different perspectives on Nongqawuse that had been generated since the mid nineteenth century. It examined the association of Sir George Grey with the rapid spread of the European cattle lung sickness in the territories inhabited by amaXhosa. The critical examination of literature indicated that the cattle lung sickness had far reaching impact in the annihilation of about 80% of the herds of amaXhosa. The peak of the cattle killing occurred after the lung sickness had spread deep into the communities of amaXhosa. The cattle culling method was executed as the last desperate attempt to save the few remaining cattle that were not infected. The reaction and the attitude of the British colonial officials indicated that the decimation of the productive capabilities of amaXhosa was viewed as a positive development to break the backbone of resistance.

Chapter Five

The Tragedy of Distorted History

"Excellent education is not enough if we do not teach them the essence of who they are. It is of paramount importance that our history should not gloss over our past whilst glorifying others."
Jongi Klaas (Reflections at the time of writing the book)

1. Subtlety of Subjective Historical Narratives

Most of what has been published and promoted as the official version of South African history, especially in the past 350 years, has been predominantly written by white males of European descent. They were in a position of privilege and power to determine the content of official knowledge following the completion of the British and the Boer conquest towards the end of the nineteenth century. Unfortunately, the African pioneers of written knowledge who started writing their version of history toward the end of the nineteenth century and the beginning of the twentieth Century were not always fortunate enough to have their work printed and published. At the helm of the institutions responsible for the production of knowledge mostly were men of European descent who were the gatekeepers. In most cases the content produced by African writers perceived to be too critical towards the colonial establishment was declined and shelved. According to Peires (1981), during the administration of Reverend Robert Henry Wishart Shepherd[1] (1888-1971) of Lovedale, which went on for twenty years, any material that was critical of the British establishment was not published.

---

1   In 1920, Reverend Shepherd was deployed in South Africa as the missionary of the Church of Scotland. In 1932, he joined Lovedale Mission as the Editor of the Lovedale Press until 1955. In 1960, he returned to South Africa to serve as the head of the Presbyterian in Alice until he died in 1971.

As a result, three manuscripts written by SEK Mqhayi (1875-1945), the gifted writer, historian and pioneer of the written language of isXhosa, perished at Lovedale during Shepherd's reign. Consequently, most of the published official history of South Africa, which prospered in the nineteenth and twentieth century, was the work of historians such as Robert Godlonton (1794-1884), George McCall Theal (1837-1919) and George Edward Cory (1862-1935). At times the written work of Godlonton and Theal in particular was not different from the official government records of historical events designed to convey glorious accounts of conquest with very little credit given to the positive contributions of Africans. Unfortunately, the essence of the historical narrative that dominated their work was largely the subtle and at times blatant glorification of British colonialism to the detriment of African history.

This trend continued until the 21st Century and prospered during the institutionalisation and maintenance of the Apartheid regime. According to Professor Ncedile Saule, the continued perpetuation of inaccurate historical narratives had a negative impact on the socialisation of African scholars. They reproduced a distorted history, often presented as the absolute truth.

A few of the history books written about the Cape colony in particular are worth highlighting, since it was the first theatre of military operations during the era of British colonial encroachment in Southern Africa. As a result, we cannot be certain whether most of what has been written is a true reflection of what actually took place. Professor Timothy Stapleton, the Canadian historian who wrote extensively on the history of Southern Africa in the nineteenth century, illustrated this observation quite well in his book *A Military History of South Africa* (2010). *"Three days after the battle Willshire reported that 150 Xhosa corpses had been left behind, three weeks later a Cape Town newspaper claimed that 500 Xhosa had been killed, and 10 years later settler Thomas Pringle stated that 1,400 had died. In 1876 Charles Stretch… wrote that 2,000 had been killed, and in the early twentieth century , historian George Cory put the figure at around 1,000"* (Stapleton 2010, 24). The various versions on what actually happened makes it difficult to know the true account of the incident. The discrepancy on the numbers varying between 150 and 2000 was probably done to downplay the sterling contribution and the heroic acts of African warriors in the battlefield.

On a similar note, with regard to the casualties in the War of Mlanjeni, the number of Africans who died is placed at around 16 000, whilst the number of Europeans who died is estimated at around 1 400. Based on the series of accounts of the deadly war, characterised by the increasingly higher number of Europeans who were killed in every military engagement from the battles of Qoboqobo to Mount Misery in Fort Beaufort /KwamaQoma, the overall number of Europeans who perished is likely to be between 3 500 and 4 000.

Premesh Lalu, a South African Professor of History in his book *The Death of Hintsa – Post Apartheid South Africa and the shape of recurring pasts*, (2009) highlights some of the fundamental challenges such as subjectivities, biases and deliberate distortions of written history. *"The discipline of history generally approaches the colonial archive with a measure of suspicion because of its supposedly inherent biases. This attitude has merely called forth greater caution in extracting the truth of the experience of the colonized, who are thought to be embedded, even buried, in the bureaucratic procedures of documenting the work of Empire in civilizing, conquering and controlling"* (Lalu 2009: 41). When one reviews primary sources of documented information written by the Europeans about their observations based on the encounters with Africans, one begins to get a sense of unwillingness to admit that Africans performed remarkably well in the battlefields. Also, to a great extent one could notice a consistent trend of uneasiness to write about military campaigns characterised by staggering figures of European casualties. Hence the War of Mlanjeni had always been omitted from the official South African history in favour of the Battle of Grahamstown where the British obtained a decisive victory.

Some of the fascinating primary sources explored in this book were the work of John *Barrow, An Account of Travels into the Interior of Southern Africa, in the Years 1797 and 1798*, published in 1801; Captain W.R. King, *Campaigning in Kaffirland or Scenes and Adventures in the Kaffir War of 1851–1852*, published in 1855 and James McKay *Reminiscences of the last Kaffir War* published in 1871. The remarkable accounts of John Barrow, in particular, are more in the nature of an expeditionary exploration of the Cape colony in order to provide true accounts to the policy makers in Great Britain. Some of the observations he made about amaXhosa have been highlighted in Chapter One of this book. Since he came as an explorer, there was a reasonable degree of objectivity in his accounts, hence his work is a living passage of incredible knowledge packaged as vivid accounts of the natural disposition and the physical characteristic of amaXhosa.

Captain W.R. King, one of the British soldiers who fought in the great war of Mlanjeni of 1850–1853, provided comprehensive emotional and graphic accounts, which were packaged as a book published in 1855 under the supervision of Professor Charles Dunfar. King narrated detailed and harrowing accounts of the brutal war, which he believed pushed the British soldiers to breaking point. His extensive work provided deeper insight into the protracted harrowing encounters and how the fighters felt about the war, fought under almost unbearable conditions. However, in one of his accounts, he made a controversial comparison of African and European dead combatants. *"The stench was intolerable...A few yards further on lay the clean picked skeleton of the Serjeant of the 12th, killed at the same time, which was recognized by the fragments of the his red coat, torn to pieces and trampled in the dirt by the hyenas and jackals, which invariably attack white in preference of black"* (King,1855.134). To what extent can one be certain that what King wrote was a true account of what happened in the battlefield if he expressed such resentment towards the dead African combatants? What if the Serjeant had died earlier on, hence he was already devoured by wild animals? From the side of amaXhosa, there were no known published accounts about what actually happened during the war. Maybe the unpublished manuscript of SEK Mqhayi that disappeared in Lovedale may had provided such stories. It remains a challenge therefore to believe that those who happened to possess the means of writing and publishing may actually have presented true accounts of what actually happened.

James McKay, was the British sergeant of the 74th Highlanders, who was brought to South Africa to reinforce the British army in the War of Mlanjeni of 1850-1853. He wrote a diary about the accounts of the war which was published in 1871 as *Reminiscences of the last Kaffir War*. In one of the incidents, he provides a characterisation of General Henry Somerset, who was Supreme Commander of the British Army during in the War of Mlanjeni in relation to his association with Khoe women. What is concerning about McKay's narrative was the usage of derogative phrases such as 'bastard Hottentots' and 'passable looking wenches.' From such highly disparaging narrative it is difficult to understand the genuine disposition and temperament of the Khoe women except being portrayed as sex objects.

One would recall that before the War of Mlanjeni, the Khoe people collaborated extensively with the colonial establishment. During the ethnic cleansing of amaXhosa in 1811-1812 they were at the forefront of the onslaught as they were the ones who located the secret hiding place of the elderly people, women and children. Nevertheless, it is astonishing that people who had been loyal to the colonial authorities for decades were described in such a resentful manner, with the use of demeaning words. His honest description of the Khoe was probably indicative of the prevailing attitude at the time.

Next, the critical interrogation of some of the influential South African History books published in the late 1980s reveals dominant narrative characterised by fragmented, glossed over and isolated accounts. The contributions and the reactions of African people to the loss of land and nationhood during the period of the British conquest of Southern Africa, are often compartmentalised. In some instances, the authors would rather conduct research on a particular group of African people and avoid historical events where Africans were engaged as a united block in the relentless wars of resistance. For the purpose of this narrative the historical books written by Professor J.D. Omer-Cooper, *History of Southern Africa* published in 1987, Professor Rodney Davenport, *South Africa A Modern History* published in 1988 and Professor Jeffrey Peires, *The Dead Will Arise: Nongqawuse and the Great Cattle-Killing Movement of 1856-7* published in 1989, have been examined.

Professor J.D. Omer-Cooper, who was based at the University of Otago in New Zealand, published a book titled *History of Southern Africa* in 1987. In the 1990's the book was prescribed for the undergraduate History students at the University of Fort Hare in South Africa. The writing style and packaging of South African by Omer-Cooper is in such a way that one could not make sense about the South African history as an intertwined unity. The history of African are isolated pockets of events presented in a very trivialising and glossed over narrative. The dispossession of land and livestock of the Khoe people as well as their displacement and dehumanization comes across as a subtle belittling narrative written in a euphemistic manner. *"Khoi communities who lost their cattle from natural causes, in warfare or after the establishment of the Dutch settlements, through trade or conflict with whites, sometimes reverted to a hunting and gathering way of life like that of the San"* (Omer-Cooper, 1987: 7). The deliberate ambiguous narrative on the plight of Khoe people is tantamount to total disregard of their agonising experiences. Yet they were subjected to systematic extermination, which was carried out for over 150 years. In the process, they lost land and livestock and their populations dwindled significantly down to a manageable size, able to provide labour for the Europeans. Omer-Cooper chose not to recognise that the Khoe people ceased being pastoralists after coming into contact with the Dutch, as they were dispossessed of their land, displaced and dehumanized. They resorted to hunting and gathering of wild fruits in order to survive on the beautiful rich land they once owned as pastoralists.

In terms of how the Khoe people were drawn into organised labour, Omer-Cooper (1987) had this to say, *"At an early stage in the development of the colony, some Khoe began to enter the employment of the freeman. Some did so because they had been deprived of their lands and cattle. Others were attracted by the prospects of material reward"* (pg 22). In this instance, he implied that entering the labour market of the colony was a free choice as well as circumstances they found themselves in. What he is not saying is that this was part of the organised Dutch establishment to dispossess and to commodify the Khoe in order to enter the labour market or perish.

With reference to the first British scorched-earth policy in Southern Africa, which was used in the expulsion amaXhosa from Zuurveld, Omer-Cooper once again glosses over this important issue. *"The authorities commissioned Captain Collins to tour the eastern frontier areas. He proposed that forcible measures should be taken to drive out the Xhosa from the Zuurveld and make the Fish River an effective frontier between the races. In 1812-12 the proposal was carried out. War was launched against the Zuurveld Xhosa and the followers of Ndlambe and the smaller chiefdoms were driven across Fish River"* (Omer-Cooper, 1887: 44). Omer-Cooper made a deliberate omission of the fact that Governor Cradock ordered Colonel John Graham to execute the ethnic cleansing of amaXhosa from the Zuurveld. Secondly, he omitted the fact that Prince Chungwa of amaGqunukhwebe was murdered on his deathbed by the British forces, along with thousands of elderly people, including women and children who could not run away.

From the few highlighted incidents, in his entire book the author omitted the wars of resistance, except the one that occurred in 1819, since it is the only war where the British army attained victory over amaXhosa. Interestingly, despite the fact that the omitted wars were the game-changers that shaped the socio-economic and political landscape of the region, were ignored. Even a cover page illustrating a white person bossing over a half-naked African sitting on the ground is an offensive perpetuation of white superiority. The book is basically a fallacious narrative of the African experiences in the face of the invading European colonialists. The author has repeatedly treated several fundamental events of historical significance to the African people in a very superficial manner. It is surprising that such a book was recommended to be studied at university level, despite the glaring shortcomings.

Professor Rodney Davenport, a retired don of History from Rhodes University, wrote a book entitled *South Africa: A Modern History* that was published in 1988, with a colourful cover of four jubilant African men. In the section on the Cape history from mid-eighteen century to the beginning of the nineteenth century, he omitted the entire ethnic cleansing event of amaXhosa in the war of 1811–1812. The only seemingly important development to him occurred in 1812, when Cradock introduced the Circuit Courts, which according to him, was a positive development even though it led to the Slagters Nek Rebellion of 1815 (Davenport, 1988). He writes about the courageous British settlers in Makhanda without providing the context on how they arrived and who owned the land before they came. Davenport goes further to portray the British settlers as victims of the relentless devastating raids that were carried out by amaXhosa, again no context is provided why the raids occurred. The fact that amaXhosa were compelled to resort to the raids in order to reclaim their confiscated livestock so that they could survive meant nothing to Davenport. Those who survived the harrowing expulsion from the Zuurveld crossed the Fish River as refugees, since their villages had been burnt down and the livestock was confiscated in order to create comfortable conditions for the white settlers who later moved in as farmers. The omission of such vital contextual information avenport is an indirect way of projecting amaXhosa as a nuisance against the progress and prosperity of the white settlers who landed on the shores of the southern tip of Africa, with no empty land and free livestock waiting for them.

To the surprise of readers, Davenport justified their hardened resentful racism towards Africans as an acceptable phenomenon in such situations. "The *1820 Settlers became acclimatised to their new surroundings...developing the physical and moral toughness and the harder race attitudes common to the inhabitants of turbulent frontier districts...* (Davenport, 1988: 44). Such deliberate omissions, decontextualized biased narrative and the glorification of people responsible for appropriation of land of the indigenous inhabitants is tantamount to arrogance of the worst kind in academic writing. He packaged a distorted history presented as the product of intellectual exercise.

Later in the same book, Davenport glossed over the brutal murder of King Hintsa. Instead he insinuated that King Hintsa was in possession of 50 000 colonial cattle, thus proving the veiled justification for Governor Benjamin D'Urban's belligerent aggression towards amaXhosa over the Kei River and the arrest of King Hintsa. Also, with reference to what triggered the War of Mlanjeni, Davenport presents a complete distortion of history by projecting amaXhosa as the aggressors. *"On Christmas Day 1850, three of the military villages in Victoria were surprised and destroyed by the Ngqika, as did Mhala, son of Ndlambe, and even the Kat River Khoi, driven to desperation by the drought and the growing insecurity of their settlement"* (Davenport, 1988: 133). In this context, Davenport omitted the fact that on 24 December 1850, it was Lieutenant Governor George Mackinnon, on instructions of the Governor Major General Harry Smith, who led a military expedition to the stronghold of Prince Sandile in Qoboqobo to either arrest or kill him. To his shock, the British army was intercepted in Boma Pass by amaXhosa fighters and subjected to a relentless onslaught. Mackinnon suffered heavy casualties and retreated in complete disarray. In this regard, amaXhosa were justified in defending themselves. What poured salt into the wound of amaXhosa was the fact that Harry Smith, who was now a governor, had been complicit in the brutal murder of King Hintsa a few years earlier. Yet Davenport decided to omit such vital contextual background that led to the destruction of settler villages. This is not just distortion but the destruction of history as a subject by hiding equally vital developments to the readers in order to portray ones recreated events of history.

Another inaccurate presentation of events involves the reasons provided for the insurrection of the Khoe people. It was not drought that drove them into the insurrection; they were deeply aggrieved by the unceremonious expulsion from the Kat River, after they had served and protected the interests of the British settlers for decades. The omission of such vital historical context portrayed the Khoe as hysterical, irrational and ungrateful people. The author trivialized their deep-seated grievance and the prejudice and resentment they were subjected to by the white settlers. In Chapter three it is mentioned that white settlers resented the fact that Khoe were excellent fighters in bush warfare, while they were protecting the British from amaXhosa.

Professor Jeffrey Peires, the celebrated author of famous books such as the *House of Phalo* published in 1981, and *The Dead Will Arise: Nongqawuse and the Great Cattle Killing Movement of 1856* which was published in 1989, has done incredible work in writing the extensive history of amaXhosa. Although he attempted to portray objective accounts based on his interaction with amaXhosa and his ability to speak isiXhosa, he was unfortunately not immune to the challenges of subjective narratives in the discipline of academic writing. In his book, *House of Phalo*, he says, *"The beauty of the D'Urban system was that it offered the settlers the prospects of vast stretches of this beautiful country virtually free as compensation for war losses'* (Peires, 1989: 123). However, according to Peires these were not his views. The statement represented the opinon of John Mitford Bowker, one of the influential leaders of the British settlers at the time. The statement was written in the context of land ownership and reselling of land as a commercial enterprise. In this regard, Bowker seemed to express admiration for the policies of Lieutenant General Sir Benjamin D'Urban, Governor of the Cape Colony between 1834 and 1838, who was complicit in the brutal murder of King Hintsa.

The question is: from whose perspective did D'Urban's system was beautiful? Whom was the book talking to in the celebration of land obtained through dispossession and displacement of the indigenous inhabitants? To an African reader, the 'beauty' of the D'Urban system was actually the sanitization of the brutality of our history of bitterness and resentment. The expression of such sentiments creates discord as it comes across as the arrogant glorification of the conquerors.

Professor Peires conducted extensive research on the history of amaXhosa including the controversial narrative of Nongqawuse. The previous Chapter explored and illustrated how problematic the Nongqawuse narrative was especially where certain events were reported out of context in disregard of the sequence of interconnected events related to Nongqawuse. Inasmuch as the intention of Peires was to focus on the essence and the history of amaXhosa as a distinct group as well as their relationships with other nations, their history of resistance in the nineteenth century remained a critical missing component. Whether that was by design or convenience the subtle strategy was probably influenced by the politics of the time to avoid delving into the protracted acrimonious wars of resistance fought over a period of one hundred years. For instance, in one of his accounts about amaXhosa and wars, he began comprehensively, presenting possible factors which may have led to the war of 1834, and then left the narrative halfway through without saying much about the actual war.

In his thesis published in 1976, Peires presented a narrative which hinted at amaXhosa as a divided people, who were always fighting each other for power and dominion and selling each other out, even to the Europeans. He implied that they were victims of their own creation, who fought all the time, with no sense of any organized system to withstand the European advancement. However, in his later work such as the House of Phalo, he did an incredible work in presenting a balanced history and went as far as acknowledging the heroic dedication of certain leaders of amaXhosa during the wars of resistance.

Johan de Villiers, in his paper published in 2003 says *"By 1811 at least 20 000 Xhosa intruders had already crossed the Fish River into the grassy Zuurveld and beyond"* (pg 2). De Villiers writes in the context of the War of Resistance of 1811–1812 in which the British executed ethnic cleansing in order to clear amaXhosa from the rich grazing lands between Xelexwa and Nxuba Rivers. Calling amaXhosa 'intruders' when trying to reoccupy their own land is astonishing. He implied that the white settlers were entitled to the land probably because they fought for it.

In essence, the serious limitations, arrogance and propaganda emerged as the key impediments in the objective writing of our history. One limitation involves rigidly stratified society, where writers tend to be conditioned by their own assumptions and prejudice in projecting the views of their own societies shaped by the dichotomies of class, race, religion and language (Wilson & Thompson, 1982). Wilson and Thompson argue that physical features, language and economy cannot be used to characterise and define the Khoe and San because "some of those who speak Bantu language are part Caucasian in physical type" (pg. 35). They further asserted that the claim that whites discovered and occupied an empty piece of land was a myth.

2. School History Textbooks: The Terrain of Contested Pedagogy

The manner in which South African history from 1652 onwards has been packaged and rebranded in the school History textbooks has always glorified the stories of the conquerors and misrepresented the accounts of the conquered. Unfortunately, this has been allowed to go on for a considerable period of time with no sort of collective efforts from all stakeholders to rectify the anomaly. The tragedy of the official South African history is the presentation of historical events in detached compartments and continued the marginalisation of the fundamental events related to African people. In most cases, the official history is packaged history in a such a way that Europeans were the saviours of the continent who brought civilization, advanced religion and liberated the natives from the shackles of darkness. What is concerning are the bold omissions of the chilling accounts of unimaginable atrocities committed by the conquerors and the systematic destruction of pre-colonial African civilizations. The deliberate distortion of South African history has been perpetuated under the cover of academic excellence, pseudo-intellectualism and the abuse of power to determine the content of official history.

The impact of decades of teaching a highly distorted history of conquest cannot be underestimated. It created deep-seated psychological scars for the conquered people. From the perspective of a recipient of harassment and persecution during the 1980s and 1990s in the South African context, one often experienced a defeatist psyche of resigned hopelessness and lack of pride in our contributions as Africans before, during and after the colonial era. Learners are compelled to master the history of conquest, whilst positive accounts of African history had been marginalised and shrouded in small components of compartmentalised biased narratives.

During the period of Apartheid in South Africa, the pedagogy of the conquered was designed in such a way that learners were expected to memorize the content whilst critical interrogation of the events was frowned upon and sometimes punishable. It required enormous courage and inner resilience to allow oneself to be subjected to the systematic mental torture and psychological humiliation to internalise the dichotomised history of us and them, civilized and savages, superior and inferior people. No wonder there was such a high dropout rate in both primary and secondary school, because of the rigid and dogmatic pedagogy provided no space for hope and creative critical thinking.

Two decades into the new millennium, almost three decades since the first South African democratic elections, and 187 years since the abolition of slavery in South Africa on 1st August 1834 (Slavery Abolition Act of 1833), it is of paramount importance to ensure that our history embodies an objective and inclusive representation of our collective stories. In this regard, the official History textbooks of the national curriculum are powerful instruments (Karpov, 2005) in determining whose history is important in the shaping the cognitive development of the 'ideal citizen' (Bertram & Wassermann, 2015). Robinson (2018) argues that history is a critical faculty in developing the consciousness of students to understand the past and be able to address the present in order to grapple with the future. Therefore, it is of paramount importance to examine the symbols, the influence and impact of the official History textbooks embedded in the national curriculum for high school as well as a few History books used at university at undergraduate level. In order to lay the foundation, we first look at a few perspectives about the essence of history and observations made about the official South African history in the national curriculum.

Vygotsky (1978) asserted that the impact of the historical textbooks in shaping the human mindset and behaviour of learners in the construction of knowledge and cognitive development can never be underestimated. Similarly, Karpov (2005) argued that textbooks are powerful psychological instruments in the use of language and images to transmit historical knowledge to learners. Therefore, the curriculum content contained in the school textbooks provides fundamental foundations in which the knowledge of learners about the past constitutes the essence of their cognitive development, including where they come from and who they are. Unfortunately, in the South African context, African students have less appreciation of history because of the manner in which it had been packaged to serve the interest of the privileged class and taught as an indisputable pedagogy.

One of the enduring psychological tragedies in the state of cognitive development of African learners is the deeply entrenched sense of both a superiority and inferiority complex because of decades of a distorted historical narrative structured on the dichotomies of the conquerors and the conquered. It is not surprising, therefore, that a significant number of learners come out of that history with no sense of cultural pride, national patriotism and strong identity. As the learners transcend to adult life, they wrestle with the essence of the educational value of the official history learnt from the school textbooks.

In essence, the classroom is meant to influence the thoughts and behaviour of learners in such a way that they must believe what they are taught as the reality of what actually happened in the past (Vygotsky, 1978 & Karpov, 2005). If they learn that the era of conquest of Africa was an inevitable phenomenon in order to bring civilization to a continent whose inhabitants were portrayed as wasteful savages, they are likely to develop defeatist and self-hating behaviour. It is therefore not a surprise that we have brought up youth with a confused sense of their own identity, less appreciation of their culture and language or lukewarm desire to contribute to the building of a nation which feels foreign to them in many respects.

If learners are taught a version of African history that is confined to the victimhood of land dispossession, displacement and dehumanization and a portrayal of Africans as people who contributed nothing to civilization, such a pedagogical process is bound to leave permanent scars and an inferiority complex. Tragically it will impact negatively on vital areas of cognitive and intellectual development in relation to how they view themselves in the context of the larger world.

If there is a collective willingness to deconstruct the decades of distorted history, then charity begins at home. In the African context in particular, we have a collective obligation to rectify this anomaly in order to instil a sense of pride to African learners, by providing opportunities for them to learn about their own heroes and heroines. In that way, they will develop confidence in themselves, believe in possibilities and see beyond the pyscho-social and economic confines in which they find themselves. History should be one of the fundamental subjects providing a learning space of empowerment, admiration and pride from learning about the gallant efforts of their African forebears. Such real history will enable the learners to develop the courage to tackle the current socio-economic and political complexities to create a better future.

The fact that the history of the War of Mlanjeni, in which united Africans stood toe to toe with the Europeans in what became the longest war of resistance against colonial encroachment in Southern Africa in the mid-nineteenth century, has been omitted from the national History curriculum is intentional. It is because African children must not learn about how their forebears fought some of the most courageous wars of resistance in case they derive courage from such knowledge to liberate themselves. Just imagine how inspiring it would be to the learners to learn about the Battle of Adwa, in which the united Ethiopian army defeated the invading Italian regiments in 1892, a historical event which marked the birth of Africanism. The continued denialism through pseudo-intellectual theories of the fact that the pyramids of Egypt and Sudan were built by Africans is a deliberate ideological position to reduce Africans to the margins of history.

The contestation about whose knowledge and perspective should embody the content of the History textbooks is also noted by Jason Nicholls (2006) from the University of Oxford, who conducted an international comparative study on the perspectives of various countries on how the Second World War is portrayed in official History textbooks. Based on the findings, Nicholls argued that the nature of engagement on how the textbooks are presented in the classroom is an important aspect. It matters whether the textbook is the "sole source of information" with a "single authoritative narrative on events or multiple perspectives are offered" (40). Are the students examined on their knowledge or critical interrogation ability? Is history about memorization of facts or interpretation and analysis of both the content and source of information?

In the South African context if one looks at some of the studies conducted on South African school History textbooks in the past 10 years, interesting observations have been made on the content and the pedagogical process in the classroom situation. For instance, Katalin Estzer Morgan (2011) conducted research that examined various Grade 11 History textbooks as part of her doctoral dissertation at the University of Johannesburg. Morgan applied various analytical tools such as hermeneutics, discourse, visual, critical and semiotic analysis in the study of meaning-making of history textbooks. In essence, her findings showed that textbooks as mediums of intellectual exercise in the teaching of History vary remarkably in the construction and packaging of official knowledge. According to Morgan, history has great potential for imaginative influence to expose students to unlimited possibilities of human potential. Morgan viewed history as a pilgrimage to understand the past in order to make sense of the present. The way in which textbooks construct information and how teachers convey it are critical aspects in the creation of new knowledge in the classroom (Selander, 2007). Morgan (2011) argued that the production of History textbooks is an intellectual exercise in the generation of knowledge meant for a classroom setting. They constitute an important form of socio-cultural knowledge, transmitted through language and images, in order to shape a particular mindset.

Morgan's analysis of the findings reiterated that textbooks play a critical role in history education as they embody an intellectual project in the teaching of History. The essence of the intellectual project in this regard is how textbooks "*mediate thinking and the development of the intellect, while addressing affective issues*" (Morgan, 2011: 286). Morgan tabled a number of recommendations in which, amongst other things, she mentions the portrayal of historical events as complex and ambiguous and allowing students to apply what they learnt, and to "*consider how external, social processes of identity construction become internalised, which in turn determines how higher functions develop and how individuals affect society*" (291). Morgan believed that authors of History textbooks should be creative as well in the interpretation and application of the curriculum.

According to her, the processes of meaning-making in the interpretation and analysis of historical facts and images are an important component in the construction of knowledge and intellectual development of learners. Morgan (2011) observed that History as a school subject is an intellectual project serving as a microcosm for the understanding of broader complex matters during the process of the cognitive development of learners. In this regard, how learners learn and think about their historical positioning in the broader spectrum of world history, impacts on their mindset, behaviour and development as citizens.

In another study, Bertram and Wassermann (2015) conducted an overview of South African History textbooks used in schools and in institutions of higher learning between 1944 and 2015. They looked at how critical concepts of nationalism and race were projected in relation to prejudice, bias, ideology and symbols of representation. In their findings, they observed that during the 1970s and 1980s the History textbooks were static as they were dominated by the Afrikaner Nationalist historiography. There was very little space provided for critical engagement. The overview showed that the period between the 1990s and 2000s witnessed rapid growth of scholarly work in History textbooks. In their conclusion, Bertram and Wassermann (2015) asserted that the production of history is not only to ensure compliance with the curriculum; it is important to interrogate the sources of information used in the writing of the History textbooks. They argued that History textbooks are the ideological embodiment of "whose history is important" in shaping the development of the "ideal citizen". According to them, the content contained in the school textbooks since their conception and distribution is influenced by political and educational processes. They concluded that history carries strong official messages in terms of what the story of the nation should embody.

The observations made by Bertram and Wassermann (2015) highlighted, amongst other things, the importance of sources of information used in the production of History textbooks and the ideological school of thought embedded in the content as critical elements in the construction of History textbooks. In the South African context, one would assume that there is a policy guideline informing the selected service providers, publishers and authors in the identification and utilization of sources to be used in the production of History textbooks. Such a policy guideline would also provide guidance on what national school of thought should inform the History curriculum.

Maposa (2016) applied a Critical Discourse Analysis (CDA) methodology to analyse four contemporary South African History textbooks. The CDA applied by Maposa entailed three dimensions of description, interpretation and explanation (Fairclough, 1995). The analysis focused on the presentation of post-colonial history. According to Maposa, African beings are presented at multidimensional levels. The findings illustrated contestations on the description of Africanness. The textbooks, according to Maposa, were ambiguous in providing a consistent definition of who is an African.

Maposa concluded that *"learners of history should, through the textbooks, develop a consciousness that enables unity, renewal and development in a postcolonial condition"* (pg 22). Inasmuch as those in power influence the dominant discourse in History textbooks, ordinary citizens should make a contribution as well.

In another study, Natasha Robinson (2018) conducted fieldwork research focusing on four racially diverse Grade 9 History classes in Cape Town as part of her PhD work. Her findings showed that although learners may be knowledgeable about the subject, they could not link the historical events to how they shaped contemporary South African society. She believed that History should be taught in a way that empowers learners to address educational, social and political problems, with a strong sense of identity. Robinson asserted that History education should create a space of consciousness to enable the learners to understand and be able to address the social challenges facing the country. The learners should be able to see the interconnection between the past and the present realities. According to her, the shortcoming of History education is the emphasis on causes and consequences of historical events but failing to reflect on the implications and lasting impacts of those events in relation to poverty, racism and discrimination and how they have shaped contemporary South African societies. Students need to understand how historical events of the past have shaped the current structural socio-economic landscape of the present.

Robinson (2018) came to similar conclusions as Maposa (2016) by elevating the role of History from merely a school subject to that of triggering consciousness; an empowerment and educational tool to address social challenges. That history should create interconnectedness between past historical events and their implications for the current socio-economic complexities. In this regard, learners should be able to link and understand how the South African history of conquest pertaining to African dispossession of the land, displacement and dehumanization led to the current skewed ownership of land in South Africa. For instance, the South African Department of Rural Development and Land Reform's Land Audit Report of November 2017 showed that Whites owned 72% of the land, including farms and agricultural holdings, followed by Coloureds at 15%, Indians at 5%, Africans at 4%, 'other' at 3% and co-owners at 1%. History should be able to empower learners to create a link between the current socio-economic disparities such as huge imbalances to the historical events which occurred from the mid-1600s. Such historical consciousness would broaden their understanding that the current structural imbalance of the South African society came as a result of centuries of domination and subjugation.

In retrospect, the questions raised by Nicholls (2006) are linked to the observations made by Morgan (2011) which positions History textbooks as intellectual projects in the generation of knowledge and creative critical thinking. Furthermore, the critical issues noted by Nicholls (2006), Morgan (2011) and Robinson (2018) remind me of an incident when I was an undergraduate History student at the University of Fort Hare. One of our History lecturers, a white male of Dutch descent, presented the highly glorified perspective of European missionaries in Southern Africa in the nineteenth century. Amongst other things, he highlighted their role in building institutions of learning, and as mediators in times of war. I raised my hand and asked for clarity pertaining to the critical perspective of Bishop Sigqibo Dwane on the controversial role of missionaries in which he noted that *"the post- missionary Christianity in Africa with its links with colonialism, capitalism and the abstract proclamation of the Gospel, has created a deep cultural confusion and left a permanent scar on the souls of the African people."* He appeared puzzled and taken aback by my question. He said, *"Is that a question or a statement?"*

At the time if you were perceived as a constant source of irritation and nuisance by a lecturer based on the type of questions you raised in the lecture room, you were sure to fail the course. On the same note, there were lecturers in other departments who encouraged and appreciated critical interrogation of the content. Unfortunately, the History department at the time had a number of conservative lecturers whose perspective had to be treated and imbibed as the sole authoritative form of knowledge. So when the lecturer asked me whether that was a question or comment, what followed were a few seconds of a passive-subtle standoff as his response was a coded language of saying *"Do you really want to ask this question and thus put me in a corner? If you do so, you will suffer the consequences. If this is just a statement, I will continue with my lecture."* I realized that if I said it was a question, he would be humiliated and would therefore make sure that I pay the price. By saying *"or a statement"*, he was basically giving me an option to exit what he perceived to be an academic duel.

My reading of the peculiar situation was correct. I responded *"No Sir, it was just a statement."* He then proceeded with his presentation as if nothing had happened. We continued interacting cordially thereafter, because I appeared to have understood my place in the classroom. I knew that although at times I would develop an urge to engage by asking pertinent questions for clarity, I had to weigh what was more important: asking critical questions or mastering the knowledge and passing the subject. At the time, the goal was to pass the subject, complete the degree and proceed with my life. My circumstances did not grant me the luxury of embarking on critical engagement as part of the academic exercise expected in an institution of higher learning, especially in a subject such as History in the South African context. The inclusion of this anecdote of my encounters as a student of history is a form of evidence in order to add value to the historical narrative (Saller, 1980)

The incident is an illustration of my observations about the process of learning history in terms of whose knowledge is regarded as official. The critical reflections of Nicholls (2006), Morgan (2011) and Robinson (2018) on what ought to constitute the content of History textbooks and the pedagogical processes present food for thought on what can be done to enhance the value and meaning of History textbooks. This can assist to provide an intellectual space of consciousness, development and empowerment. What Nicholls (2006), Morgan (2011) and Robinson (2018) also attempted to illustrate is that we may have reasonably well-balanced textbooks, but the manner in which the content is presented is pivotal in the transmission and understanding of knowledge. They concluded that how the historical content is approached, who is teaching the history, to which group of students, and for what purpose, are all critical elements of the process.

What we have demonstrated so far is the realization that History textbooks are a highly contested intellectual space in terms of whose history is important in shaping the cognitive development of learners (Karpov, 2005) and in the development of a particular consciousness in their conceptualisation of the past and present (Bertram

& Wassermann, 2015; Maposa, 2016). Morgan (2011) made bold assertions on how school History textbooks have the power to shape the mindset and behaviour of learners in the construction of knowledge and cognitive development. Robinson (2018) took the argument further by noting that school History textbooks should enable learners to create a connection in terms of how the events of the past impact on current socio-economic realities. Next, we will conduct a critical interrogation of subjective narratives from a position of privilege.

3. Contested Narratives in South African History Textbooks: Dominant Voices, Content Coverage, Key Characters and Major Events

Nicholls (2003) utilises various forms of analysis such as historiographical analysis, visual analysis, question analysis, critical analysis, structural analysis and semiotic analysis. In addition, Pingel (2010) provides various forms of analytical methods such as hermeneutics analysis, linguistic analysis and discourse analysis.

The focus on the critical analysis of South African History textbooks is centred on the volume of coverage of South African and African history compared to world history as well as what aspects of South African history are covered. Also, to what extent the South African history between the seventeenth century and twentieth century portrayed the accounts of the key role players at the time. Further, to establish the extent of coverage of the South African precolonial history. For purposes of this exercise one will conduct a critical examination of the official South African History textbooks. The analytical approach will look at whose voices and accounts are packaged in the content contained in official South African History textbooks; what is the extent and the nature of the content coverage is, how the key characters are characterised and which major historical events are covered or omitted. These aspects are critical in enabling one to understand the nature of the content contained in the History textbooks.

Morgan (2011) made the crucial observation that History textbooks are an important domain in which socio-cultural knowledge is transmitted in order to develop a particular mindset. Similarly, Bertram and Wassermann (2015) asserted that History textbooks embody the ideological pillars of "whose history is important" in shaping the intellectual development of the envisaged citizens. That is why it is deemed imperative for the purposes of this book to conduct a critical interrogation of the current South African History textbooks in particular.

3.1 Whose Knowledge Matters?

In the context of the highly diverse South African society, it matters whose dominant voices are accommodated in the construction of history content. It matters whether the packaging of the History textbook is a domain of the few dominant authors or a terrain which provides space for authors from diverse backgrounds considering the complexity of history and the composition of different nationalities. When such a vital educational space, meant to influence the body of knowledge, the understanding of our history and the cognitive development of SA learners, is allowed to be the domain of a few selected voices over a long period of time, this poses a serious challenge in terms of whose history is being taught.

For the purposes of this book, official History textbooks used from Grade 8 to Grade 12 were identified that are still used in 2022 as part of the national curriculum of the South African Department of Basic Education. Table 1.1 provides a list of the official History textbooks as well as information about the authors, the publishers and the period in which they were in circulation.

The dominant authors in these text books are B. Johanneson, the co-author in four textbooks for Grades 8, 9, 10 and 11; M. Fernandez, who co-authored textbooks for Grades 10, 11 and 12; M. Friedman, the co-author of textbooks for Grades 9 and 11; P. Ranby, who co-authored textbooks for Grades 8 and 9; and Y.Seleti, the co-author of textbooks for Grades 10 and 12. The fact that from Grade Eight to Grade Twelve , the History textbooks are written by the same authors, from one publishing company, is problematic, because it suggests a monopoly on what is contained in the national curriculum. Such a monopoly is not reflective of the diverse South African populations and therefore does not provide different perspectives on the content.

Table 5.1:　　Current High School History Textbooks

Title	Authors	Publication Date	Publisher
Focus on Social Sciences Grade 8	P. Randy, E. Potenza & B. Johanneson	2006 and 2008	Maskew Miller Longman
Focus on Social Sciences Grade 9	P. Randy, B. Johanneson & M. Friedman	2006 and 2010	Maskew Miller Longman
Focus History Grade 10	B. Johanneson, M. Fernandez, B. Roberts, M. Jacobs & Y.Seleti	2011 and 2012	Maskew Miller Longman
Focus History Grade 11	M. Fernandez, M. Friedman, M. Jacobs, B. Johanneson & J. Wesson	2012 and 2013	Maskew Miller Longman
Focus History Grade12	M. Fernandez, L. Wills, P. McMahon, S. Pienaar, Y.Seleti & M. Jacobs	2013	Maskew Miller Longman

Surely there are other capable academics and writers who, given an opportunity, would have contributed diverse perspectives in the packaging and presentation of historical content? The fact that some of these authors have been allowed to be dominant voices since 2006 is unacceptable.

3.2   Anomaly of Foreign Content

In *The History Focus Grade 10* (Johanneson, Fernandez, Roberts, Jacobs & Yeleti, 2012), about 50% of the book provides a comprehensive history of the European conquest, the French Revolution and world powers in the 14th and 15th centuries. The coverage of South African History is presented in small fragmented portions, descriptive list of nationalities and the history of conquest by the Dutch and the British in Southern Africa. The book gives the impression that both the world and the Southern African history in the past five centuries revolved around the rise and the consolidation of the European conquest. The illustrious history of the great civilizations and formidable kingdoms that existed in Africa in pre-colonial period has not been properly covered.

The presentation of South African history is characterised by a shallow and superficial list of kingdoms that appear to have existed in the distant past, with less historical significance and contextual interconnectedness between the kingdoms. Despite the fact that there are extensive primary sources of information available on the indigenous history of South Africa, it occupies a very small portion of the Grade 10 textbook.

In terms of how far back the current History textbooks go in covering South African history, only the *History Focus Grade 10* goes as far back as 1750. There is no account of South African history and civilizations that existed in the pre-colonial period. No effort has been done to cover the comprehensive history of the Khoe and San people in the textbooks from Grade Eight to Grade Twelve. The history of the Khoe and San during the period of Dutch colonialism and the systematic extermination of the indigenous groups between the mid-1600s and the beginning of the 1800s has been omitted. Probably it was omitted because of the uneasiness to narrate how the Dutch settlers subjected the Khoe and San to systematic dispossession, displacement, dehumanization and commodification. The period was so brutal that there were institutionalized commandos created and financed to carry out the systematic annihilation of the Khoe and San people.

In essence, the coverage of South African history is characterised by superficial, unbalanced and Eurocentric narrative. The glaring omissions of the history and the demise of the Khoe and San people is worrisome considering the fact that they occupy a unique place in the history of South Africa as the indigenous inhabitants of the rich beautiful land. In the context of the British conquest of the Cape Colony, some of the defining events, such as the ethnic cleansing of amaXhosa in 1811–1812 have been omitted.

Table 5.2: Content coverage in the form of major themes covered in Grade 8 to Grade 12 South African History Textbooks

Textbook	Topic
Focus on Social Sciences Grade Eight (8)	• French Revolution (*16 pages*) • Industrialization (*28 pages*) • British Conquest and Resistance (*26 pages*) • Conquest of Africa (*26 pages*) • Ideas and Technologies (*18 pages*)
Focus on Social Sciences Grade Nine (9)	• German Human Rights Issues in the 1940s (*24 pages*) • World Human Rights Issues after World War Two (*12 pages*) • Apartheid in South Africa (*42 pages*) • Nuclear Age & Cold War (*18 pages*) • Issues of our time (*21 pages*)

Textbook	Topic
Focus History Grade Ten (10)	• World Around 1600 (*26 pages*) • European Conquest Between 15th and 18th Centuries (*36 pages*) • French Revolution (52 pages) • South Africa transformation after 1750 (*42 pages*) • Colonial Expansion After 1750 (*92 pages*) • South African War (*48 pages*)
Focus History Grade Eleven (11)	• Communist Russia,1900–1940 (84 pages) • Capitalism in the USA 1900–1940 (50 pages) • Ideas of Race in the late 19th & 20th Century (58 pages) • Nationalism: South Africa, the Middle East and Africa (110 pages) • Apartheid South Africa, 1940s–1960s (62 pages)
Focus History Grade Twelve (12)	• Cold War (74 pages) • Independent Africa (74 pages) • South African Civil Resistance in 1950s to 1980(115 pages) • Coming to democracy in South Africa and the past (63 pages) • End of the Cold War (56 pages)

The Grade Eight and Nine Social Sciences textbooks are structured in such a way that they cover both the Geography and History components equally. For purposes of this exercise, we are focusing only on the History section of each book.

The History section of the Grade Eight textbook is essentially about the conquest of both South Africa and the continent at large and what happened in France. From such a basic level, one would have expected the textbook to cover the history of African civilization, such as the building of the Pyramids, the era of the great Kingdom of Mapungubwe, and many other topics. Instead, it provides a deliberately distorted perspective, as if the history of Africans started with colonialism. Grade Eight learners are influenced to believe that the continent had no history prior to the arrival of Europeans in Africa. They are denied the opportunity to learn about the rich Africa history and how the African forebears contributed to some of the greatest eras of civilization in Africa.

In reference to the Grade Nine textbook, there is coverage of contemporary South African history with reference to Apartheid. However, the book omits the historical fact that Apartheid did not happen in isolation. There were world powers who supported it in the context of the Cold War, hence after the fall of the Union of Soviet Socialist Republics (USSR), the great political dispensation was followed by the de-escalation of some of the longest civil wars in Africa, the unification of Germany and the intensification of the negotiations between the National Party and the African National Congress in South Africa.

The section "issues of our time" has a sub-section titled "the effects of globalisation on Africa." In this regard, one would have expected the book to focus on the effects of colonialism in Africa and the continuation of exploitation of the continent. Also, it is interesting that the authors chose to talk about the genocide in Rwanda, while they ignored the cases of genocide in Namibia carried out by the Germans, the systematic annihilation of the Khoe and San people in the period between the mid-1650s and late 1800s, and the ethnic cleansing of amaXhosa in 1811-1812. Probably it is because the the leading authors are of European descent, who found it convenient to write about African genocide committed by Africans on other Africans. None of the textbooks, from Grade Eight to Grade Twelve, cover the genocides committed by Europeans on Africans. This echoes the earlier concern raised that the national curriculum of the school History textbooks cannot be left in the hands of a few authors, no matter what reasons have been provided to justify such an anomaly and monopoly to determine the content of the history textbooks.

Next, in the Grade 10 textbook, the first theme "The world around 1600" has two chapters on Asian Empires, a chapter on European societies between 1300 and 1600 and one chapter on the African Songhai Empire. The question is: why did the authors not provide two Chapters on the African Empire instead of two chapters on Asian empires? Was it because there was no available information or was African history perceived to be less significant than non-African history? Ordinarily, one would expect that African history deserves more coverage, especially for South African students, who are part of the African continent.

One wonders what the rationale was for dedicating 52 pages to the French Revolution in Grade Ten, when the learners had already studied the French Revolution in Grade Eight. Why was it necessary for it to be repeated? What value did it add for South Africa learners? Why did the authors not choose the events and the leading figures in the wars of resistance against colonialism in Africa? Grade Eight African learners are exposed to very little information about their own history and about their forebears in the textbooks. To a large extent, the textbooks contain content about events in Europe and the Europeans in Africa. If one looks at the theme "South African War", this is about the war between the Dutch and the British, following the discovery of minerals in South Africa. Why did the authors omit the War of Mlanjeni the second-longest war fought in Southern Africa in the mid-1800s, in the then Cape Colony in the triangle between Gqeberha, Graaf Reinet and Gcuwa? This was an important war in the history of African resistance against European domination in Southern Africa, in which the African royal leadership led united African groups against the British and the Dutch forces for over three years of deadly engagement.

The Grade Eleven textbooks cover a repeat of the Apartheid theme in 62 pages which had been covered in 42 pages of the Grade 9 History textbooks. The sub-topics covered in both instances overlap quite significantly. Why are such topics repeated as if there are no other important historical events in South African history? Under the sub-theme "Ideas of Race in the late 19th & 20th Century", Chapter Three presents graphic images of how the Nazi Germans implemented the race theories against non-Europeans in Germany. Was it necessary to go into such great detail? In what ways does it empower the learners? What value and whose interests does the section serve in the South African context?

In conclusion, the coverage of history in the South African History textbooks is largely centred on European content, to a point that many of the themes are repeated in different grades. The coverage of both South African and African history is superficial, highly selective and limited.

3.3   Portrayal of Key Characters

Chapter Seven of the Grade Eight history textbook *Focus on Social Sciences* (Ranby, Potenza & Johanneson, 2008), which focuses on industrialisation, portrays the British imperialist Cecil John Rhodes as an innovative philanthropist. *"After a disagreement over who controlled the diamond fields, Britain took them over in 1872"* (Ranby, Potenza & Johanneson, 2008:144). This creates a false impression of what actually happened because after the discovery of diamonds, the British were even more determined to exert their power as an extension of their conquest in South Africa, especially in key strategic regions with minerals.

The statement that *"His policy was equal rights for every civilised man south of the Zambezi"* (Ranby, Potenza & Johanneson 2008:145) is contrary to a later statement that *"Rhodes changed the law of the Cape to allow the vote only to those who owned property worth 75 pounds a year"* (Ranby, Potenza & Johanneson 2008:145).

Furthermore, the reference to *"every civilized man"* is a loaded one in the context of the era of conquest in which the standard of civilisation was Anglicisation to the norms and belief systems of the British colonial establishment.

On page 145, the book shows a portrait of King Lobengula suggesting that he was a fly caught by Cecil Rhodes the Chameleon. The South African Grade Eight history pupils are brainwashed with powerful symbolism of European superiority and African inferiority. One cannot believe that

Eurocentric history is perpetuated in the 21ˢᵗ Century under our watch.

The claim that *"Africans wanted to work for cash wages to get guns or farming implements, or to earn money to pay the traditional bride price or lobola"* (Ranby, Potenza & Johanneson, 2008:146) is contrary to the earlier statement that when Rhodes was the Prime Minister of the Cape, he introduced the Glen Grey Act of 1894, which compelled Africans to become commodities of cheap labour in the mines. The authors either did not apply their minds when making such a reductionist and insensitive statement, or deliberately trivialised the plight of African people. What the authors deliberately omitted is that Africans were dispossessed, displaced, dehumanized and commodified, and they were subjected to compulsory labour to serve the imperial interests in Southern Africa. Such an overt distortion of history in the 21ˢᵗ Century is incomprehensible. It is tantamount to arrogance and disrespect of the real history of the African people.

In the next section of the same book, on page 147, the authors claim that working in the mines was glorified as a form of higher status in the African communities. There is a glorification of the inhuman forced migrant labour system, which destroyed the essence of African families.

3.4   The Extent of Distortions and Omissions

The historical sociological posture is based on the premise that the dominant historical narratives had a significant impact in shaping the cognitive understanding and theoretical conceptualisation of our distorted history. The tragedy of decades of institutionalized history of conquest is that it created the socialisation of Africans as inferior beings in relation to Europeans, who were projected as heroic conquerors and saviours of the continent. We cannot underestimate the extent of the deep-seated psychological and the sociological scars and how the official dominant narrative of a distorted history impacted negatively on the African learners in particular. The African learners are made to believe that their ancestors were half-tamed savages with no potential to think, whilst Europeans are often portrayed as saviours of the continent.

The reality that the Europeans arrived on the shores of this continent with a clear objective to conquer, exterminate and grab the land, livestock and resources to the catastrophic detriment of Africans, is glossed over with dominant narratives of missionaries and white settlers who brought civilization to the continent. The Africans are often portrayed as victims of their own limitations in the form of the highly-glorified narrative of Nongqawuse. In actual fact the previous Chapter demonstrated that Nongqawuse was a euphemism for the colonial biological weapon of mass destruction, which was the cattle lung sickness meant to destroy the productive capability of amaXhosa. The colonial establishment and white settlers resented amaXhosa for their heroic resistance, especially after the devastating war of Mlanjeni between 1850 and 1853.

The institutionalised colonial narrative of a history centred on the false doctrine of European superiority and imagined African inferiority was perpetuated for decades under the guise of Euro-centric academic knowledge, taught in schools, colleges and universities. One way or another, African children and students were made to imbibe a history curriculum meant to make them think that they were inferior and to act as such, whilst the Europeans continued to entrench themselves as the superior race in full ownership of the land and the resources.

The tragic impact of how the institutionalised distorted history shaped the cognitive nature, the socialisation and the identity of African people up to the present societies is undeniable. That is why renowned academics such as the late Professor Mbulelo Mzamane advocated the importance of setting up systems to embark on a cognitive decolonization process. The reason why the official history is not at the top of our agenda as Africans is because of the impact of its defeatist approach on our psyche.

At the beginning of the 20th Century, pioneers of African intellectualism such as S.E.K Mqhayi attempted to write history from the African perspective, shaped by their history, experiences and reflections of their world. Unfortunately, the colonial establishment, which possessed the means of publication of knowledge, regulated the African narratives and discarded any writing perceived to be critical of the colonial regime. The lamentable role played by Reverend Robert Henry Wishart Shepherd who was of Scottish descent, as a gatekeeper of knowledge production at the Lovedale Press in Alice is indicative of the draconian colonial policies, which stifled the generation of African knowledge. Besides other unknown cases, S.E.K. Mqhayi lost three valuable manuscripts which were never published. Generations were denied the opportunity to learn about what actually happened without relying on fragmented pieces of a subjective colonial narrative.

There are defining historical events in the context of African wars of resistance against the European encroachment which are either deliberately omitted, glossed over or distorted from the dominant Euro- centric narrative about the interactions between the Africans and the Europeans between 1652 and 1879.

As it has been mentioned in the previous chapters, one would like to reiterate that the, the painful history of the Dutch systematic institutionalized extermination of the Khoe and San at an industrial scale which occurred over a period of 150 years, has been omitted from the South African history textbooks. Next, the first British ethnic cleansing of amaXhosa that was executed in 1811 -1812 between Nxuba and Xelexwa Rivers is almost the forgotten history. Also, the brutal murder of King Hintsa is part of our history that requires the respect and recognition it deserves. The defining war of Mlanjeni from 1850 to 1853 had been marginalised. Instead, the Anglo-Boer is regarded as the great South African war. The story of Nongqawuse requires proper re-examination in order to place it into proper perspectives in the context of the other related events which occurred at the time.

The reconceptualisation of the Frontier Wars in the chapter two is anchored on the premise that calling the African wars of resistance *Frontier Wars* is a classic example of the Eurocentric narrative, which implies that these wars were fought over the contestation of borders, thus placing the white settlers and the colonial establishment on the same setting as the Africans who owned the land. This is a blatant and arrogant distortion of history. Firstly, these wars were not fought over border disputes. For instance, when Governor Cradock and Colonel Graham launched an unprovoked attack on amaXhosa in the ethnic cleansing of 1811 to 1812, this was not a contestation of a border but a direct and premeditated colonial intention to kill, displace and dispossess Africans.

Secondly, amaXhosa would rarely declare war against the colonialists. In most cases, the colonial establishment would embark on an unprovoked war of displacement with the intention of occupying a particular piece of land and amass the livestock in the process. In April 1829, General Henry Somerset and Colonel Andries Stockenström launched a military onslaught with the clear intention of removing Prince Maqoma and his people amaJingqi from the Kat River, currently known as KwamaQoma, because the white settlers wanted to occupy what was seen as rich land with easy access to water. In essence, the Africans were forced into these dreadful wars with European, hence they had no option but to fight back in order to resist the calamitous colonial encroachment. Therefore, in the context of this section, it is more appropriate to redefine these wars as Wars of Resistance.

If one reads some of the accounts of white settler historical narratives, they often portray depressing accounts about Africans as half-tamed savages, who were wasteful and self-destructive, thus presenting a deceitful justification for their conquest and extermination. It requires strong mental resilience to sift through the fractured narrative, cloaked under the guise of academic knowledge. Sifting through the fragmented history of Africa in the past 500 years that is contained in many history books is often an emotionally draining exercise for an African reader, because there are few documented moments of celebrated heroism except a series of harrowing accounts presented as the supposed official history of Africans.

Most written accounts of SA history are characterised by distressing accounts of decades of institutionalized enslavement of Africans as instrumental commodities of capitalism for the enrichment of Europeans. These accounts are followed by the protracted wars of African resistance against the European conquest. Despite the subsequent period of political liberation of the continent, the resources of Africa are still owned, managed and utilized by foreign powers, as Africans are navigating the possibilities of total emancipation and ownership of their land and the means of production.

To those who aspire to read, study and write about the history of the continent, where do they start? What sort of inspiration can one obtain to master the art of writing objective history from the plethora of cynical narratives that leave the reader with a negative and defeatist impression? Critical comparative analysis over a spectrum of diverse primary and secondary sources is imperative in order to identify the historical moments of inspiration and heroism and, more importantly, to develop a broader analytical understanding of what actually happened.

Matoti (1990) acknowledged that bias, prejudice, omission and commission are dominant features that have often emerged from research based on textbook analysis. Issues of accuracy and fairness in the presentation of historical events are often ignored in pursuit of particular interests.

Having noted that, it remains a challenge to compile a precise reconstruction of early South African history because of the compromised nature of available primary sources of information. The challenge is further compounded by concerns about deliberate distortions and omissions of vital information as well as the impact of deep-seated subjective narratives. Unfortunately, we have limited means to know and to understand what actually happened in the past. Peires (1981) acknowledges that one of the greatest challenges in attempting to provide precise accounts of what happened in the past is that the "more distant the event, the harder it is to grasp" due to the quality and the reliability of original sources of information.

4. Taking a Pause

The fact that the packaging of the historical content of South African History textbooks has continued to be dominated by a few authors over a long period is an anomaly that has to be rectified. The fact that the dominant authors of these history textbooks are people of European descent has impacted negatively in shaping the content. The dominance of the highly celebrated content of European conquest in South African history is bound to negatively influence the cognitive, intellectual development of leaners and thus impact negatively on the construction of their identities.

The minimalising of both South African and African history, whilst providing substantial detail of European history, is not accidental. This is a deliberate distortion of history that is still happening in the 21st Century, under our watch as ordinary South Africans, academics and practitioners of knowledge production.

The glaring omissions from the official school History textbooks for Grade Eight to Grade Twelve is very concerning. African accounts for some of the greatest civilizations such as the construction of the Pyramids by Africans, the notable Kingdoms and Empires of Africa such as the Kingdom of Axum in Ethiopia, Kingdom of Wagadu in Ghana, Kingdom of Mali, Songhai Empire (covered in the textbooks), Kingdom of Zimbabwe, Kingdom of Mutapa in Southern Africa, Kingdom of Congo and the Benin Empire.

Considering the impact of our distorted history, we cannot deny its consequences in the socialisation of Africans as a conquered nation, often portrayed as having contributed nothing to world civilisation. Therefore, it is of paramount importance to consider revisiting the impact and symbolism created by colonial names. Firstly, certain colonial names bestowed in honour of particular individuals who caused so much pain and horror to the African people should be reconsidered for replacement as a form of atonement, healing and recognition of our painful history. It remains an anomaly that names associated with individuals known of the worst inhuman brutality are still in use in South Africa and other parts of the world. Secondly, the current content of official knowledge in South African history should be considered for review in order to reflect balanced narratives of what actually happened in the past. Continuing to teach such history is tantamount to the disregard of the national aspirations and fundamental pillars of nation building. Lastly, there should be special efforts conducted to unpack and celebrate African languages, locally produced innovations of culture, heritage and history. In conclusion, excellent education is not enough if we do not teach learners the essence of their heritage and history.

5. Conclusion

One of the fundamental aspects examined in chapter one was the critical interrogation of the natural disposition of amaXhosa and what enabled them to fight one hundred years wars in the triangle. The critical examination revealed that they were led by visionary generations of decisive royal leaders who were far ahead of their time in the realization of the imperatives of nation-building and sustainability through integration of the defeated nations and maintenance of alliances with formidable neighbouring kingdoms. What enabled them to sustain the deadly wars was their ability of adaptability in the face of an enemy with superior firepower, leveraged on their productive capabilities and dictated the rules of military engagements by taking advantage of their rugged terrains. The royal aristocracy remained the centre that kept the nation together, hence amaXhosa were able to withstand the existential threats of foreign domination.

King Hintsa emerged as the epitome of the African royal aristocracy whose extraordinary aura and unique mantra of leadership influence reignited amaXhosa to avenge his unceremonious departure. The British colonial leadership and the military commanders were certain that the fall of the supreme royal aristocrat of amaXhosa on the waters of Nqabarha River will break the backbone of resistance. To their shock, the British army was overstretched beyond its capabilities on the agonising war fought on the mountains of Mathole. The false declaration of victory by Sir Benjamin D'urban was an act of desperation to accept the humiliating defeat by Prince Maqoma. The victory in the battlefield was the demonstration of the collective resolve of amaXhosa.

The agonising War of Mlanjeni (1850-1853) led by the decisive royal leadership was a defining moment where African people drew a line on the sand by taking a collective stand against the British encroachment in Southern Africa. Hence it remained the longest and the deadliest conflict in the history of wars of resistance in Africa. Some of the lessons learnt from the War of Mlanjeni was the collective will to take a stand and the ability to adapt the military strategies in the face of the deadly British firepower. As they continued fighting the British army over the decades they improved their strategies as they learnt lessons and gained ascendency in the battlefields. Chapter two mentions that they avoided facing the British army on open terrains, operated in small agile regiments to launch surprise targeted ambushes, rotated their army in order to sustain the war and deployed informers in strategic positions to monitor enemy movements.

The critical re-examination of the dominant distorted narrative of Nongqawuse phenomenon in the wider context of the wars of resistance between amaXhosa and the British establishment was an attempt to provide new African perspective. The critical review indicated that the primary objective of the colonial constructed skewed compartmentalised narrative of Nongqawuse was to isolate it from the context of the sequential interconnected events that occurred prior and during the Nongqawuse period. At the core of the relentless wars of resistance was the realization that the ownership of fertile land and thousands of cattle were the foundations of productive capabilities which enabled amaXhosa to sustain the protracted wars. The destruction of the fundamental pillars of resistance became an absolute necessity after the devastating War of Mlanjeni which drained the resources of the British Empire. The landing of the highly contagious European cattle lung sickness which decimated about 80% of the cattle of amaXhosa was not an accidental phenomenon. This was a continuation of the war in the form of a biological weapon which was hidden under the highly celebrated narrative of Nongqawuse that was meant to portray amaXhosa as victims of their own creation.

In conclusion, the contribution of this book to the new African perspective is anchored on some of the bold assertions made pertaining to the systems of conquest and continued entrenchment of the distorted narrative. Some of the hidden triggers of the wars of resistance was the controversial role of Reverend John Ayliff the Wesleyan Missionary, who emerged as the key enabler of the British conquest in the context of the fall of King Hintsa and the exodus of amaMfengu from Gcuwa to Ngqushwa in May 1835. The book offered the recontextualization of what used to be defined as Frontier Wars in the context of the wars of resistance, dispossession, displacement and dehumanization of Africans. It presented the compelling comprehensive examination of the War of Mlanjeni in a way that has never been done before making use of primary sources of the eye witness accounts. Finally, the critical review of the distorted Nongqawuse phenomenon and the comprehensive re-examination of the South African secondary school history textbooks are attempts towards the decolonization of the South African historiography.

Bibliography

Adhikari, M. 2010. *A total Extinction Confidently Hope for : The Destruction of Cape San Society Under Dutch Colonial Rule, 1700-1795. Journal of Genocide Research* (2010), 12 (1-2) March-June, 19-44. https://doi.org/10.1080/14623528.20 10.508274

Advertiser (quoted in *Cape Frontier Times*, Graham's Town, March 22, 1853.)

Ayliff, J. & Whiteside, J. 1912. *History of Abambo (Fingos).* Butterworth: Gazette Printers.

Alexander, J.E. 1837. *Narrative of a Voyage of Observation Among the Colonies of Western Africa in the Flagship Thalia and of a Campaign in Kaffirland on the Staff of the in Chief in 1835.* London: Henry Colburn Publisher.

Andreas, C.B. 2005. *The Spread and Impact of the Lung sickness Epizootic of 1853-57 in the Cape Colony and the Xhosa Chiefdoms.* South African Historical Journal, 53 (2005),50-72. https://doi.org/10.1080/02582470509464889

Barrow, J. 1801. *An Account of Travels into the Interior of Southern Africa in the years 1797 and 1798: Including Cursory Observations on the Geology and Geography of the Southern Part of the Continent, the Natural History of Such Objects as Occurred in the Animal, Vegetable and Mineral Kingdom, and Sketches of the Physical and Moral Character of the Various Tribes of Inhabitants Surrounding the Settlement of the Cape of Good Hope.* London: A. Strahan Printers. https://doi.org/10.5962/bhl.title.101950

Bergh, J.S. & Visagie, J.C. 1985. *The Eastern Cape Frontier Zone, 1660-1980. A Cartographic Guide for Historical Research.* Durban: A.G. Oberholster.

Bertram, C. & Wasserman, J. 2015. *South African History Textbook Research – Review of the Scholarly Literature. Yesterday and Today,* Volume No 14, December 2015. https://doi.org/10.17159/2223-0386/2015/nl4a7

Bezdrob, A.M.D. 2011. Winnie Mandela: A Life. Johannesburg: Penguin Random House South Africa.

Binckes, R. 2013. *The Great Trek. Escape from the British Rule: The Boer Exodus from the Cape Colony, 1836. 30.* Wynberg: South Publishers (Pty) Ltd.

Brinton, W. 1977. *History of the British Regiments in South Africa 1795 -1895.* Department of Extra-Mural Studies. Cape Town: University of Cape Town.

Campbell, J. 1815. *Travels in South Africa. London:* Black and Parry Publisher.

Cape Frontier Times, Graham's Town, April 5, 1853.

Cape Frontier Times, Graham's Town, May 10, 1853.

Cradock-Graham, N.D.RCC, VIII, p. 160. *Private communications from Graham, 2 Jan. 1812, RCC, VIII, p 237.*

Coetzee, C. 2000. *The Unfortified Military Villages of Sir Harry Smith 1848-1850.* Edited and revised by Tony Westby-Nunn. Cape Town: Westby Nunn Publishers.

Coetzee, C. & Westby-Nunn, T. 2019. *Forts of the Eastern Cape & Sir Harry Smith's Fortified Military Villages.* Cape Town: Westby Nunn Publishers.

Cory, G.E. 1919. *The Rise of South Africa. A History of the Origin of South African Colonisation and of its Development Towards the East From the Earliest Times to 1857. Volume III. 1834-1838.* London: Longmans, Green and Co LTD.

Cory, G.E. 1926. *The Rise of South Africa. A History of the Origin of South African Colonisation and of its Development Towards the East From the Earliest Times to 1857. Volume IV. 1838-1846.* London: Longmans, Green and Co LTD.

Cory, G.E. 1930. *The Rise of South Africa. A History of the Origin of South African Colonisation and of its Development Towards the East From the Earliest Times to 1857. Volume V. 1847-1853.* London: Longmans, Green and Co LTD.

Crais, C.C. 1992. *The Making of the Colonial Order White Supremacy and Black Resistance in the Eastern Cape, 1770 –1865.* Johannesburg: Witwatersrand University Press.

Davenport, T.R.H. 1988. *South Africa: A Modern History.* Bergvlei: Southern Book Publishers.

Dekker, N. 2016. *Maqoma's Last War the Sinking of the Birkenhead.* Kuilsriver: Amava Heritage Publishing Pty Ltd.

De Villiers, J. 2003. Colonel John Graham of Fintry and the Fourth Cape Eastern Frontier War, 1811-1812. South African Journal of Military Studies Vol.31 No.2. https://doi.org/10.5787/31-2-150

Fairclough, N. 2010. *Critical Discourse Analysis. The Critical Study of Language. London:* Taylor & Francis Ltd.

Fernandez, M., Friedman, M., Jacobs, M., Johanneson, B. & Wesson, J. 2012. *History Focus Grade 11.* Second Impression 2013. Cape Town: Maskew Miller Longman (Pty) Ltd.

Fernandez, M., Wills, L., McMahon, P., Pienaar, S., Seleti, Y. & Jacobs, M. 2013. *History Focus Grade 12.* Cape Town: Maskew Miller Longman (Pty) Ltd.

Graham's Town Journal, January 11, 1853.

Graham's Town Journal, February 20, 1835.

Graham's Town Journal, April 16, 1853.

Graham's Town Journal, April 30, 1853

Graham's Town Journal, June 12, 1835.

The Guardian, Manchester, February 1852.

Johanneson, B., Fernandez, M., Roberts, B., Jacobs, M. & Seleti, Y. 2011. *History Focus Grade 10.* Third Impression 2012. Cape Town: Maskew Miller Longman (Pty) Ltd.

Jordan, A.C. 1940. *Ingqumbo Yeminyanya.* Alice: Lovedale Press.

Karpov, Y. 2005. *The Neo-Vygotskian Approach to Child Development.* Cambridge: Cambridge University Press. https://doi.org/10.1017/CBO9781316036532

King, W.R. 1855. *Campaigning in Kaffirland or Scenes and Adventures in the Kaffir War of 1851–1852* (Second Edition) London: Sanders and Otley, Conduit Street

Lalu, P. 2009. *The Deaths of Hintsa – Post Apartheid South Africa and the shape of recurring pasts.* Cape Town: Human Science Research Council Press.

Landau, S.P. 2010. *Popular Politics in the History of South Africa, 1400–1948.* Cambridge: Cambridge University Press. https://doi.org/10.1017/CBO9780511750984

Legassick, M. 2010. *The Struggle for the Eastern Cape 1800 – 1854.* Democracy in Africa Vol 1. Johannesburg: KMM Review Publishing.

Le Vaillant, F. 1790. *Travels into the interior parts of Africa : by the way of the Cape of Good Hope in the years 1780, 81, 82, 83, 84, and 85.* London: Printed for G.G.J. and J. Robinson. https://doi.org/10.5962/bhl.title.101583

Majeke, N. 1952. *The Role of the Missionaries in Conquest.* Society of Young Africa. Johannesburg: Published by African People's Democratic Union of Southern Africa. *(Author's original name Dora Taylor).*

Maposa, M. 2016. *The Construction of the African Being in South African History Textbooks. Journal of Education*, No.65, 2016. https://doi.org/10.17159/i65a01

McKay, J. 1871. *Reminiscences of the last Kafir War.* Grahamstown: Glanville and Co, High-Street.

Meintjes, J. 1971. *Sandile the fall of the Xhosa Nation.* Natal: TV Bulpin Publishers.

Mellet, P.T. 2020. *The Lie of 1652.* Cape Town: Tafelberg.

Milton, J. 1983. *The Edges of War: A History of Frontier Wars (1702 -1878).* Cape Town: Juta & Co, Ltd.

Mnguni, "Hosea Jaffe" 1952. *Three Hundred Years.* Unity Movement History Series. Cape Town: New Era Fellowship Publisher.

Mqhayi, S.E.K. 1914. *Ityala Lamawele*. Alice: Lovedale Press
  Publisher.

Mostert, N. 1992. *FRONTIERS The Epic of South Africa's Creation And
  The Tragedy of the Xhosa People*. New York: Alfred A. Knopf.

Mutwa, 1966. *Africa is My Witness*. Johannesburg: Blue Crane Books

Nicholls, B. M., Charton, N.C. & Knowling, M. 1998. *The Diary of
  Robert John Mullins 1833 – 1913*. Grahamstown: Rhodes
  University, Department of History.

Nicholls, J. 2003. *Methods in school textbook research. International
  Journal of Historical Learning, Teaching and Research*, Vol. 3,
  No 2. https://doi.org/10.18546/HERJ.03.2.02

Nicholls, J 2005. *The Philosophical Underpinnings of Textbook
  Research.* Paradigm Journal of the textbook Colloquium, 3
  (1), pp. 25–35.

Nicholls, J. 2006. *Are Students Expected to Critical Engage
  with Textbooks Perspectives of the Second World War?
  A* Comparative and International Study. *Research in
  Comparative and International Education*, Vol, 1,Issue
  No.1,2006. https://doi.org/10.2304/rcie.2006.1.1.5

Ndletyana, M. 2008. (Ed.) *African Intellectuals in 19th and early 20th
  century*. East London: Commissioned and funded by the
  Amathole District Municipality and National Heritage
  Commission.

Nyamende, A. 2010. *The Conception and Application of Justice in
  S.E.K. Mqhayi's Ityala Lamawele. Tydskrif. letterkunde.*
  Vol.47 No.2 Pretoria Jan. 2010. https://doi.org/10.4314/tvl.
  v47i2.60621

Offenburger, A. 2009. *The Xhosa Cattle-Killing Movement in History
  and Literature. History Compass*. Volume 7, Issue 6/p 1428–
  1443. https://doi.org/10.1111/j.1478-0542.2009.00637.x

Omer-Cooper, J.D. 1987. *History of Southern Africa*. Claremont:
  David Philip Publisher (Pty) Ltd.

Owen, D.R. 1994. *Ubukhosi Neenkokeli : A Directory of Eastern Cape Black Leaders, From C.1700 To 1990. Grahamstown:* Albany Museum New History Series.

Patin, E., Lopez, M., Grollemund, R., Verdu, P., Harmant, C., Quach, H., Laval, G., Perry, G.H., Barreiro, L.B, Froment, A., Heyer, E., Massougbodji, A., Fortes-Lima, C., Migot-Nabias, F., Bellis, G., Dugoujon, J.M., Pereira, J.B., Fernandes, V., Pereira, L, Van der Veen, L., Mouguiama-Daouda, P., Bustamante, C.D., Hombert, J. & Quintana-Murci, L. (2017). *Dispersals and Genetic Adaptation of Bantu-speaking Populations in Africa and North America. Science,* May 5, 2017. https://doi.org/10.1126/science.aal1988

Peires, J.B. 1981. *The House of Phalo.* Johannesburg: Ravan Press.

Peires, J.B. 1987. *The Central Beliefs of the Xhosa Cattle-Killing.* Journal of African History. Vol. 28 No.1 (1987), pp. 43-63. Cambridge University Press. https://doi.org/10.1017/S0021853700029418

Peires, J.B. 1989. *The Dead Will Arise Nongqawuse and the Great Cattle Killing Movement of 1856-7.* Johannesburg: Ravan Press (Pty) Ltd.

Pettman, C. 1920. *South African Journal of Science.* Cape Town 1909. Volume 17, No. 3, 352.

Phela, N.S. 2017. *Examining the Unseen Reasons Behind the Xhosa Cattle Killing. An Interactive Archive of Exemplary First-Year Writing Projects.* (Retrieved 20 June 2021) www. University of Notre Dame. https://freshwriting.nd.edu/volumes/2017.

Phillipson, D.W. 1976. *Archaeology and Bantu Linguistics. World Archaeology.* Volume 8. No.1. *Archaeology and Linguistics.* Taylor & Francis, Ltd. https://doi.org/10.1080/00438243.1976.9979653

Pollock, N.C. 1954. *The Town of Alice, Cape Province. Geography Academic Journal of the Geographical Association.* Vol. 39 No. 3. July 1954. Taylor & Francis Lt.

Ranby, P, Potenza, E. & Johanneson, M. 2006. *Focus on Social Sciences Grade 8*. Eighth impression 2008. Cape Town: Maskew Miller Longman (Pty) Ltd.

Ranby, P, Johanneson B. & Friedman M. 2006. *Focus on Social Sciences Grade 9*. Tenth Impression 2010. Cape Town: Maskew Miller Longman (Pty) Ltd.

Raper, PE. 1989. *Dictionary of Southern Place Names*. 2nd Edition, Johannesburg: Jonathan Ball Publishers.

Rees, W.L. 1892. *The life and Times of Sir George Grey, K.C.B. Volume One*. London: Hutchinson & Co. Library of the University of Wisconsin

Republic of South Africa, Department of Rural Development and Land Reform. 2017. *Land Audit Report. Phase II: Private Land Ownership by Race, Gender and Nationality*. Pretoria: Government Publishers.

Robinson, N. 2018. *The Way History is Taught in South Africa is Ahistorical – and that's a Problem*. The Conversation. Academic Rigour Journalistic Flair.

Rubusana, W.B. 1911. *Zemk' inkomo Magwalandini*. Second Editon (First Edition 1906). Messers Butler & Tanner the Selwood. London: Printing Works Frome.

Mqhayi, S.E.K. 1983. *Ukuphela Kwetyala*. In: Satyo, S.C (Edit) *Amazinga Eembongi Xhosa Anthology*. Johannesburg: Educum Publishers.

Saller, R. 1980. *Anecdotes as Historical Evidence for the Principate*. Vol.27, No.1. pp.69–83. Cambridge: Cambridge University Press. https://doi.org/10.1017/S0017383500027352

Saks, D. 2005. Hunting Maqoma: *The Second Waterkloof Campaign, October – November 1851. Military History Journal Vol. 13. No. 4.*

Shakespeare, W. 1599. *Julius Caesar*. Oxford: Oxford University Press.

Soga, J.H. 1930. *The South Eastern Bantu (Abe-Nguni, Aba-Mbo, Ama-Lala).* Johannesburg: Witwatersrand University Press.

Solilo, J.P. 1922. *Mthandi Wesizwe.* In Satyo, S.C. (Ed.) *Amazinga Eembongi Xhosa Anthology.* Johannesburg: Educum Publishers.

Stapleton, T.J. 1994. *Maqoma: Xhosa Resistance to Colonial Advance, 1798-1873.* Johannesburg: Jonathan Ball Publishers.

Stapleton, T.J. 2016. *Maqoma the Legend of a Great Xhosa Warrior.* Cape Town: Amava Heritage Publishing, 2016.

Stapleton, J.T. 2010. *A Military History of South Africa. From the Dutch-Khoi Wars to the End of Apartheid.* Santa Barbara: Praeger Security International.

Stretch, C.L. (Ed.) 1988. *The Journal of Charles Lennox Stretch.-LE Cordeur, Basil* (Ed) Grahamstown: Maskew Miller Longman.

Stubbs, T. 1978. *The Reminiscences of Thomas Stubbs including men I have known.* (Edit) WA Maxwel & RT McGeogh. Grahamstown: Rhodes University.

Theal, G.M. 1904 *History of South Africa from 1846 to 1860.* London: Swan Sonnenschein & Co.

Theal, G.M. 1912. *Documents Relating to the Kaffir War of 1835.* London: Government of the Union of South Africa.

Wilson, M. & Thompson l. (Edits) 1982. *A History of South Africa to 1870.* Cape Town: David Philip Publishers (Pty) Lts.

Yekela, D.S. 2006. *The Death of Chungwa "the Addo Bush Affair".* Alice: Lovedale press (PTY).

Vygotsky, L.S. 1978. *Mind in Society.* Cambridge, MA: Harvard University Press.

Unpublished Thesis

Dowsley, E.D. 1932. *An Investigation into the Circumstances Relating to the Cattle Killing Delusion in Kaffraria.* Master's Thesis. Grahamstown: Rhodes University.

Goedhals, M.M. 1979. *Anglican Missionary Policy in the Diocese of Grahamstown under the first Two Bishops, 1853-1871.* Master's thesis. Grahamstown: Rhodes University.

Matoti, S.M.1990. *An Analysis of Some School History Textbooks With Special Reference to Styles of Concept Presentation.* Master's thesis. Grahamstown: Rhodes University.

Maxengana, N.S. 1989. *The Causes of the Eight Frontier War (The War of Mlanjeni 1850 – 1852).* Bachelor of Arts Honours thesis. Alice: University of Fort Hare.

Morgan, K.E. 2011. *Textbooks as Mediators in the Intellectual Project of History Education.* Doctoral thesis. Johannesburg: University of Johannesburg.

Peires, J.B. 1976. *A History of the Xhosa 1700–1835.* Master's thesis. Grahamstown: Rhodes University.

Spicer, M.W. 1978. *The War of Ngcayechibi 1877- 8.* Master's thesis. Grahamstown: Rhodes University.

Owen, D.R. 1994. *Ubukhosi Neenkokeli : A Directory Of Eastern Cape Black Leaders, From C.1700 To 1990. Grahamstown:* Albany Museum New History Series.

Yani, S. (2018) *Isixhosa Interpretations of the Nongqawuse Saga: Oral Narratives and Theatrical Performances of the Nongqawuse Story.* Doctoral thesis. Cape Town: University of Cape Town.

Conference Paper in Published Proceedings

Selander, S. 2007. 'Designs of democracy in contemporary
learning resources. In: M. Horsely,M. & McCall, J. (eds),
*Peace, Democratization in Textbooks and Educational
Media: Proceedings of the* Ninth International Conference
on Textbooks and Educational Media of International
Association for Research on Textbooks and Educational
Media in Norway and Australia.

Public Presentations

Saule, N. 2017. Prof Ncedile Saule's King Hintsa Memorial Lecture
presented at Butterworth Christian Centre, organized by
King Hintsa TVET College, Kingdom of amaXhosa and
three Municipalities of Mnquma, Mbhashe and Amathole.
https://xhosaculture.co.za/king-hintsa-memorial-
lecture-2

Oral Knowledge

Professor Ncedile Saule: Contribution of oral knowledge to the
names and nuances of the history of amaXhosa.

Electronic Material

Bikitsha, M. 2019. *AmaMfengu. Re-thinking Fingoism/Fingoness:
Contextualizing Hintsa's approach, the 1835 "Fingo Vows"
and its effect to the progressed socioeconomic development
of the Eastern Cape in the 183 years, with a view to Mfengu
identity (an act of who you are), and self-determination.*
(Retrieved 15 November 2022) https://www.sahistory.org.
za

Szymanowski, F. 1988. *Aerial Image of Fort Frederick.*(Retrieved 10
September 2021) https://commons.wikimedia.org

Electronic Online Websites

https://archive.org/

https://books.google.com

https://inflationcalc.co.za/

http://news.bbc.co.uk/2/hi/uk_news/1309216.stm

http://www.capetown.at/heritage/history/voc_simon.htm

https://www.un.org/en/genocideprevention/index.shtml

https://www.sahistory.org.za/

https://en.wikipedia.org/

google.com/books

https://xhosaculture.co.za/

https://fortress.maptive.com

https://iziduko.wordpress.com